Tom Worthington's
CIVIL WAR

Tom Worthington's
CIVIL WAR

*Shiloh, Sherman, and
the Search for Vindication*

JAMES D. BREWER

McFarland & Company, Inc., Publishers
Jefferson, North Carolina, and London

The present work is a reprint of the softcover edition of Tom Worthington's Civil War: Shiloh, Sherman, and the Search for Vindication, *first published in 2001 by McFarland.*

LIBRARY OF CONGRESS CATALOGUING-IN-PUBLICATION DATA

Brewer, James D.
    Tom Worthington's Civil War : Shiloh, Sherman, and the search for vindication / by James D. Brewer.
      p. cm.
    Includes bibliographical references and index.

    ISBN 978-0-7864-7377-9
    softcover : acid free paper ∞

    1. Worthington, Thomas, 1807–1884. 2. Shiloh, Battle of, 1862. 3. Sherman, William T. (William Tecumseh), 1820–1891. 4. United States. Army. Ohio Infantry Regiment, 46th (1861–1865). 5. Worthington, Thomas, 1807–1884 — Trials, litigation, etc. 6. Trials (Military offenses) — United States. 7. Ohio — History — Civil War, 1861–1865 — Regimental histories. 8. United States — History — Civil War, 1861–1865 — Regimental histories. 9. Soldiers — Ohio — Biography. I. Title.
E473.54.B75   2013
973.7'31—dc21   00-068705

BRITISH LIBRARY CATALOGUING DATA ARE AVAILABLE

© 2001 James D. Brewer. All rights reserved

No part of this book may be reproduced or transmitted in any form or by any means, electronic or mechanical, including photocopying or recording, or by any information storage and retrieval system, without permission in writing from the publisher.

On the cover: Drawing of Worthington from one of his pamphlets; burial site in the Worthington family plot.

Manufactured in the United States of America

McFarland & Company, Inc., Publishers
  Box 611, Jefferson, North Carolina 28640
    www.mcfarlandpub.com

Contents

List of Illustrations vii
Preface 1

PART I

CHAPTER ONE. The Early Years 7
CHAPTER TWO. West Point Years 13
CHAPTER THREE. Citizen-Soldier and the Mexican War 29

PART II

CHAPTER FOUR. To Punish Insurrection 49
CHAPTER FIVE. "In Virtue Worthy" — Worthington at
 the Battle of Shiloh 77
CHAPTER SIX. Fallout from Shiloh 111

PART III

CHAPTER SEVEN. Court-Martial of Thomas Worthington 137
CHAPTER EIGHT. In Search of Honor 173
CHAPTER NINE. After the War 183
CHAPTER TEN. Conclusion 203

Notes 215
Bibliography 227
Index 235

List of Illustrations

Map 1.1 8	Map 5.8 100
Photograph 1.1 9	Map 5.9 101
Photograph 2.1 16	Photograph 5.5 103
Photograph 2.2 26	Map 5.10 104
Photograph 3.1 34	Map 5.11 105
Map 3.1 39	Map 5.12 107
Map 4.1 54	Photograph 6.1 114
Photograph 4.1 60	Photograph 6.2 120
Photograph 4.2 62	Photograph 6.3 121
Map 4.2 72	Photograph 6.4 133
Map 5.1 78	Photograph 7.1 138
Map 5.2 80	Photograph 7.2 141
Map 5.3 82	Photograph 7.3 160
Map 5.4 87	Photograph 7.4 170
Map 5.5 91	Photograph 8.1 178
Photograph 5.1 94	Photograph 9.1 186
Photograph 5.2 95	Photograph 9.2 187
Map 5.6 96	Photograph 9.3 192
Photograph 5.3 97	Photograph 9.4 200
Map 5.7 98	Photograph 10.1 207
Photograph 5.4 99	Photograph 10.2 212

Preface

The Civil War was both a defining period in the history and fabric of the United States and a life-changing event for the men who fought it. Costing many lives from battlefield death and disease, the conflict also changed the quality of life for those countless men who were wounded. The physical wounds were debilitating and devastating enough, but the psychological wounds of the Civil War often compounded the physical. For some veterans this mental agony far outlasted the effects of a minié ball in the leg or an amputated arm.

Such is the story of Tom Worthington, whose personal, psychological war had barely begun at the time of the surrender of Confederate forces at Appomattox, Virginia, in April 1865. This book examines the life of Thomas Worthington (1807–1884) and the events that changed a man destined for wealth, stature, and greatness into an angry, bitter old veteran who spent his life, his fortune, and his sacred honor trying to scrub from his name the stain of shame.

This book will relate the facts of Worthington's life, including his education, his military service, his court-martial and removal from the Union Army, his claims of malfeasance on the part of prominent Army leaders, and his efforts in later life to tell his version of the truth about the Battle of Shiloh. From these facts will emerge a portrait of a man very much a product of his early nineteenth-century environment — an educated man, born of a prominent family, whose life became a cauldron of controversy and bitterness. The reader will learn of Worthington's claims against famous military men like Ulysses S. Grant and William T.

Sherman, and will understand why those claims are important. Also, the reader will examine Worthington's treatment at the hands of his peers, his commanders in the U.S. Army, President Abraham Lincoln himself, and Worthington's own family and friends. And perhaps most important of all, the book will demonstrate what Worthington did to himself.

Because Tom Worthington outlived his siblings, never married, left no direct descendants, and spent much of his life as a recluse, reconstructing his life has often been a bumpy journey along a winding trail replete with controversy, surprising discoveries, and dead ends. While Worthington's many postwar pamphlets and Civil War writings have existed in various libraries around the country since the 1870s, these works have languished on dusty shelves for want of critical examination. Yet if Worthington's claims about General William T. Sherman are true, or even partially true, they represent new information that should be considered when forming a twentieth-century understanding of Sherman the soldier, the Battle of Shiloh, and the Civil War.

I first discovered the postwar writing of Tom Worthington in 1984 while preparing a brief paper for the U.S Army Armor Officer Advanced Course at Fort Knox, Kentucky. Having grown up in west Tennessee some 35 miles from the Shiloh National Battlefield Park, I possessed more than a passing knowledge of that battle, and upon reading an abstract of one of Worthington's pamphlets, I became intrigued by his claims and determined to do a paper on them.

When I ordered the work through interlibrary loan, I was shocked to receive the actual pamphlet, yellowed and brittle, instead of a photocopy. Something about handling that old publication tweaked my sense of fairness and challenged my love of history.

My initial study was limited to simply outlining Worthington's claims and presenting their overall importance, if true, to the outcome of the Battle of Shiloh, April 6–7, 1862. But once I had finished the paper, the matter refused to be dismissed from my mind, and for the next decade and a half I found myself frequently drawn back to this crotchety old Ohio colonel's story and his serious allegations against one of the heroes of the Civil War, General Sherman.

My Army duties during this period included a tour as assistant professor of English at Worthington's alma mater, the U.S. Military Academy in West Point, New York. While teaching there I gathered primary source material on Worthington as a young cadet. The more material I found, the more determined I became to discover further information about one of the strangest characters the Civil War produced. In short, the Tom

Worthington story needed to be not only investigated but also added to the growing body of historical information on the Civil War.

Worthington's story also interested me because of my preferences in research and writing. Having been a magazine journalist writing about Civil War history for almost a decade and having done a book on Civil War cavalry raids (*The Raiders of 1862*) in 1997, I discovered that my personal interest in writing history involves looking into stories that would not otherwise be told. I enjoy telling stories that focus on smaller, lesser-known aspects of that terrible conflict, yet still offer a broader lesson to apply to our overall understanding of war itself and the men who fight it. In other words, I have little interest in writing the thirtieth book debating the wisdom of Pickett's Charge or the twenty-fifth book guessing whether the South would have defeated the Union Army at Shiloh if Confederate General Albert Sidney Johnston had lived. Choosing the Worthington story, therefore, was no contest.

My quest led me through the archives at West Point, through the records of the Ross County Historical Society, and back to the Worthington family home at "Adena" in Chillicothe, Ohio. I searched through the National Archives in Washington to recover Worthington's court-martial record, his military service record, and the collection of queries and documents he submitted to the War Department in an attempt to clear his name. Returning to the Shiloh National Battlefield Park, I walked every step of ground that Worthington's unit, the 46th Ohio Volunteer Infantry, occupied during the battle. I charted angles of fire, measured lines of sight, and assessed battle positions. I applied an experienced military eye to Worthington's claims, and this book represents the compilation of the facts from that study.

The work will focus upon the following topics:

- •žWorthington's early life and the events that shaped his world view and his later behavior during the Civil War and its aftermath
- •žWorthington's claims regarding the behavior and actions of General William T. Sherman leading up to and during the Confederate attack at Shiloh on Sunday morning, April 6, 1862
- •žSherman's actions against Worthington in response to Worthington's charges
- •žWorthington's efforts to expose what he believed to be the wrong done to him and the truth about Sherman's actions while in command at Shiloh and during the months following the battle

The first part of the book will detail Worthington's early years in Ohio, his years at West Point, his service as a citizen-soldier in the 1840s, his Mexican War service, and his life during the period leading up to the Civil War. In this part, a picture will emerge of Worthington's early influences and his developing character.

The second part of the book will provide a close examination of the first day of the Battle of Shiloh. The focus will be upon (a) the actions of the 46th Ohio Infantry and its tenacious Colonel Worthington relative to the Sunday morning attack, and (b) Sherman's behavior leading up to and during that attack. Many fine works have been written detailing the Battle of Shiloh in its entirety, and it is beyond the scope or intent of this volume to replicate those detailed works. But until now, outside of general mention in the broad histories of Shiloh, no scholars have closely examined Worthington's claims in light of the terrain, the emerging historical evidence, and the events following the battle.

Part III of the book presents the court-martial of Tom Worthington and examines his lifelong efforts to vindicate himself and to hold General Sherman accountable for wrongs Worthington believed were done not only to him personally, but to all the Union soldiers who fought at Shiloh.

It is appropriate at this point to acknowledge some of the people who assisted me with the formidable task of collecting resources and information on the reclusive Tom Worthington. Those individuals include, but are not limited to: Mr. Alan Aimone, Special Collections, U.S. Military Academy Library, West Point, New York; Mary Anne Brown, site manager at Adena (home of Governor Thomas Worthington, Sr.), Chillicothe, Ohio; Pat Medert, Ross County Historical Society, Chillicothe, Ohio; the late George Reeves, superintendent, Shiloh Military Battlefield Park; Judy Stephenson, Armor School Library, Fort Knox, Kentucky; Charlotte Wells, Walpole, Massachusetts; and the ladies of the Ross County Genealogical Society, Chillicothe, Ohio.

James D. Brewer
December 2000
Elizabethtown, Kentucky

PART I

CHAPTER ONE

The Early Years

THOMAS WORTHINGTON, SR.

In central Ohio, Thomas Worthington High School enjoys a modern-day reputation as the home of both an excellent academic curriculum and a fiercely competitive sports program. Such characterizations are appropriate since the man for whom this institution is named was one of the brightest, most politically competitive men in Ohio history. Known as the Father of Ohio Statehood, Thomas Worthington guided Ohio's emergence into statehood like a shepherd guides a flock, and he has been nearly idolized over the past 200 years.

The Worthington family emigrated from Cheshire, England, in the early 1700s. The branch of the family that would eventually produce Thomas Worthington, Sr., and his son Tom, the subject of this book, settled in Virginia. Thomas Worthington, Sr., was born on July 16, 1773, in Jefferson County, Virginia (now part of West Virginia). Orphaned as a young boy, he found himself being raised rather loosely by his three older brothers and appears to have requested that a guardian be appointed for himself and his sister (Brown 1). Worthington came under the guardianship of General William Darke, one of many Virginia revolutionary war soldiers who received a land bounty in an area of the West known as the Virginia Military Reservation. General Darke, a man who served in the Virginia convention that approved the U.S. Constitution, ensured that Thomas Worthington, Sr., received the standard education for the time. Following his preparatory studies, Worthington spent some time at sea

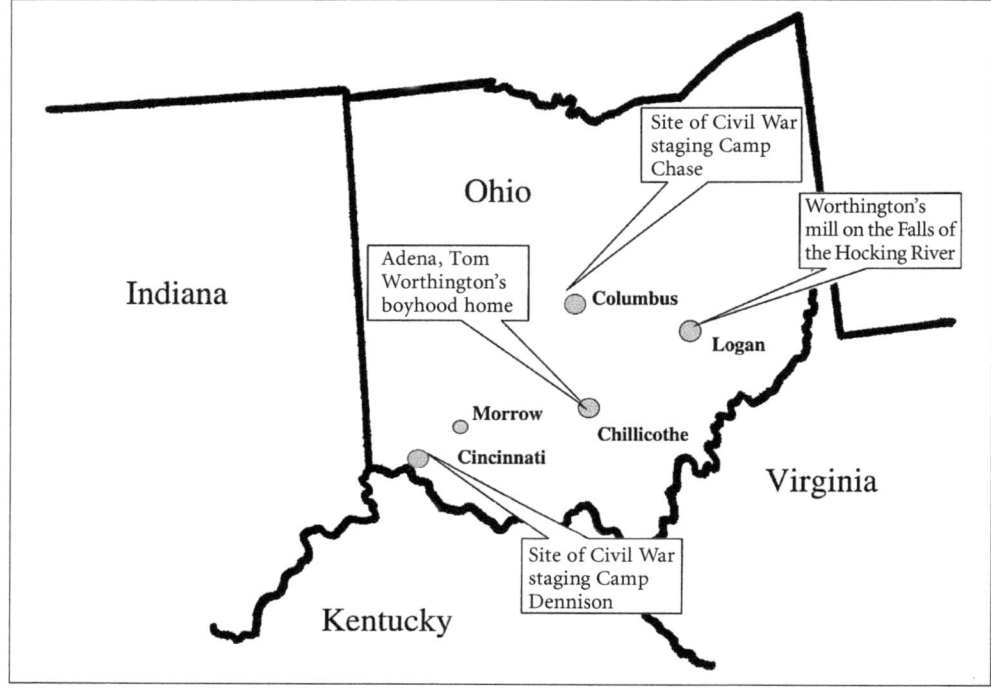

MAP 1.1 Important Ohio locations in Worthington's life.

and then returned to Virginia to study surveying. Acknowledging Worthington's skills in surveying, Darke, elderly and unfit for the arduous journey required to survey the land he had received for his military service, determined that Worthington would go west into what is presently Ohio and complete the survey (Galloway 210–211).

Thomas Worthington must have surely fallen in love with the land Darke sent him to survey, for upon his return to Virginia, he arranged to purchase the land from Darke and proceeded to move his family to Ross County, Ohio, in 1798. To the pioneer village of Chillicothe, Worthington was accompanied by Dr. Edward Tiffin, who would become Ohio's first governor (Galloway 210–211). Also joining Worthington on his trek into what then was called the Northwest Territory were a number of recently freed Negroes. Abiding by the Ordinance of 1787, which prohibited slavery in the Northwest Territory, Worthington had freed the people he held as slaves in Virginia, brought with him those who chose to leave, and provided for those who did not, according to the law regarding emancipation in Virginia.

PHOTOGRAPH 1.1 "Adena," now a state historical site, was the Chillicothe home of Governor Thomas Worthington and his family (photograph by author).

Settling into the quality farming land near the Scioto River, Worthington began to build a family business in farming, milling, stock, and shipping (Sears 23). He soon received appointment as a major in the militia and as the deputy surveyor of the Northwest Territory; thus from his earliest arrival in the territory, Thomas Worthington had money, power, and position.

The senior Worthington set about building the only plantation-style home and farm to be found in Ohio, naming his 5,000-acre estate "Adena." The Federal-style home, designed by Benjamin Latrobe, a man employed as a surveyor by Thomas Jefferson and considered the first professional American architect, was completed in 1807. In his diary entry of September 18, 1811, Worthington stated that Adena is a name given to "places remarkable for the delightfulness of their situations." In fact, the view from the front of Adena is the same panorama that is depicted on the Great Seal of Ohio (*Ohio History* 1).

That a prominent man should have an elegant home was nothing unusual at the time, but the elaborate nature of Adena, with its suggestion of the southern aristocracy, caused some to question why he would build such a home. Perhaps Worthington's sights were already set on a successful political career, for when asked why he built Adena, Worthington replied, "That Mrs. Worthington [Eleanor] and I might be able to entertain our friends as we did in our old Virginia manor-house" (Galloway 211). Worthington understood the importance of image: through the doors of Adena over the next 20 years would pass some of the most distinguished men and women in the history of Ohio and in the country, including a number of the Indian chiefs of the Northwest Territory.

Amid this pastoral scene — a scene laced with the comings and goings of men and women of tremendous stature and importance — Tom Worthington was born on March 18, 1807. In a family that would ultimately produce ten children, Tom would grow up amid expectations to affirm the family motto: *Virtute Dignus Avorum* ("in virtue worthy of one's ancestors"). Thus, from his birth until he left home for advanced schooling, Tom Worthington's life would be shaped by the profound influences of a frontier existence, emerging statehood, politics, pride, and particularly the overwhelming charisma and personality of his father.

CARRYING ON THE FAMILY NAME

Before Tom was born, his father had been a delegate to the state constitutional convention in 1803 and was elected as a Republican to the U.S. Senate. During Tom's boyhood, his father would serve as governor of Ohio from 1814 to 1818, then as canal commissioner from 1818 until his death, remaining in his later years active in state government as a member of the Ohio House of Representatives (*Bioguide*). According to Mary Anne Brown, site manager at Adena, Governor Worthington may best be described as a Democratic-Republican, or what some have called a Jeffersonian Democrat. A frequent house guest of Thomas Jefferson, Worthington, like many people in southern Ohio, tended to align himself more closely with the political and cultural ideals of Virginia and Kentucky,[1] as opposed to people from northern Ohio, who more closely identified with New Englanders (Brown 1). Though young Tom had many siblings,[2] he seems to have been particularly close to his father and must have surely emulated the mannerisms and behaviors of a man so thoroughly immersed in the business of politics and power. Many of the characteristics that in later life would define Tom Worthington's relationships with other people may be seen in descriptions of his father. The elder Worthington was "impetuous by nature and had a quick temper," and his career was marked by his being "constantly irritated by the weakness and indecision of his contemporaries" (Sears 35). Indicating what is perhaps a pattern of family dissatisfaction with military bureaucracy, the senior Worthington had his own run-ins with those he thought would deny him his due rank and position within the state militia. Holding a commission as a lieutenant colonel, he resigned that commission when the position he was promised in the Ross County Militia was awarded to another man. The decision was based, so Worthington was told, on his "lack of combat experience" (Sears 36–37). The tendency to believe that his military expertise was ignored or wasted would later haunt his son, as would another personality trait described by Alfred B. Sears in his book *Thomas Worthington: Father of Ohio Statehood*: "He was inclined to be a little smug and supercilious at times and was too often disdainful of his critics" (147).

Thomas Worthington was a man of numerous interests and pursuits, managing to balance a demanding public life with the requirements of running a farm, a mill, and several other business enterprises. It was into this frenetic lifestyle that young Tom Worthington and his siblings were born and expected not only to participate, but to thrive. When their father was the U.S. senator from Ohio, the family lived in Washington. Worthington seemed not at all certain that the capital environment was conducive to his children's development. While the elder Worthington sought to obtain for them the best schooling possible, he worried about their spiritual upbringing as well, declaring:

> As to the morals and manners of my poor boys ... I am convinced that nothing of the frippery of this world will satisfy the soul. Religion alone, pure religion can only do so and the youth who believes and acts on this belief will never fail in after life to feel the greatest consolation from it [Sears 172].

Young Tom would not demonstrate at any point in his life his father's penchant for religion as the primary path to success.

Chapter Two

West Point Years

What does a young man of 16 do with his life when his father has held a position in the state militia, his father's guardian was a celebrated revolutionary war soldier and later commanded a Virginia regiment in the Northwest Territory, and his older brother attended West Point? He does what many of his landed contemporaries did — he attends West Point for a quality education in mathematics, engineering, foreign languages, and rhetoric, pays his dues as a soldier, then applies his education to improving the quality of life for himself and those around him.

When Tom Worthington was ten years old, in 1817, his eldest brother, James, became the first family member to attend the U.S. Military Academy at West Point. But he resigned after two years and did not graduate due primarily to his father's designs on James to assist him in meeting the demands of the family business and a political life that taxed his time and efforts during the period 1817–1819. During the time that James was at West Point, the elder Thomas Worthington wrestled with a decade-long controversy over the rechartering of the National Bank. Part of the difficulty rested in "whether a branch of the National Bank which had been authorized for Ohio should be opened in Chillicothe or in Cincinnati" (Sears 201). While actively lobbying in Philadelphia and Washington on behalf of Chillicothe (an act that got him roundly criticized in the Cincinnati newspapers), Thomas Worthington took the occasion to visit Cadet James at West Point. The fact that such an accomplished public servant was present at the academy prompted the leadership to ask Worthington to address the corps of cadets.

But as proud as he might have been that James was attending the academy, Worthington saw an ever-increasing need to have the young man back in Ohio. The load of Worthington's public service over the banking issue, coupled with the growing workload of promoting legislation in support of the Ohio canal system, had caused his own business interests to suffer for lack of attention. Sears points out that although Worthington's business and estate interests were "fairly well" supervised during his many absences, "they did not flourish as they did when he was home and able to give them his constant attention" (114). The idea that both Worthington and his wife, Eleanor, "paid a price" for their public service might well be extended to James.

Business and political considerations seemed to have prompted in Worthington a change of heart relative to offering his son up for military service. He came to the conclusion that he did not intend his son "for the Army in times of peace," indicating that he believed the academy a school for "dissipation and idleness" when the country was not at war (Jared Mansfield 1). Many of the elder Worthington's letters to James during his time at West Point appear harsh and demanding. Mary Anne Brown, site manager at Adena, indicates that the governor's letters "pounded on James for failing to write home regularly and for neglecting his familial duties" (Brown 1). Initially, Worthington sought a solution to bringing James home short of resignation, and he attempted to call in a favor by prevailing upon then–Secretary of War John C. Calhoun to allow his son a furlough. Calhoun, in an effort to support Governor Worthington, wrote on James Worthington's behalf on August 14, 1819, to Sylvanus Thayer, superintendent of the U.S. Military Academy: "If you can grant the furlough desired, conformably to the regulations, I wish it to be done; otherwise, you will permit Cadet Worthington to resign" (Calhoun 1). But regulations are regulations, and the military academy, not unlike its approach to business today, saw no reason to grant special considerations to Cadet James Worthington regardless of whom his father happened to be. So James Worthington's resignation took effect on August 30, 1819, and he threw himself into assisting his father in business affairs. By the summer of 1822, James was employed as one of the surveyors locating the "best and cheapest" routes for the proposed waterways in the Ohio canal project (Sears 225).

James' younger brother, Tom, would enroll at the military academy four years later, at the age of 16 years and four months; and the fact that James did not complete his course of study might have motivated Tom Worthington not only to outperform his brother but perhaps, more important, to uphold the family name and meet the expectations of his father (*Official Register* 6).

In the Company of Greatness

A prominent young man from a wealthy family, whose father was formerly a U.S. senator and the governor of the state of Ohio, would quite naturally find himself in the academic company of men of tremendous talent and potential. Such was the case with young Tom Worthington and his contemporaries at West Point, New York. When Tom enrolled at West Point on July 1, 1823, his fellow plebes (freshmen, or fourth-class cadets) included men whose names were to be inextricably linked to the coming Civil War:

- žLeonidas Polk of North Carolina, later known as the "Bishop General of the Confederacy"
- žNapoleon Bonaparte Buford of Kentucky, later an instructor at the academy and field commander under Generals Grant and Pope
- žPhillip St. George Cooke of Virginia, author of the 1862 version of *Cavalry Tactics*
- žGabriel J. Rains of North Carolina, veteran of the Seminole War and the Mexican War and a Confederate general in charge of the Confederate Torpedo Bureau

Already at the academy upon Worthington's arrival was a third-class cadet whose military actions in the coming Civil War would contribute to young Tom's life-changing ordeal at the Battle of Shiloh: Albert Sidney Johnston. That Worthington not only met Johnston, but knew him, is not surprising, given that all four classes totaled approximately 200 cadets.

The West Point where Tom Worthington spent the next four years of his life was a small, cozy, near-pastoral scene compared to the sprawling complex of buildings present today. An 1825 map of the area indicates three primary buildings in use at the time—a four-story North Barracks, a three-story South Barracks, and the Academy Building, where cadets attended classes. Each of these buildings was made of stuccoed stone, and together they surrounded the drill field, a flat plain that extended from the buildings to a lofty overlook of the Hudson River. Also surrounding or near to the plain was the Old Washington Headquarters House, the Mess Hall, Kosciuszko's Cottage, and miscellaneous supply buildings (Gardner 3). Considering the historical relevance of Fortress West Point during the American Revolution, the intrigue of Aaron Burr and Major Andre's treasonous map in his boot, and the legacy of previous graduates, Tom Worthington surely felt the pressure to succeed and uphold the

PHOTOGRAPH *2.1* Major Robert Anderson, the "hero of Fort Sumter," was Tom Worthington's roommate at West Point (Library of Congress).

family name as he went about the day-to-day activities of a cadet. Those activities, shown in Table 2.1, were highly structured and usually quite monotonous.

Table 2.1

Sunrise to 7 A.M.	Study
7:00 to 8:00	Breakfast
8:00 to 11:00	Recitations
11:00 to 12:00	Lectures and recitations
12:00 to 1:00 P.M.	Dinner
1:00 to 2:00	Recreation
2:00 to 4:00	Study, laboratory, and drawing
4:00 to sunset	Military exercise
Sunset to ½ hour later	Supper
½ hour past sunset to 9:30	Study
9:30	Tattoo and roll call/Lights extinguished
10:00	Rooms inspected[1]

Source: *Gardner 12*

Making it through that first year at West Point proved particularly challenging for most cadets, thus when in January 1824, the first critical examination had eliminated those unable to meet the standard, Worthington must have been quite pleased to find his name on the superintendent's list of cadets ordered to "attend at 3 o'clock to-morrow afternoon at the Post Adjutant's Office for the purpose of receiving their warrants" (Gardner 18).

During the first two years of his education, Worthington had, for at least part of the time, a roommate who was also destined for the history books. A proslavery, upper classman from Kentucky shared the rudimentary cadets' quarters with Tom, and by 1860 this man would rise to the rank of major with the 1st U.S. Artillery. In 1861, history and circumstance would select him and his two-company contingency at Fort Moultrie, South Carolina, for a most perilous and fateful duty. Ordered by the Buchanan administration to make a decision that would seem to dictate war or peace, the officer would move his men into the unfinished Fort Sumter and there receive the bombardment that many would argue began the Civil War (*Civil War Homepage*). The officer's name was Robert Anderson, and Tom Worthington ate, drank, shared a room, and trained with him for more than a year.

In Worthington's second year at West Point, he was joined by a young plebe named Jefferson Davis, and in his third year at West Point, a plebe named Robert E. Lee arrived from Virginia on July 1, 1825.

West Point cadets were not allowed the opportunity to return home until their third summer at the academy, so Tom Worthington spent two years on the Hudson, his only comfort from family coming in the form of letters from loved ones at home in Ohio. Yet even in his third summer, when he might have returned home, Worthington was already demonstrating an independent streak that would characterize how he related to the rest of his family for his entire adult life. He elected not to go home that summer, citing "reasons I shall state when I see you [his brother James] which I hope will be in a few days" (Worthington 24 June 1826). Worthington was expecting his brother, then en route to New York, to visit him at West Point that summer. In the same letter, Tom indicated that most of his family would be traveling during June and July, his mother "leav[ing] home for Saratoga [New York] on or about the 15th July," [2] his father on the road, and his "sisters ... at Troy [New York]"[3]. Perhaps Worthington figured that even if he took a furlough, no one would be at home at Adena for him to visit.

Tom's eldest brother had maintained contact with the faculty he had left behind upon his resignation from West Point in 1819. In his June 24th letter, Tom indicated some of the individuals James might expect to see upon the occasion of his visit.

> Wotenvlict [is] here [and] you will probably see him. I saw Whelock a few days since who is very anxious to see you but will leave the Point for the south before you arrive. Maitland will be shortly but perhaps not before the middle of July.

Closing his letter, Tom offered a passing observation about the quality of Ohio cadets now attending the academy and tinged his comments with some added guilt should his brother decide not to visit while in New York:

> Our state is not doing very well but more of this when I see you. Try and be here on the 4th unless you would rather be in New York.
>
> Your affectionate brother
T. Worthington

EARLY CONTROVERSY

An incident occurred in the Class of 1827 demonstrating that Tom Worthington showed some unusual restraint in righting perceived wrongs.

The Tom Worthington who emerged during and after the Civil War did not exert his normal feisty behavior relative to a mini-scandal in the Drawing Department in 1826. Some cadets had availed themselves of a technique for scoring well in drawing class that involved "tracing the outlines of their drawings upon the models given them to be copied," according to Lieutenant Colonel Thayer, superintendent of cadets (Gardner 14). Thayer, ever a stickler for honor and integrity, considered this "an attempt at gross deception." Several cadets, including Phillip St. George Cooke and Leonidas K. Polk, took exception to the marks they received in drawing— marks, no doubt, rendered lower than the cadets expected as a result of the tracing activities. But rather than taking their grievance to the superintendent, they jumped the chain of command and appealed in a letter directly to the Secretary of War. Not surprising, the Secretary of War's response on February 8, 1826, fully supported Thayer's determination and the instructor's marks for the cadets and roundly chastised the complainants as losing "sight of the obligations under which they entered the Military Academy" (Gardner 15). That Worthington was not a party to this grievance seems out of character with the brashness he would demonstrate in later years. Still, his letter dated February 6 (written before the cadets had received the Secretary of War's reply) to his brother James, then in Paris, France,[4] indicates that he, too, had a complaint about his standing in class relative to drawing instruction:

> Circumstances are so peculiar with respect to my standing in philosophy and drawing that I cannot possibly do more than keep my place and in drawing I shall probably fall. Between the 1st of September and the examination we went through a course of pencil drawing but between this and June we [did] Topography, and judging from my writing, heaven knows where I shall be in this branch [Worthington 6 Feb. 1826].

The "peculiar" circumstances he mentions were likely a result of the tracing controversy, and Worthington might have been one of the errant tracers himself. The letter has almost a tone of preparing the reader for possible bad news on the grades front. But while Tom may not have been a party to the appeal to the Secretary of War regarding drawing marks, he still maintained his characteristic sense of pride and self-worth relative to his standing in chemistry. In the same letter, sent to France in care of Monsignor J. C. Barnet, Counsel American, No. 14 Rue Plumet, Paris, he wrote:

> The affair which hangs most heavily on my mind will commensurate first ... the result of the last examination by which I was 6th in

> chemistry, 13th in philosophy, and 20th in drawing. In chemistry I had a right to expect to be put head of my class although from the peculiar circumstances in which I was not I did not expect a higher place than 5th. In consequence of the illness of both principal professors in Chemistry we did not commence the study of it till the 1st Nov at which time I was in the 2nd section ... [but] ... before the commencement of the examination when I was transferred to the 1st [section] and the only week I was marked in that section any work was also the maximum, so that at the examination my marks were higher than those in any of the class though I had not received most of those marks in the 2nd section [Worthington 6 Feb. 1826].

He went on to suggest that because he was switched from one section to the other, he encountered examination questions for which he had not been adequately prepared. Still, with all his misgivings about grading and testing, Worthington acquitted himself well enough to maintain a high standing in his class. Later in his letter he soberly observed that "there have been 130 in my class, there are now 46."

In addition to Tom Worthington's somber observations about grading, his February 1826 letter to James also showed the young cadet's breadth of knowledge and currency in world events. He discussed the appointment of Richard Andrews as minister to Colombia and suggested that the individual submitted for appointment as the U.S. representative to Panama would likely not be confirmed:

> This may result I am sorry to say from the hostility of that body to the administration ... and also from our unwillingness to take what would [be] an active part in the affairs of countries whose independence has not yet been acknowledged [Worthington 6 Feb. 1826].

In closing his letter to his brother, Tom mentioned several books that would "be of service to me in my next years course which I should like to have and perhaps it may be in your power to bring them." He mentions Dupin's *Voyages*, another work in the realm of polytechnic, and Tredgold's *Carpentry*. Whether or not Tom ever received these books from his brother is unknown. Just before mailing his letter to James in Paris, young Tom added a postscript that read: "We have just heard of the death of Alexander of Russia." That Tom depended greatly on the advice, counsel, and friendship of his brother seems apparent from the tone and content of his letters while at West Point.

During the period 1825–1826, the elder Thomas Worthington's health began to fail. He had been prone most of his life to attacks of bilious fever, or what he called "inflammation of the bowels" (Sears 233). Realizing that his father and his grandfather had died of the same illness (likely an affliction of the gall bladder or perhaps a gastric ulcer), the elder Worthington sought treatment at Saratoga Springs, New York. But he found little relief, and his bilious attacks became increasingly severe.

Still attempting to remain active in the business of the canal commission in Ohio, the elder Worthington wrote to Tom, now a third-year cadet, at West Point in December 1826. The letter was one of encouragement, not unlike many Tom had received from his father, yet it reflected a somewhat melancholy tone, which indicates that Governor Worthington sensed that he might not get many other opportunities to write due to his declining health. Governor Worthington indicated that he had learned much about life and that he hoped to share what he had learned "if [his] life is spared" (Governor Worthington, 24 Dec. 1826). In response to one of Tom's earlier letters stating that Ohio boys had not fared well in their performance at West Point, Governor Worthington wrote:

> I am very sorry that Ohio has been unsuccessful and am convinced it has been the folly of the parents more than the want of capacity of the child.... We must let others do as they will [and] attend with strict attention to ourselves and leave no exertion untried or duty unperformed [Governor Worthington, 24 Dec. 1826].

From this letter it is clear that at their last meeting the elder Worthington had been rather direct in his admonishment of Tom with "frank and serious advice"— advice Tom was less than enthusiastic about receiving. "The severest lessons of adversity ... never fail to teach us wisdom generally [received] with impatience and unthankfulness," Governor Worthington wrote.

The father knew the son's nature all too well, for in his letter Governor Worthington sounded a warning that, if heeded from his West Point years forward, might have spared Tom Worthington much of the heartache and sorrow of his later life:

> I have often told you that nothing is so important to any one as a complete control of temper and actions united with a benevolent heart and disposition. ... I think on the whole we do ourselves injury by meddling officiously in the affairs of others or by our folly with unbridled tongues give others an opportunity if not an invitation to meddle in our affairs. The first [thing] to be done therefore is to govern our tongue which indeed is included in

a great measure in the gov[ernment] of temper tho[ugh] I have known men of very bad temper who could be silent when anger raged within [Governor Worthington, 24 Dec. 1826].

As if young Tom needed any more pressure to succeed, or to follow in his father's footsteps, Governor Worthington continued:

> If the Lord spares my life to the time when you are to be inducted into the duties of the station which you so kindly and affectionately offer to fill to relieve your Father now beginning to be worn down with business ... I feel very desirous you should use every exertion to get as high in your class as possible and as far as you can in conduct [Governor Worthington, 24 Dec. 1826].

ACADEMIC PERFORMANCE

In June 1827, the first-class cadets (seniors) at the U.S. Military Academy underwent their general examination. Based upon the result of that examination, and on the record of their conduct during the four years on the Hudson, the students were ranked in order of merit on two scales: examination performance and conduct. For a key to understanding Tom Worthington's encounters and difficulties in later life, one has only to examine closely the prophetic results of his academy rankings and record.

As a result of the general examination in June 1827, Thomas Worthington graduated 12th in a class of 40 cadets. The only future Civil War leaders of note who ranked ahead of Worthington were Leonidas Polk, 8th in the class, and Napoleon Buford, 6th in the class (*Official Register* 6). Table 2.2 offers a detailed breakdown of the results of Worthington's general examination, listing his actual scores against his possible scores.[5]

Table 2.2
Tom Worthington's General Examination Scores

	Possible Score	*Actual Score*
Math	300	210
French	100	51
Natural Philosophy	300	248
Drawing	100	63
English	300	277
Chemistry & Mineralogy	200	182
Rhetoric & Moral Philosophy	200	167

	Possible Score	Actual Score
Tactics	200	160
Artillery	100	88
Conduct	300	100

Source: *Register of Merit, 1817–1835*, vol. 1.

Tom Worthington could be described in modern military parlance as tactically and technically proficient. With the exception of his performance in French and his low scores for conduct, Worthington demonstrated to the satisfaction of the U.S. Military Academy faculty his worthiness to graduate and be commissioned as a second lieutenant. His knowledge of tactics would be expressed later in the publication of a drill manual in support of volunteer troops readying themselves for action in the Civil War. His ability in rhetoric would be shown in the many publications he produced after the war as he sought to purge the shame he had brought to the family name. His conduct scores, however, may be most revealing of all the records, and thus, they bear a bit more scrutiny.

MILITARY CONDUCT

Receiving demerits for inappropriate conduct at the U.S. Military Academy is no difficult task. Few cadets ever make it through that institution without their fair share of behavioral blemishes. One exception to that rule was Robert E. Lee, but then Lee was an exceptional man on multiple levels. Just as the military academy maintains the academic records of all cadets, the institution also archives the ancient, yellow-paged volumes that catalog the behavioral record of cadets. The *Record of Delinquencies, 1822–1828*, lists in painful detail every demerit a cadet received during his four-year odyssey.

In spite of Governor Worthington's charge to his son to "get as high as possible and as far as you can in conduct" in his December 1826 letter, young Tom Worthington's delinquency record is characterized by the sheer length of its entries. Where the delinquencies of most cadets are listed in two columns on a single, long ledger page, Cadet Worthington occupies his page *plus* one and one half other pages. Lest one be too hard on Cadet Worthington, it is important to remember that delinquencies, which result in demerits at the military academy, are quite often calculated overreactions to everyday events designed to remind a cadet exactly who is in charge and to regulate every aspect of the cadet's life. The "break a man down to build him up" concept found in modern military basic training was then, and to a great extent remains, a critical part of forging a civilian into a soldier. A demerit, therefore, might be received for something as trivial as looking the wrong way at the wrong time, sewing a button on crooked, or inadvertently addressing an upper classman without the proper courtesy. But demerits can also apply to more serious offenses, such as dereliction of duty or absence without leave. Usually, a series of more weighty offenses results not in demerits, but in removal from the military academy. The fact that Tom Worthington was not removed from the academy and did, in fact, graduate, would argue that none of his offenses were that grievous. Yet from the record of his delinquencies, one can note a pattern of behavior that later in his life would plague Worthington.

The record book shows that virtually all cadets at this time had petty demerits, e.g., forage cap improperly worn, bed not made, being out of order, or improper absence. But Worthington had *more* of these citations than most of his contemporaries. He was once arrested and confined for two days, charged with being "absent from duty and going to bed too soon." Keep this event in mind and determine later in the story, when more is revealed about him, whether or not it is hard to imagine Tom Worthington saying, "To hell with that, I'm going to bed!"

Table 2.3 lists some of the recurring demerits for which Worthington was cited.

Table 2.3
Recurring Demerits for Cadet Tom Worthington

> Out of order at inspection
> Out of order at parade
> Visiting in study hours
> Out of order at mounting (guard)
> Gross neglect of duty — inattention at drill
> Grossly unmilitary conduct on artillery drill
> Replying (inappropriately) to an officer
> Inattention at parade
> Inattention in guard mount
> Absent from parade without orders

Worthington's behavior raises some serious questions. Were his actions indicative of the immaturity of carefree youth? He was, after all, barely 16 upon his admission to the academy. Did he believe that since his father had been a senator and a governor that he should be held to a different standard of behavior? Was he emulating his father's smugness or prideful nature? Or did Tom Worthington simply possess a general disdain for authority? Time and the eroding effect of life experiences would tell.

"A Longing, Lingering Look Behind"

Having been ill throughout the winter of 1826–1827, the elder Thomas Worthington realized his time was nearly at an end. In his diary he complained of frequent abdominal attacks that seemed to have rapidly aged him (Brown 1). Still, he insisted on accompanying some boats he had built to New Orleans in the spring of 1827, growing increasingly ill throughout the trip. After delivering the boats in New Orleans, he arrived by ship in New York on May 15 following a 35-day voyage. The elder Worthington was near death. Cadet Tom Worthington requested and received a leave of absence from the academy and traveled the roughly 50 miles to the city. He found his father in critical condition at the American Hotel. Thomas Worthington, Sr., was moved to another location, and Alfred Sears indicates in his book that young Tom "was in constant attendance, spending several hours with him almost every day" (Sears 234). But Tom could not remain with his father indefinitely, as the requirements for study and graduation from West Point drew him back up the Hudson. His father's illness must have weighed heavily upon Tom as he underwent his final examination during June. The fact that he scored as well as he did is a reflection of his determination and perhaps in some measure is a tribute to the influence of his father and older brother.

Mississippian's Charge to the Cadets

Part of the graduation exercises for the Class of 1827 consisted of an oration delivered on June 20 by the Honorable Thomas B. Reed of Mississippi. As the country edged closer to Civil War by the 1850s, an address by a southerner like Reed might well have been met with controversy in later years. But while the seeds of national division were ripening even in 1827, the open animosity that so characterized the later years had yet to reveal itself. Reed's address provides a piece of oratory representative of the period, laced throughout with classical references and foreign allusions sure to strike a familiar chord among the young cadets who had

Photograph 2.2 The Worthington family plot at Grandview Cemetery in Chillicothe, Ohio. (Photograph by author)

studied the classics for the past four years. His remarks, designed to inspire men like Tom Worthington, referred to the graduates as "a college of young gentlemen, educated by the government, and who may justly be considered the present pride, and the future support and glory of the country" (Reed 1).

Is it any wonder that Tom Worthington and his fellow cadets felt themselves worthy of the respect and gratitude of the nation? Records indicate that 38 cadets graduated and received their commissions as brevet second lieutenants and felt ready to take on the world.[6] Worthington, because of his ranking of 12th in his class, received one of the coveted engineer branch designations which offered him a status above his fellow cadets who were branched in artillery and infantry.

Reed sought to charge and inspire the cadets in his address, saying, "You will consider yourselves a 'holy brotherhood,' associated together, to fulfill the highest destinies which can be entrusted to man" (Reed 37).

Yet even with such a charge, many of the graduates of the Class of 1827 would serve only an initial period of duty with the Army, choosing to return to civilian life. Perhaps the modest Army pay and the perpetual slowness of promotion led many of them to leave the service. Some, though certainly not all, would answer the clarion call to return to the Army during the war with Mexico, and a still smaller group — then in advanced age — would volunteer their services in the Civil War. But the day they graduated on the plain at West Point would be the end of an era in their lives and the last time many of them would see each other — at least as allies and friends. Young Tom Worthington heard Mr. Reed of Mississippi sum it up all too well in the closing lines of his address:

> The moment of freedom from academic constraints, may appear to you a moment full of joy; but believe me, in after life, you will look back upon those scenes with a lively enthusiasm, especially if misfortune should overtake you in the career of life. But be assured, your country will every where meet you with approbation, and open to you the prospects of useful and honorable pursuits.... You will cast, I know, a "longing, lingering look behind," when you leave the Academy at West Point; but go "where duty calls you," and improve, as I know you will, the advantages you have enjoyed [Reed 39–40].

Tom Worthington would leave West Point a classically educated, politically aware, militarily skilled man. He would take to heart Reed's declaration that his country would meet him with respect and opportunity, but he would also immediately encounter some of the misfortunes Reed described. For, within hours of his graduation, Tom received news of his father's death.

The elder Thomas Worthington, statesman, governor, and source of inspiration and strength to his wife and family, died in New York on June 20, 1827, the same day that his son Tom graduated from the Military Academy. The elder Worthington's body was returned to Ohio, and he was buried in a lot northwest of Adena (Sears 235). The family later bought lots 34 and 35 in Grandview Cemetery in Chillicothe on July 25, 1853, and the governor's body was moved there. On the spire monument to the governor, along with the name of his wife and the names of his children, are inscribed the words "Noble in Principle, Pure in Morals, Exalted in Patriotism." The family would purchase two more adjacent cemetery lots, 45 and 46, on May 21, 1860, where other family members would be laid to rest near Governor Thomas Worthington.

CHAPTER THREE

Citizen-Soldier and the Mexican War

After his commission as a second lieutenant at West Point in July 1827, Tom Worthington was assigned to the 4th U.S. Artillery at Fort Monroe, Virginia.[1] One year later he resigned his commission and returned to Adena where, assisting his eldest brother, James, Tom Worthington threw himself into the administration of his late father's farms, mills, mines, and shipping interests in Ross, Hocking, and other Ohio counties (McCormick 28). Worthington chose to return to Ohio and apply his valuable West Point education to the pursuits of a farmer and businessman. At the time of the elder Worthington's death in 1827, the family owned some 15,000 acres of land and numerous town lots. Those land possessions, combined with various business enterprises, amounted to an estate conservatively valued at $150,000 (Weisenburger 130). Unfortunately, the late Governor Worthington had maintained very little liquid capital, and throughout his life, he seems to have had difficulty paying his bills. The early Ohio frontier functioned largely on a barter economy. "Anything and everything that had an intrinsic value was received and paid out" (*Hocking Sentinel* Sept. 1994, 33). But as the population grew and settlement increased, so did the use of currency in the conduct of business. Following the governor's death, the family spent almost 12 years trying to settle the estate and meet the demands of a host of creditors holding liens against the Worthington family for debts and services rendered. During the decade of the 1830s, the late governor's wife, Eleanor Swearingen Worthington, was compelled to operate on a tight budget with the emphasis being on "hanging on to the home place" at all costs (Brown 1).

STRIKING OUT ON HIS OWN

Upon his father's death, Tom had inherited land in Hocking County along the Falls of the Hocking River, near the village of Logan (see Map 1.1), a town his father had platted (*Hocking Sentinel* Sept. 1994, 33). As management of the property and mill required more and more of his time, Tom left Adena in 1834 and settled on his land near Logan. But occupying the land and the mill was one thing—keeping up the taxes and paying off the debts accrued by his father was another. The next ten years presented Tom with a constant struggle to hold on to his property. When he moved to the mill at Logan, Worthington was "not worth a cent and [had] no personal possessions worth naming" (Worthington 11 Feb. 1839). To get started, he borrowed $6,000 from, among others, his uncle James Swearingen (his mother's brother). But Tom's behavior over the next few years demonstrated the immaturity and restlessness of youth; consequently, by the end of the decade he found himself in the embarrassing position of potentially losing his property. Tom's financial circumstances were clearly as much the result of his own bad decisions and personal indulgences as the residue of his father's indebtedness. Early in the decade he lost several thousand dollars in bad deals for wheat and flour, and from 1831 through 1837 Worthington "lost a large amount by betting occasionally at Faro tables as a rapid way of making money." He made the curious assertion that his gambling was "by no means a habit" and that his wagers had been strictly to make money for his business, since, according to his view, he did not engage in "private gambling" (Worthington 11 Feb. 1839). During these wild years, Tom had infrequent communication with Swearingen, and he dodged payment of his debt until, faced with the possible loss of everything, he seemed to reach a crossroads in his life. Writing to his uncle in 1839, he attempted to provide him partial payment on his debt and tried to keep him regularly informed of his efforts at managing his property. "Dear Uncle," Worthington wrote:

> I hope you will excuse my long letters and bad writing but my situation is so critical and the stake involved so great that I could not pay up. Please write and say what the amount owed you from the estate is and also the amount of your judgement against me [Worthington 17 Jan. 1839, 3].

As late as 1839, portions of Worthington's property were still being contested in probate over claims against canal construction debts initiated by his father, and his hold on his remaining property was so precarious as to require intervention in his debt relief by the Ohio Senate and House of Representatives, which acted, no doubt, out of respect for the legacy of his late father. Worthington eventually got portions of the estate released based upon a House resolution that required him to give "bond and warranty" against the property (Worthington 17 Jan. 1839). By February 1839, Worthington was busy trying to convince his creditors of both the gradual improvement of his financial situation and the validity of his overall approach to managing the property. "I have not treated you as I ought," he wrote Swearingen in 1839, adding, "I shall be able to raise in cash $2,000 to $3,000 and give satisfactory evidence of my ability to meet the last amount of the 1st of April." Laying out a detailed plan of how he intended to repay his uncle, he wrote, "I have had with me for two years a Virginian from Hampshire County named Lyons whom I have always found intelligent, active, and honest." With Lyons, Worthington set up a work arrangement in which Lyons would run the mill and take a percentage of the profits, and Worthington would designate a portion to be sent regularly to the Lancaster and Chillicothe Bank for deposit in repayment of Swearingen (Worthington 27 Feb. 1839).

Confessing his errors in a letter to Swearingen, Worthington insisted, "I have altered my conduct and manner of doing business and have placed myself in a fair way to be out of trouble within a year or in two more at the farthest." Between 1837 and 1839 he had managed $10,000 in improvements at the Falls near Logan, and in his letter to Swearingen he cited his efforts as "judiciously laid out and yielding an abundant return" (Worthington 11 Feb. 1839).

During the late 1830s, Worthington family letters and diary accounts indicate that his mother and siblings viewed Tom as the problem child of the family. Their writings show clear concern for the direction of his life. In addition to gambling, young Worthington had also developed an unhealthy affinity for liquor, and the family had, undoubtedly, witnessed the volatile mixture of the two in Tom's behavior. Gambler, heavy drinker, and debtor — these were descriptions characteristic of people *other* than Worthingtons. During the heyday of his wildness, Tom's behavior prompted his sister Elizabeth Worthington Pomeroy to write to their mother in June 1836, "Tom paid us [a visit] while here. Will his restless spirit ever be controlled in this world? I was glad very glad to see him, little of his time however was spent with me" (Wells *Miscellaneous* 2). Another sister, Margaret, echoed the family sentiment toward Tom when she recorded in her diary entry of October 14, 1836, "Met Tom in the street. He is just recovering from a severe fall — My poor brother, he is involving himself [in gambling and drinking], I fear irretrievably, and will take no caution or word of advice" (Margaret Worthington, 49). By December of that same year Tom's situation had worsened, and he had returned to Adena to try and pull himself together. "Tom has been here two days," Margaret noted in her diary, "being weaned [from alcohol]" (Margaret Worthington, 97). In his letter of confession of mismanagement to Swearingen in 1839, Worthington noted that "James and others ... did not expect [Swearingen] would be willing to wait any longer for the amount which has been owed [him] for so long." Because of the shame of his long-standing debt, Worthington admitted he "never could bring himself to speak to" Swearingen regarding his debt until "compelled by necessity" (Worthington 11 Feb. 1839).

Despite his attempt to turn his life around, by the winter of 1839 Worthington's decade of hard living began to take its toll on his health as well as his livelihood. Several family letters from 1839 indicate that Tom looked sick, yet, as one notes, he still managed to stop at Pearl Street to visit a saloon. In 1834, Tom Worthington's younger brother Albert Gallatin Worthington had died, and the family might have figured that unless he changed his lifestyle, Tom might be next. "[Tom] is feverish," Margaret's husband, Edward Deering Mansfield, wrote on October 3, 1839. "I wonder at his running about in this way. He thinks he has done very well this summer — but he has some difficulties to settle with the Trust Company. So goes the world" (Wells *Miscellaneous* 3). It appears his financial and behavioral problems continued at least until 1841, when his sister Margaret wrote that Rufus King would travel to Logan and "endeavor to free Frank [Tom's younger brother] from any engagements into which poor Tom has entangled him" (Wells *Miscellaneous* 3).

Citizen-Soldier

Although Worthington's return to civilian life had meant financial struggle and behavioral problems, the old adage "once a soldier, always a soldier" proved true. Worthington wasted little time after leaving active duty before affiliating with the local militia. While still living at Adena he entered the Ohio Militia at the rank of sergeant, though he might have expected his position upon enlistment to be considerably more reflective of his education and experience. He was, after all, a son of the former governor and a recent West Point graduate. But the state militias of the 1800s were no more free of politics than many Army National Guard organizations are today. Worthington's Jeffersonian political heritage might not have enhanced his favor among the Whigs and Democrats well-entrenched in the Ohio Militia system. In fact, Worthington suggested some years later that he was overlooked for promotion and position in the militia due to his "not belonging to 'the Party'" (Worthington 26 Nov. 1847). He was most likely referring to the Whig Party, given that party's hawklike behavior surrounding the war with Mexico. Still, Worthington's talents as a soldier did not go unrecognized, for by 1829 he had advanced to the rank of sergeant major, a position he held until 1831, when he was promoted to major in the Ohio Militia. At last he was an officer again, and he revealed his dissatisfaction at having to toil his way through the ranks in an 1847 letter updating the roster of graduates at the U.S. Military Academy: "As you see from a 2nd Lt of Artillery I went down to a militia sergeant" (Worthington 26 Nov. 1847).

Although Worthington claimed that politics held him back in his promotions, politics had not held back his brother James. For even though James Worthington failed to graduate from West Point, he, too, served in the militia and had by 1832 risen to the rank of major general. James' rank in the militia, coupled with the fact that he would also serve in the Ohio General Assembly from 1831 to 1840, likely counterbalanced any political handicaps Tom Worthington faced (McCormick 28). But along with the possible benefit of his brother's influence came additional pressure to succeed, and now instead of only living in his father's shadow, Tom was under his brother's shadow as well.

Even in his move to Hocking County, Worthington did not lose touch with his militia activities. While he oversaw the successful operation of the mill, Tom managed to get promoted to lieutenant colonel in 1837, to colonel in 1839, and finally to brigadier general of the Ohio Militia in the latter months of 1839. Tom Worthington must have felt some sense of validation. He had returned to his native Ohio not only to be successful as a civilian businessman (though he came close to losing it all), but he also rose through the ranks of the Ohio Militia from sergeant to brigadier general in only ten years. Still, his success with the militia was tempered by his view of such duty as second-class service. When submitting information for the roster of West Point graduates, Worthington added a footnote to his letter:

> I have thought [it] proper to intimate that I do not wish or intend such a statement of my militia *honor*[2] as I have set forth — It would of course be sufficient to append to my name as a — "Brigadier 1838" [Worthington 26 Nov. 1847].

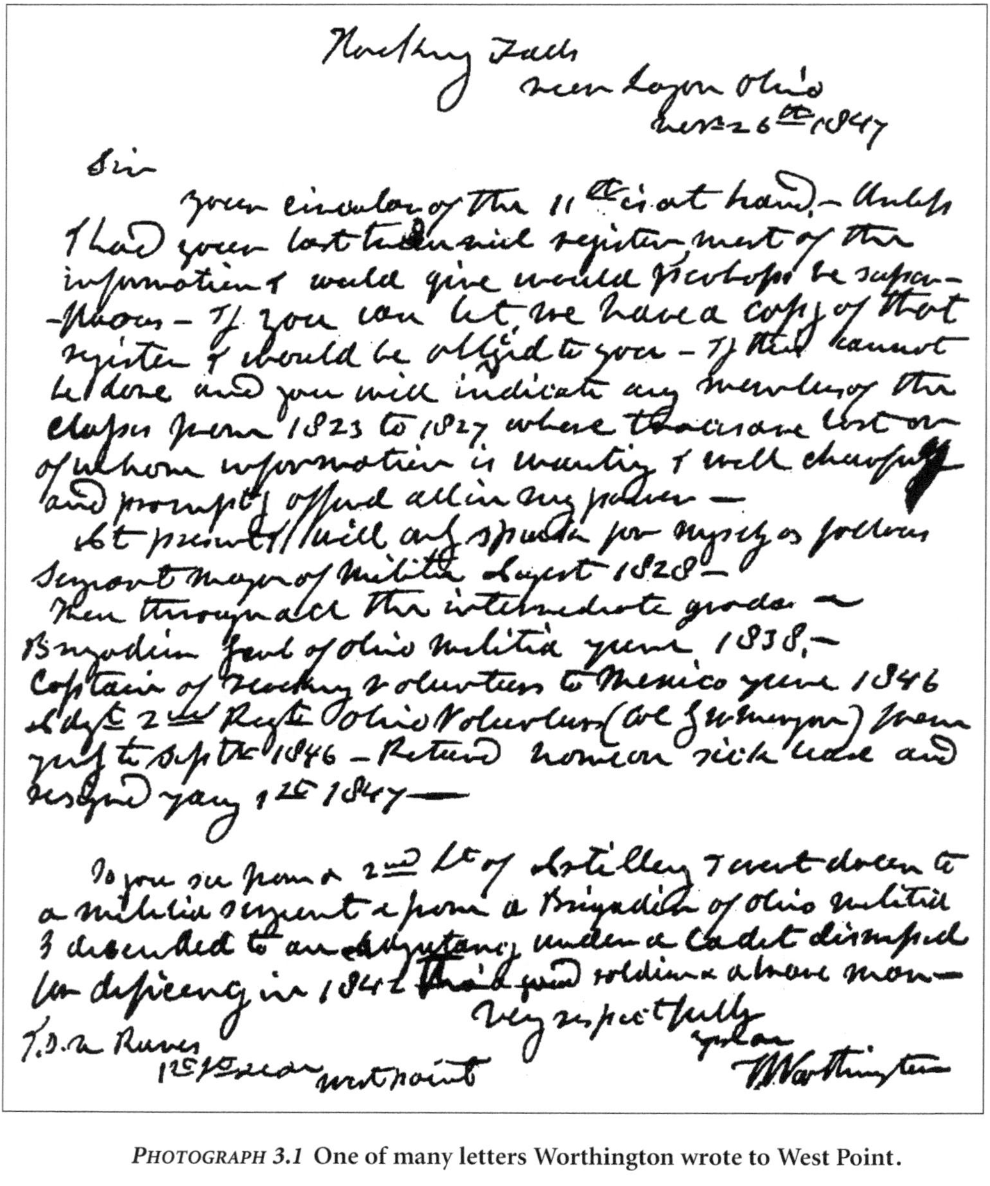

PHOTOGRAPH 3.1 One of many letters Worthington wrote to West Point.

It was not uncommon for West Point graduates, or those affiliated with regular Army service, to look down on volunteers and militia organizations as inferior in skill and potential. Worthington, like many of his contemporaries, held to that view and not completely without cause. In reality, most militia units could not approach the discipline or the tactical skills of regular Army troops. They met irregularly, their equipment was most often outdated or inferior to that of the standing Army, and their promotion system was fraught with political patronage.[3] It is interesting to note that Worthington did not mind West Point historians mentioning he was a brigadier general, even if it were in the Ohio Militia. The compilers of the roster of West Point graduates entered Worthington's entire record anyway, including his time as a lowly sergeant in the militia.

In 1840 Tom Worthington was a proud, class-conscious man. Born into a family with money, power, and status, he expected nothing less for himself. Some historians have attempted to downplay the divisions in class and social status among frontier (Ohio was then still classified as frontier) communities. Francis P. Weisenburger in *The Passing of the Frontier*, writes, "In rural Ohio before 1850, class distinctions were relatively unknown or unemphasized. Variations in wealth, however, were never wanting" (129). In this rather idealized concept of frontier equality, Weisenburger fails to recognize that the primary determinant of social class is *money*. One need not be a student of Karl Marx to realize that any notion of variations in wealth not leading to variations in class is absurd. While the frontier did impose a certain equality of life across the broad spectrum of society (e.g., most everyone hauled water, most everyone built fires, most everyone made clothes), families like the Worthingtons, by virtue of their wealth, considered themselves a cut above the average citizen.

But family notoriety did not necessarily guarantee financial success, and Worthington continued to struggle during the 1840s just to hold on to his land and business in Logan. As late as 1845 the treasurer of Hocking County was still threatening to sell at public auction some 44 acres of Worthington's land near Logan for $1.39 in delinquent taxes (*Hocking Sentinel* March. 1995, 20). Weather extremes hurt Worthington as well, for in the spring of 1846 a flood "washed away a great part of" his mill works, costing him over $10,000. Worthington felt the disaster would "likely put the finishing touches to [his] ruin" unless he could get help from the state of Ohio (Worthington 21 May 1846). Yet even amid his battle to stave off the gaunt face of poverty, Worthington maintained his sense of class and status. He had been raised with a belief in public responsibility, and in the Worthington tradition men like Tom were expected to assume positions of leadership in the community. He simply could not allow financial setbacks and business complications to stand in the way of his destiny. While he did not choose to emulate his father's role in politics, Tom exercised the leadership responsibilities of being a Worthington through the Ohio Militia. He would soon have an opportunity to further demonstrate that leadership as the relations between the United States and Mexico deteriorated through the early 1840s.

WAR WITH MEXICO

On April 25, 1846, General Mariano Arista sent Mexican troops across the Rio Grande and ambushed a squad of U.S. Dragoons under the command of Captain Seth Thornton. In what became known as the Thornton Affair, 14 Americans died immediately, and two others subsequently died as a result of wounds received in the fight. Provoked by this attack and escalating controversies over land rights and settlement in the Southwest,[4] the Congress of the United States, at the prompting of President James K. Polk, declared war on Mexico on May 13, 1846. While many Whig politicians opposed the action as hasty and opportunistic, the majority of the public found themselves solidly behind the decision once they learned that American blood had been shed.

Despite serious reservations among many Ohio politicians and leaders (chief among them Governor Mordecai Bartley) about the wisdom of engaging in a war with Mexico, the people of Ohio geared up to support the call of men to arms. Governor Bartley officially called for troops on May 20, 1846, appealing to the "gallant and spirited sons of Ohio" to support the Federal government:

> Let it not be said that when our country appeals to the courage and patriotism of the citizen soldiers of Ohio for aid, that that aid was not promptly rendered [Weisenburger 448].

Worthington immediately "on the breaking out of the war ... reported to the War Department that [he] was ready for any service for which [he] might be detailed" (Worthington 6 Nov. 1847). He clearly had in mind being called back to active service and being restored to a regular Army rank befitting his position and experience. But despite his offer of service, the War Department did not offer him a commission. In fact, his overture seems to have been completely ignored. Here was the country on the verge of a monumental military undertaking, yet it did not seem to need the services of a West Point graduate. Despite Washington's ambivalence, Worthington was as much caught up in the war fervor as any man, and he resolved to take leave of his now-successful milling and farming business for the service of his country. He might have reasoned that, with James having not finished West Point and now fully involved in managing the Worthington business legacy, only *he* could step forward in the military realm to continue the Worthington reputation for leadership.

While Worthington's offers of service with the regular Army were being rebuffed, several battles of the war with Mexico were already taking place. The first major battle, an artillery duel at Palo Alto eight miles north of the Rio Grande, had occurred on May 7 with the Mexicans withdrawing south after suffering heavy casualties. The following day, the U.S. Army under General Zachary Taylor again fought the Mexicans at Resaca de la Palma and defeated them. By May 18 the Mexicans had been forced to withdraw from Matamoros. Congress, meanwhile, had authorized thousands of volunteer troops to be mustered and deployed for 12 months' service, thus providing Worthington with another chance to get into the war.

"Everywhere demonstrations were held to further enlistments" (Weisenburger 448), and while men in the state began flocking to the colors, Tom knew that enlisting as a private in someone else's regiment would not have been a display of patriotism worthy of a Worthington. So, when Democratic politician Thomas L. Hamer was commissioned early that summer as a brigadier general for his efforts at raising the 1st Ohio Volunteers, Tom Worthington probably expected to receive the same treatment. This was, after all, the first war in which graduates of the U.S. Military Academy would participate, so Worthington believed he would be called upon to contribute. His offer of regular service had been ignored, he believed, because he did not belong to "the party." His status as a brigadier of the Ohio Militia had provided him neither a pathway to a commission in the regular Army nor appointment by the governor to a position similar to that obtained by Hamer. In a letter to West Point he wrote, "I have not been called on while Cadets dismissed [from the military academy] for deficiency of talent or bad conduct have been appointed Col[onels]" (Worthington 6 Nov. 1847). Exactly which officers he referenced as being dismissed is unknown, but without doubt Worthington considered himself snubbed by the War Department and by the political-military hierarchy of his own home state. Thus, Tom enlisted in the 2nd Regiment, Ohio Volunteer Infantry, on May 27, 1846, at the rank of first lieutenant, but he immediately set about raising his own company, the Hocking Volunteers, based out of Logan, Ohio, "because in his view 'no one else in the county would do it'" (McCormick 28). Organizing the company on or about June 23, 1846, Worthington's command, made up of men who enlisted for one year of service, eventually became part of the 2nd Ohio Infantry. With the raising of a company, Worthington was appointed captain. He then immediately ran for the elected position of colonel of the regiment and lost to G. W. Morgan. Morgan immediately recognized the value of having a West Point–educated officer under his command, and he appointed Worthington adjutant of the regiment, a position he held throughout his service in the war.[5] But even in this role, Worthington chafed under the saddle. In a letter to West Point after the war, he wrote that he "raised a company of Ohio volunteers for the War with Mexico and for the purpose of having his company accepted [and] [he] served as Adj[u]t[ant] of 2nd Ohio Regt of Volunteers" (Worthington 8 Feb. 1850). Despite what appears to be a sacrifice on Worthington's part on behalf of the company he had raised, Worthington never considered an adjutant appointment satisfactory in view of his position, background, and rank. He believed that he was more qualified to be the colonel of the regiment than was Morgan. In describing his situation, Worthington wrote:

> As you see from a 2nd Lt of Artillery I went down to a militia sergeant & from a Brigadier of Ohio Militia I descended to an adjutancy under a Cadet dismissed [from the military academy] for deficiency in 1842 tho' a good soldier and a brave man [Worthington 26 Nov. 1847].

This rather backhanded compliment to his regimental commander, Colonel Morgan, is typical not only of the personality and pride that Worthington would exhibit in service during the Mexican War, but it is indicative of the behavior that would lead him into confrontation and disgrace during the Civil War. In addition to his bitterness at having lost to Morgan in the election for colonel of the regiment, he was most certainly jealous of Morgan's rank, a rank attained without graduating from the academy. Worthington held contempt for Morgan's "volunteer" status as well.

The summer of 1846 offered a lull in the fighting and allowed time for the arrival of thousands of volunteer soldiers to the desert Southwest, including Worthington and the 2nd Ohio. Worthington and the men of the 2nd Ohio Infantry assembled at Camp Washington near Cincinnati. There they drilled and departed July 9, 1846, on a three-week journey to Mexico, landing at Brazos de Santiago. Even with his military education and a year of service with the 4th U.S. Artillery, Tom Worthington seems caught up in the same war fever as the other volunteers—fever enough to actually believe he was going away on a great adventure. But whatever he might have believed about the coming romance of war, his view would soon be tempered with the harsh realities of campaign life. Worthington, like thousands of other citizen-soldiers, would discover that:

> The romance of war was dispelled by the realities of the soldier's life in a strange and often inhospitable environment. Soldiering in Mexico [as adjutant to a regiment of volunteers] was vastly different from marching before an admiring citizenry back home [Johannsen 86].

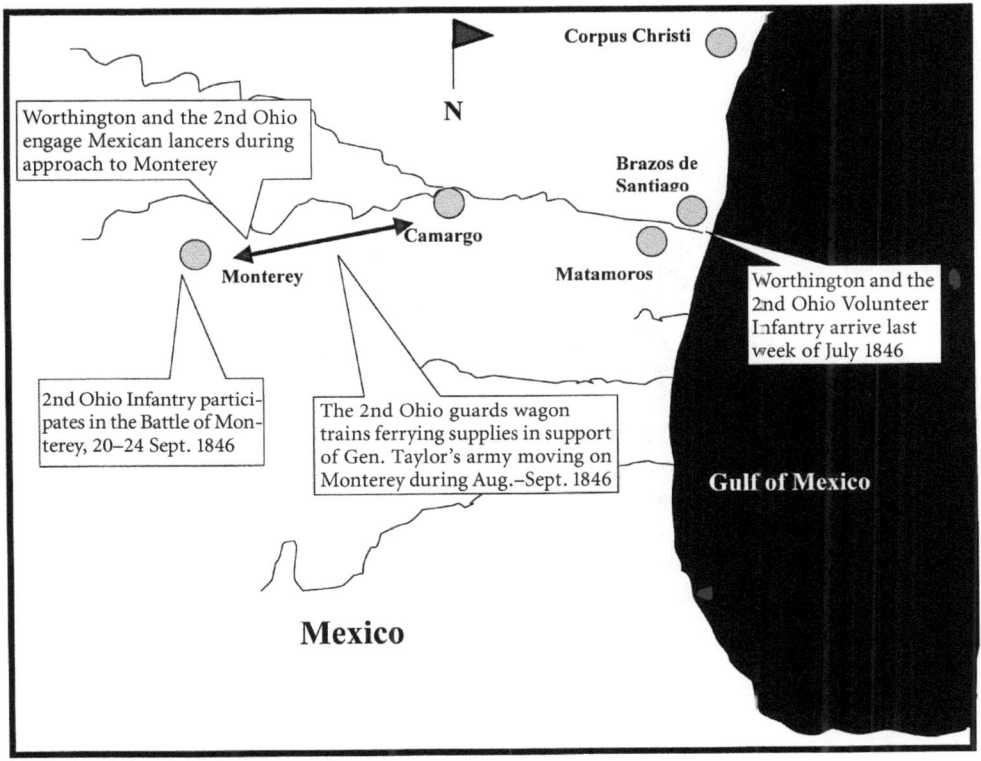

Map 3.1 Worthington's service with the 2nd Ohio Volunteer Infantry during the Mexican War.

MOVEMENT TO THE FRONT

From Brazos de Santiago, Worthington and the men of the 2nd Ohio Volunteer Infantry marched inland toward the small town of Camargo. They quickly discovered that central Ohio and northern Mexico reflect extreme topographical and climatic differences. From drilling with his men on a courthouse lawn in midwestern spring weather, Worthington found himself marching up to 18 miles a day with the desert sun beating down. Sand blew in his face and ground in his boots, and he was continually needing and wanting more water than he had available. "Men dropped from the ranks, seeking shelter under trees or among the bushes, not caring whether they lived or died" (Johannsen 87), and while Worthington might have fared somewhat better as a staff officer, he still had to endure the march. He would have been subject to most of the same physical privations—"faces ... swollen and blistered, lips cracked, and feet swelled [and] bruised"—as his fellow line soldiers (Johannsen 87).

That summer, the Army's tacticians were writing checks that their Quartermaster Corps could not cash: the Army could not match its need for transportation of supplies with the resources necessary to move them. The Mexicans had withdrawn almost 100 miles south of Matamoros to consolidate and occupy a strong defensive position in Monterey. For want of logistical hauling capability, the U.S. forces under General Taylor were still sitting in the vicinity of Matamoros when the 2nd Ohio Infantry and other volunteer units arrived to join the fight. Taylor determined that the next staging area deeper into Mexico would be a small town called Camargo, and he set about ferrying supplies from Matamoros to Camargo and marching his Army south. Because Camargo constituted Taylor's base of supplies, he believed guarding the area was important enough to require considerable troop strength, and he felt that the supply line between Camargo and his eventual target, Monterey, would be constantly at risk from Mexican marauders.

A significant part of the duty of protecting Taylor's supply line fell to the 2nd Ohio Infantry, so during August and September Worthington's duties consisted of guarding supply trains and conducting escort duty from Camargo to Monterey. His regiment occupied positions at Ceralvo, Marin, and Punta Aguda.

The maladies of Army life on the march that most likely plagued Worthington were the digestive ailments, particularly since the susceptibility for such ran in his family. Although the Army sought to institute a steady ration supply system, the nature of the terrain coupled with the sheer distances involved made food supplies erratic and often tainted. The hardtack, or hardened biscuits, issued by the government in the ration cycle were quite often infested with worms. The unsuitability of these rations and the horror expressed in the letters home from Mexican War soldiers describing "break[ing] a biscuit [and] see[ing] it move" would appear again as a major problem during the Civil War. When rations did make it through, in addition to hardtack, they consisted of pork, bacon, flour, salt, vinegar, beans, and coffee (Johannsen 88). But often the flour was infested with bugs and the pork was so salty as to be inedible, particularly considering the lack of water. What soldier, except one near starvation, would eat a slab of extremely salty pork for his evening meal when he was uncertain of the availability of water during the next day's 15–20–mile march?

Given Worthington's predisposition for abdominal difficulties, the sporadic and undependable nature of Army food, and the sanitary conditions of a unit on the march, Worthington suffered from stomach problems for a large part of the campaign. But Tom was by no means an exception, for in the Mexican War disease cost U.S. forces seven times the number of casualties as battle deaths. Imagine the disappointment and frustration of the many young men who hurried off to the glory of fighting for their country only to be laid up with amoebic dysentery and diarrhea. Makeshift hospitals in places like Jalapa, Perote, and Puebla were littered with soldiers too sick to continue the march. Worthington, too, would suffer from disease, but he did manage to complete the campaign into Mexican territory and participate in one major battle at Monterey.

To See the Elephant

Despite his training at West Point, his duty with the 4th U.S. Artillery, and his service in the Ohio Militia, it was September 1846 before Tom Worthington would "see the elephant," a phrase that soldiers primarily used to refer to actually going into combat. But in many senses, to "see the elephant" also included the rigors of camp life or being on Army duty in general.

As the 2nd Ohio Infantry made its way toward Monterey, it found itself surrounded by a Mexican Army force of lanceros under General Mariano Paredes. They formed a hollow square (the classic defense for infantry against cavalry) and continued marching toward Monterey "fighting as they advanced." Colonel Morgan sent a rider forward to request reinforcements as the regiment pressed on amid hit-and-run attacks by the lanceros. As darkness approached, the men of the 2nd Ohio heard cannon fire toward their front, and "the theory seemed to prevail that it was the enemy's battery" (*Hocking Sentinel* Sept. 1991, 31). In the failing light of day, the soldiers observed a battery rumbling through the dust and unlimbering before their regiment, specifically in front of Company D, the regiment Worthington had raised from Hocking County, Ohio. Colonel Morgan ordered Captain Abram Seifert, the man who had assumed command of Company D upon Worthington being made regimental adjutant, to "prepare your company to lead a charge and take that battery." Company D had fixed bayonets and were on the verge of executing a charge when an officer peering through his field glass realized that the artillery was friendly. "A shout went up that made the welkin ring" as the regiment realized reinforcements had arrived. The enemy lanceros retired from the field, and the 2nd Ohio pressed on toward Monterey (*Hocking Sentinel* Sept. 1991, 31).

At the Battle of Monterey the 2nd Ohio performed a follow-in-support role within General Taylor's operations, and while the soldiers saw action, they did not constitute the primary assault force. But soon after the Battle of Monterey, Tom Worthington had experienced enough of the war with Mexico. As he stated in a letter to West Point, he "returned [to Ohio] on *sick leave* from Camargo in October 1846" with what he described as Rio Grande fever (Worthington 8 Feb. 1850).[6] Sick soldiers returning to their home state were not uncommon during this war, for the absence of proper field medical facilities, coupled with the harsh climate, made it more beneficial for the Army to discharge sick men and send them home than to keep them on duty. Worthington was not technically discharged upon his return to Ohio, but he eventually submitted his resignation "on account of sickness contracted in service" effective January 1, 1847 (Worthington 8 Feb. 1850). Worthington used the period from October through December to recuperate, and he seems to have had intentions of returning to the war once he regained his health. Even after submitting his resignation, he "offered to serve again in Feb[ruary] 1847," but his offer was "not accepted" (Worthington 8 Feb. 1850). Again Worthington had been rebuffed, and while it is unclear whether his February 1847 offer of service was rejected by the regular Army or by the volunteers, it must have been far more than Worthington was willing to stand. In his commentary on his Mexican War service, he showed dissatisfaction with both his assigned duties and with the command structure. It seems unlikely that Worthington actually longed to return to the deprivations of camp and march life, particularly if he felt he was not being employed to the best use of his talents. "It was easy to die in battle," Johanssen writes, regarding Mexican War soldiers in his book *To the Halls of the Montezumas*, "but to waste away with sickness; to be crushed by the blows of an unseen enemy ... to feel that your name will occupy no place in the bright scroll of fame" might have been more than Worthington was willing to tolerate (90). His dissatisfaction with his role as adjutant, together with the prognosis for little opportunity at the kind of command position he believed he was qualified to fill and another rejection of his offer of service would have been more than enough to keep Worthington home in Ohio. In a letter to West Point in 1850, Worthington candidly wrote:

> My trip to Mexico was an accident and a great mistake — It cost me many thousand dollars, tho[ugh] if I could have got into the regular service, I would have served through the war — Regular officers were generally out of place with volunteers [Worthington 8 Feb. 1850].

Why Worthington referred to his Mexican War service as an "accident" is unclear. Perhaps he realized that he had, against his better judgment, allowed himself to be overcome with war fever. Yet raising a company of soldiers is certainly a willful act, in that one does not generally stumble into such a command. It might have been a mistake in the sense that Worthington did not get from the experience what he sought (i.e., fame, military success), but it hardly seems to have been an "accident." The adventure did, no doubt, cost Worthington a great deal of money. He, like many who raised companies, shouldered much of the cost of equipment and transportation. He bore this cost willfully, at least in the recruiting and deployment phase, and being a businessman he must have surely anticipated the expense. The fact that he was a businessman, albeit a struggling one, whose absence was reflected in the financial performance of his endeavors (milling and farming), accounts for some of the thousands that his Mexican War service cost him. He later claimed that the Mexican War service "cost him a lawsuit involving the patrimony of 1,800 acres of land" (McCormick 29).

Yet beyond the financial cost of his participation, and perhaps more than the physical maladies that sent him home, Worthington did not like being a West Point–educated officer serving as an adjutant for a non–West Point graduate in a unit composed of volunteers. The War Department's rebuff of his offer to serve as a regular Army officer at the outbreak of the war still annoyed Worthington, and while he might have been sick enough to justifiably return to Ohio, he would not have been sick enough to remain there had the War Department reversed itself and offered him a regular commission. His comment, "I would have served through the war" suggests that as a regular officer either (a) he wouldn't have gotten sick — a ridiculous interpretation, or (b) his sickness would not have been great enough to cause him to resign his commission. This statement casts serious doubt on Worthington's motivations for resigning from the 2nd Ohio Infantry.

Did Worthington have a legitimate complaint about how he was utilized in the 2nd Ohio Infantry? An examination of the officers in the five regiments and various independent companies that Ohio furnished in the Mexican War shows an interesting pattern. Among all the officers from Ohio, five had graduated from West Point, and some, as Worthington claimed, had attended but not graduated (see Table 3.1).

Table 3.1

Officer	Unit	Rank/Position	Postwar
Alexander M. Mitchell	1st Ohio Inf.	Colonel of the Regiment	Died Feb. 28, 1861, at St. Joseph, MO

Officer	Unit	Rank/Position	Postwar
James Findlay Harrison	1st Ohio Inf.	Adjutant (Captain)	Later served as a colonel of U.S. volunteers in the Civil War
Thomas Worthington	2nd Ohio Inf.	Adjutant (Captain)	Later served as a colonel of U.S. volunteers in the Civil War
Samuel R. Curtis	3rd Ohio Inf.	Colonel of the regiment	Maj. Gen. U.S. volunteers in the Civil War
William Irvin	5th Ohio Inf.	Colonel of the regiment	Died Oct. 1852 at Port La Vaea, TX

Three out of the five West Point graduates who served with the Ohio volunteers came to be colonel of their respective regiments, while Worthington himself had to settle for an adjutancy. That experience left a sour taste in his mouth (Wilcox 681–685).

Between May 1846 and December 1847, the War Department sent some 23,556 regular Army recruits to Mexico. U.S. volunteers numbered 67,905. Ohio furnished almost 4,000 volunteers, and of that number 424 were discharged because of disability, 18 were killed in battle, 218 died of disease, and 435 deserted. While he achieved no great military success, Tom Worthington was fortunate simply to have survived. For of those discharged for disability or sent home because of illness, three-fourths died before they reached home (Mansfield 351–357).

Thomas Worthington had hoped to gain public recognition from his Mexican War service. He had spent his own money, accepted a lesser position to further his own company's standing, gone into combat with the enemy at Monterey, and suffered from the diseases of campaign life. But despite his posturing and positioning, he never rose above the rank of captain. "Circumstance," Worthington declared in a letter to West Point, "'that unspiritual god of misdirection' knocks all our calculations into fits" (Worthington 8 Feb. 1850).

For the next ten years, Tom Worthington resumed his quiet life in Ohio. His mother, Eleanor, passed away in 1848, and his sister Elizabeth Worthington Pomeroy, youngest of the Worthington daughters, died in

1852. Tom, then in his early forties, remained unmarried. Finding a woman willing to put up with the emerging arrogance and cantankerous behavior apparently proved quite difficult. McCormick, in his article "Worthington vs. Sherman," offers a revealing assessment of Worthington at this point in his life. Despite his growing financial stability, as reflected in his land and assets valued at over $20,000 in the 1850 census, "one senses that he had a rather bitter, antisocial attitude" (McCormick 29). And although 48-year-old Sarah Fisher and her daughter, Anne, lived in Hocking County with Tom during the early part of the decade of the 1850s, her role seems to have been simply that of housekeeper. Fisher and young Anne left Tom's Hocking County residence by 1856, and Tom's lifestyle began to resemble that of a recluse about that time.

While no evidence exists that at this point in his life he even continued his affiliation with local or state militia organizations, Tom Worthington did remain ever the faithful West Point graduate. He corresponded regularly during the 1850s with academy officials attempting to maintain a roster of cadets, their whereabouts, and their exploits. In his letters to West Point, Worthington seems genuinely interested in keeping up with fellow cadets and with making sure the academy does not forget him. He was even concerned, more than 20 years after his graduation, that his scores had been properly recorded.

> I hope I may regularly receive your [West Point's] merit roll and I would be much obliged to you if I could find my standing in the last year's courses of 1827 including French — I never knew what it was and I was called away after a brief examination alone — on the 16th June to my father's death bed [Worthington 8 Feb. 1850].

Although he indicated that he was "not quite clear of the botheration of lawsuits," Tom Worthington's financial situation appears to have stabilized toward the latter part of the 1850s. His personal correspondence contained none of the dire predictions of financial ruin present in his previous writings; in fact, he indicated that he was "better off than ever before and thankful to the omnipotence that things are not much worse with me than they are" (Worthington 25 Apr. 1856). Yet despite his improving business situation, Tom often remained on less than cordial terms with the remainder of the family. After James Worthington's wife, Julia, died in 1856, Tom was chastised for distancing himself from the family's grief. Another sister, Margaret, had written him a "savage letter" railing against his insensitivity and failure to answer one of Julia's letters in the days before she died. Rather than responding with compassion or contrition, Tom wrote to another sister, Ellen, in April 1856, "She [Julia] lived ten years longer than I ever expected" (Worthington 25 Apr. 1856) — a reply not crafted to endear himself to his siblings.

So Tom Worthington, financially on his feet and working his land and mill in Hocking County, effectively closed himself off from the remaining members of his family. This self-imposed isolation would last until the end of the decade when war drums would once again stir Tom's martial spirit.

PART II

CHAPTER FOUR

To Punish Insurrection

"MY LIFE ... HAS BEEN A BLANK"

During the late 1850s Tom Worthington moved from the mill complex near Logan, Ohio, in Hocking County to the village of Morrow in Warren County, Ohio. He made his home at "Yamoyden" with his sister Margaret (Maggie) and her husband, Edward Deering Mansfield, on their property along the Little Miami River. A rich, fertile area, Warren County soil allowed Tom to continue working in agriculture. But while he had finally rejoined part of the family and while he appears to have left his bankruptcy and business woes behind him in Logan, Worthington still considered his life as falling far short of the fame and excitement the Worthington name had engendered in the past. "My life for the last ten years has been a blank," Worthington wrote to George Cullum at West Point in 1860,[1] "and I have nothing to add to the last report except that I am now a farmer and grower of fruit trees in this county" (Worthington 29 Feb. 1860). Worthington, now a man of 52 years, might have considered his life dull when he wrote that letter in 1860, but he was slightly more than a year from encountering the defining moment of his life and the lives of many of his contemporaries.

During the rush toward sectional confrontation in the fall and winter of 1860, the people of Ohio were far from united in their view of how the Union should respond to South Carolina and the states likely to follow it into secession. But when Fort Sumter came under fire from the Confederate States of America on April 12, 1861, northerners and southerners alike who had sought to avoid war saw their hopes rapidly fading.

> Over that bitter weekend Northerners recast their pattern of thinking, abandoned the pathetic hope that compromises and evasions might do for a few more years, and ended the confusion and disunity of the preceding months with a wholehearted response to Lincoln's call for volunteers [Roseboom 379–380].

Among those responding to that call was Tom Worthington who "threw aside pruning knife and spade," "called meetings by printed bills over the whole county," and organized a company of volunteers from Warren County (Worthington *Brief History* 1). Memories of his indignation at being underutilized in the Mexican War and the financial setbacks he suffered in raising the Hocking County company were overshadowed by the patriotism running through Ohio. In an attempt to further "his advancement in the Army,"[2] Worthington started for Washington on April 15, but he stopped in Cincinnati en route. Worthington would write after the war that he was "detained by an urgent request from the citizens to publish a manual of Infantry Tactics, as there were none to be had" (Worthington *Brief History* 1). Tom seized this opportunity to emerge from a life that he admitted had been "a blank" for the past ten years and immediately set about to write and publish a drill manual for use by the many volunteer forces then rushing to enlist in various companies and regiments throughout Ohio. Since no publisher was willing to risk money on such a venture, Worthington fronted the money for publication himself in what he called "the duty of a West Point graduate educated by the government for such emergencies" (Worthington *Brief History* 1). Perhaps he realized that the Civil War would be his final opportunity to meet the expectations of the Worthington family and achieve the greatness for which he believed himself destined. He launched immediately into action, contacting Applegate & Company, Number 41, Main Street, Cincinnati, and contracting with them to publish *The Volunteer's Manual, No. 1*.[3] The drill manual was a monumental undertaking, which Worthington "compiled from U.S. Standard Authorities" and produced with the help of Major Sidney Burbank, Lieutenant P. T. Swaine, and Captain R. W. Johnson of the regular Army. But the opening page leaves no doubt who is the primary author of the document: "T. Worthington, A Graduate of West Point, and Late Gen. 2nd B[rigade], 7th D[ivision], O[hio] M[ilitia]." The manual was issued in two volumes, with the second, *The School of the Company*,

Four. To Punish Insurrection 51

to follow "in a few days" (Worthington *Volunteer's No. 1* 2); and, indeed, Worthington published *The School of the Company* in May. In the preface to the second volume, where Worthington is the only author listed, he wrote:

> The idea for dividing the *Tactics* [into two volumes] occurred to me nearly twenty years ago, but the law for militia musters being repealed in 1845 or '46, and being deeply engaged in business, the whole matter passed from my attention till national affairs assumed their threatening aspect last winter" [Worthington *Volunteer's No. 2* iv].

Worthington had apparently conceived the idea of breaking Hardee's *Tactics* into "three or four" separate volumes in February 1861, but he indicates that his entire library with the exception of a couple of books was destroyed by fire (Worthington *Volunteer's No. 2* iv). He believed that by issuing the *Tactics* in parts,[4] the "orderly sergeants" could focus only on what they needed; giving them the entire volume tended to distract their attention, lose time, and "discourage them from an attempt at a thorough mastery of the drill." Hardee's *Tactics* at the time cost approximately $1.50 to $2.50, more, Worthington believed, "than most volunteers [were] willing to afford." His version, he claimed after the war, cost "but one-third that of the official [Hardee's] copies" (*Volunteer's No. 2* iv). Worthington was not pleased with the way Ohio soldiers had been mustered and, in his opinion, haphazardly trained. He blamed some of the inefficiency on the fact that militias did not organize and train "in every ward and township" as they had prior to 1845. He believed that all able-bodied men "from sixteen to sixty" should be enrolled in the militia. Worthington never hesitated to criticize inefficient leadership and generally believed he knew a better way to do business. But his observations about the value of a well-organized and constantly trained militia would prove true not only in the Civil War but in future conflicts as well. Tom Worthington's insistence upon solid, deliberate training and preparation according to established tactics and procedures reveals his West Point experiences. But his unwavering notion that he knew the "right" way things were to be done would within a year bring him afoul of his leadership. Still, the crusty old colonel had a more realistic grasp of the preparations needed for neophyte soldiers and the likely horror of the struggle to come than many of his contemporaries:

> If there is war with the South, it will be a *war of giants*, for which we should be prepared. They are ruled by a frenzy. To this we should oppose calmness and discipline, only to be attended by

industry and efficient perseverance [Worthington *Volunteer's No. 2* iv].

Playing heavily upon his West Point experience and the connections he had maintained to the institution over the years, Worthington had his manual read and approved by other graduates who, he stated, "most cheerfully recommend it to the Volunteers of the Union as a correct, cheap, and convenient assistant in that Military Instruction so essential in the present extremity of our national affairs" (Worthington *Volunteer's No. 1* 1). Worthington went directly to Cincinnati and published the manual with his own funds because he found that although "patriotic devotion to the Union" was abundant in the city, "organization and instruction seemed an immediate necessity" (Worthington *Volunteer's No. 1* v). The manual was "intended more especially for the Home Guards of Cincinnati," but Worthington clearly saw the need to act fast and provide such instruction among the many companies being raised throughout the state to "crush treason ere its terrible fruits of bloodshed and disunion [could] attain maturity" (Worthington *Volunteer's No. 1* 6).[5] He dedicated the first volume "to the Christian and the Soldier, Robert Anderson, an Old Roommate and Benefactor at the U.S. Military Academy" (Worthington *Volunteer's No. 1* iii).

Worthington and the people of Cincinnati had good cause for speedy action. By the morning of April 18, some 20 of the independent companies throughout the state had already been organized into two Ohio regiments (Roseboom 383). The fact that many of them lacked uniforms or equipment did not weaken their intent to defend their sovereign state against secessionist invaders. Thus, Ohio Governor Dennison and his legislative body had the considerable challenge of letting contracts for services and outfitting the thousands of men rushing to volunteer for service. The capital at Columbus was awash with recruits spilling over from nearby Camp Jackson (later called Camp Chase) four miles west of the city, so Governor William Dennison established Camp Dennison near Miamiville on the little Miami Railroad north of Cincinnati. The first regiments to occupy Camp Dennison found that

> there was no tent or hut, and not even a board of which to make a shelter — nothing but corn fields and wheat fields. There were no shade trees, not as much as a hickory sprout in a fence corner [Bogan 71].

As new units arrived on a daily basis, many of them trained without weapons to get a head start on learning drill movements in anticipation of the arrival of arms.

Worthington lived only a short distance away in Morrow, and when the supply of drill manuals had been exhausted, he believed that the situation called not only for him to create his *Volunteer's Manual* to bring order out of chaos but for his personal presence as well. Worthington must have been basking in the limelight. Truly the man of the hour, at least in his own mind, no challenge to successfully raising an army was too great for Worthington to offer assistance. When the adequacy of the water supply at Camp Dennison became critical due to the ever-increasing numbers of men, Worthington spent his own money and called upon his experience and his family's knowledge of canals to devise a water supply system to support the camp. He suggested often after the war that he was "accidentally" involved in a contract for the water supply at Dennison, but the idea that Worthington would "accidentally" get involved in anything seems to run counter to his personality. Tom might have seen an entrepreneurial opportunity. He later claimed that his quick action, which included putting up his own money, "prevented an expense to the government of more than $20,000"— money that Worthington would spend the rest of his life trying to recover from the government. But his patriotic, if not business-motivated, decision cost him something more important than money. He had to delay his trip to Washington, where he hoped to influence his assignment within the Army (Worthington *Brief History* 2).

Since Cincinnati was far from being a secure city and southern Ohio far from offering a secure border, Worthington and men like him had ample reason for concern that forces be organized and trained quickly. The state of Kentucky's response to the disintegrating Union was anything but certain; and with prosouthern sentiment alive and well within the city itself, Worthington's overtures of assistance appear to have been well received. Whitelaw Reid writes, "The position of the state between foreign territory on the north, and four hundred miles of slave territory on the south, caused immediate apprehension for her safety" (Reid, *Ohio*, Vol. 1, 370–371). "The sympathies of Cincinnati were strongly with the South," writes Anna McAllister, since many of the leading families of the city were related to their slaveholding neighbors in Kentucky:

> The position of the Queen City, situated as it was on the Ohio River ... was particularly critical. Its location and immense wealth invited attack and exposed it to greater danger than any other large city in the North [McAllister 307].

Perhaps because of his lack of success during mobilization for the Mexican War, Tom Worthington would not again depend upon raising a

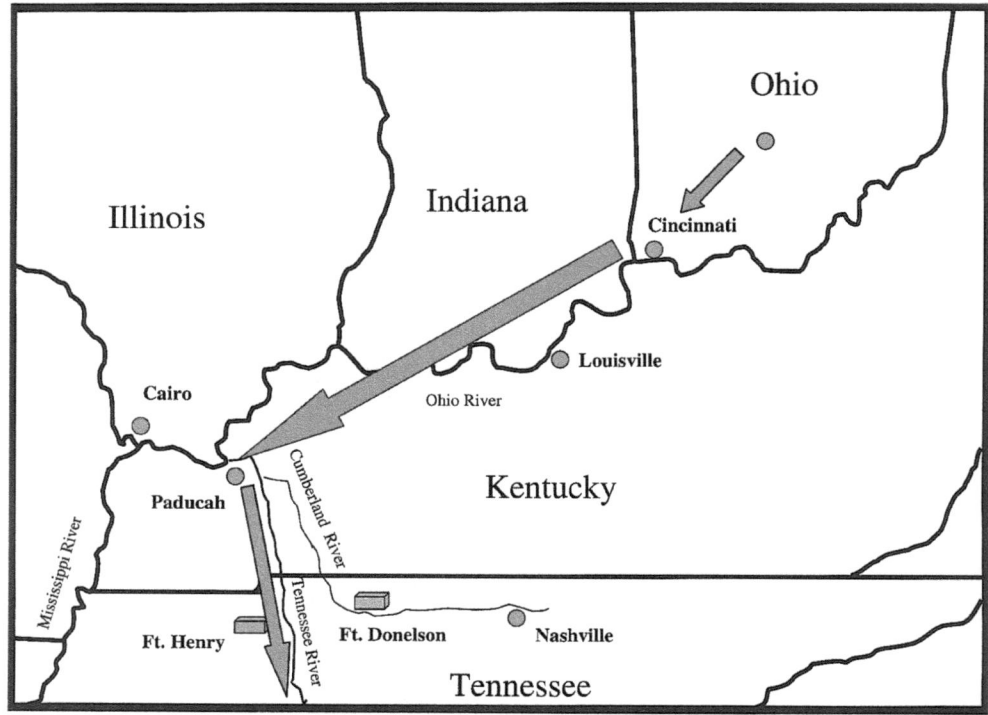

MAP 4.1 Deployment of Colonel Tom Worthington's 46th Ohio Volunteer Infantry.

company of volunteers and running for election as colonel as the sole means of attaining the command position he believed he deserved. When, on July 22, President Lincoln responded to the Federal disaster at Bull Run by calling for 500,000 volunteers for three years, Worthington saw his opportunity (Reid, *Ohio*, Vol. 1, 378). In an action reminiscent of his offer of services to the regular Army prior to the Mexican War, Worthington traveled to Washington to lobby in person for authorization to raise his own regiment. Unlike the outcome of his previous offer of service, Worthington received on July 29, 1861, authorization from Secretary of War Simon Cameron to raise a regiment of volunteers for the government. The fact that Worthington did not go through Governor Dennison for his authorization reflects the residual political struggle that he believed had so hampered his potential during the Mexican War. Whether Worthington called in some favors on behalf of the family name and his father's reputation in Washington or whether he relied on West Point connections for a favor remains uncertain. But the fact that he chose to go outside the normal channels to obtain a commission created friction in Ohio. Concerning the reaction he faced upon his return from Washington, Worthington wrote that because his "course of proceeding to get into the service was irregular," he "met with little active assistance and some positive opposition from the Executive of Ohio [Gov. Dennison]" (McCormick 29). Even without the "active assistance" of Governor Dennison, Worthington was hardly alone in his patriotic fervor and desire to serve the Union. By the close of 1861, Dennison would report that 77,845 soldiers had signed up for a three-year hitch to fight against the Confederacy (Reid, *Ohio*, Vol. 1, 378).

46TH OHIO VOLUNTEER INFANTRY DEPLOYS

From August 1861 through February 1862, Thomas Worthington raised and trained the 46th Ohio Volunteer Infantry, composed mainly of men from Franklin, Van Wert, Fairfield, and Licking counties. The command structure of the 46th Ohio consisted of T. Worthington, colonel, Warren County; C. C. Walcutt, lieutenant colonel, Franklin County; William Smith, major, Van Wert County; Jack Neil, adjutant, Franklin County; E. Giesy, quartermaster, Fairfield County; and J. B. Foster, sergeant major, Franklin County.

Work began at Camp Lyon in Worthington, Ohio, where Worthington drilled his men in the movements he had published in *The Volunteer's Manual*. He was officially mustered into the 46th as a lieutenant colonel "to fill an original vacancy" on October 23, 1861, to serve a period of three years. He was appointed colonel on January 28, 1862, "to fill an original vacancy," indicating that he was, indeed, the first colonel of the regiment (*Military Records* 4). From Camp Lyon on the Olentangy River, Worthington and his 46th Ohio moved to Camp Chase, just west of Columbus, where they remained until February 18. When the 46th Ohio, along with a dozen other regiments, received orders on February 18 to report to General William T. Sherman at Paducah, Kentucky, Worthington immediately fired off a letter of introduction to none other than Sherman's boss, Major General Henry W. Halleck, commanding the Military Department in St. Louis, Missouri. It is often the case that, with impending military orders, rumor is the vanguard of reality, so Worthington probably knew to whom he was about to be assigned even before the official word arrived. The language of his letter implies such foreknowledge and seems to represent his effort to influence the final decision as to the division commander to which he would be assigned:

Feb 18th 1862

Dear Sir

    I am a graduate of 1827, 6th and 7th in Engineering and Artillery as on the last   course — twenty years in the Ohio Militia (Brigadier since 1834) and a volunteer in the Mexican War — now Col. 46th Regt OVI and ordered to Paducah and to report thence to you. My appt. date July 29, 1861.

    I am, as far as I know, an "older not a better soldier" than any man in your dept. and a higher graduate, Buford and Sherman, excepted. Gen. [Ormsby M.] Mitchell is my *Military Friend* and if with the welfare of the service I should prefer to be in his division. I am an old bachelor of 54, very homely in all my ways, requiring but half a soldier's ration for my subsistence, and I am by habit actively employed 16 hours or over in my 24. The war is, I hope soon[?] over, but I may yet offer and hope that you may try me. I have a regt well drilled and officered for militia, which has supposed much from the men — the numbers not having over 850 effective men about 100 being absent or [on] sick leave and recruiting service. I am perfectly willing to serve wherever and under whomever ordered, and trusting you will find[?] a[?] proper place.

Major Gen. Halleck
  St. Louis.

                                  T. Worthington
                                  Col. 46th OVI
                        [Military Service Records 29]

    The 46th Ohio disembarked from Camp Chase at 3:00 P.M., February 18, on the train for Cincinnati, where they loaded aboard two steamers. Tom's older sister, 61-year-old Sarah Worthington King Peter,[6] lived in Cincinnati. Married to Rufus Peter, a man of considerable means, Sarah spent her time organizing and working as a nurse for several Catholic relief organizations, such as the Good Shepherd Sisters, the Sisters of Mercy, and the Sisters of Charity. On the night Tom entered Cincinnati, Sarah attempted to find him. "I went down to the boats," she wrote, "and searched half an hour through the throng for him but in vain" (Sarah Worthington, 19 Feb. 1862). She was rather annoyed that he had not come by her house to visit, but it is doubtful that Tom had time for anything other than looking after his men. Worthington and his 46th Ohio Infantry spent the next three nights and two days en route down the Ohio River. The boats were small and the troops crowded, but they seemed to enjoy the novelty of it all. A man in the 48th Ohio described a scene likely mirrored by Worthington's men, indicating that when they came out on deck in the morning, "The sun rose beautifully, but the air was cold.... we spread out our blankets and lay down in the sun to enjoy our free ride" (Bering and Montgomery, 1).

They docked at Paducah, Kentucky, on Thursday night, February 20,[7] and Worthington found Sherman's headquarters and reported to him. On the following Saturday morning, the remainder of the 46th Ohio went ashore to its campground, located about one mile down river from Paducah on "a new piece of ground, on a high bluff" that afforded them "a fine view of the Ohio River" (Zook 2).[8] Below them, the soldiers could see some 30 or more steamboats swarming about the landing at Paducah, and they must have surely realized that the thousands of troops arriving and disembarking indicated a major offensive brewing. Over the next few days, Colonel Tom Worthington had his men improve their camp amid a steady, drenching rain. The men wrote letters home, evaluated the usual gossip and false rumors of battles won or lost around the country, and took their turn on picket duty. It was here at Paducah that some of Worthington's men saw their first dead soldier. Private Christian Zook of Company F, 46th Ohio Infantry, described the reaction of the men:

> Some of our boys, while hunting along the river for boards [to floor their tents], found a dead man. He was a soldier and it is supposed that he got drunk and was drowned or died. They found over 50 dollars in money in his pocket and gave it to the Col [Worthington]. He may have been poisoned and perhaps lying there several weeks. I believe they buried him [Zook 6–7].

Camped adjacent to Worthington's regiment was the 40th Illinois Infantry under the command of Colonel Stephen D. Hicks. Hicks, during the initial encampment at Paducah, commanded the brigade consisting of his own 40th Illinois Infantry, Worthington's 46th Ohio, and Morton's Indiana Battery of Light Artillery.[9] Worthington soon determined that Hicks was not a soldier worthy to be his peer, much less his commander. Hicks was "an old Illinois militia officer, a benevolent and brave man, but proud and obstinate, as he was ignorant of and opposed to strict military discipline" (Worthington *Report* 11).[10] Where Worthington imposed strict West Point–style discipline on his raw troops, Hicks appears to have done just the opposite. Hicks "professed great contempt for regular officers and army regulations," according to Worthington, and paid little attention to the overall discipline of his men while encamped next to Worthington's regiment at Paducah. Upon visiting the 46th Ohio pickets, Worthington noticed that Hicks' men nearby were often sitting in small groups, arms stacked, clustered around fires, and playing cards—sometimes with Hicks himself looking on. Forsaking his father's advice about meddling in the affairs of others, Worthington brought up the behavior to Hicks, who dismissed Tom as being too hard on his own men and behaving like a "stiff and stately regular." When he reported Hicks behavior to Sherman, Worthington's concerns were dismissed, and he was ordered to allow Hicks to "proceed in the regularly irregular militia routine, or no routine at all" (Worthington *Report* 12). Sherman's unwillingness to hold Hicks and his regiment to a better standard of discipline seems curious considering: (a) his disastrous experience at Bull Run with volunteers and his subsequent distrust of them; (b) his observation while in Kentucky in November 1861 regarding the poor readiness of volunteer units; and (c) his declaration that he would "never allow [himself] to be in command" until he could "see daylight ahead" with reference to drill and discipline (Thorndike 135).

Hicks' lack of military discipline, while bothersome to Worthington, was likely not half as troubling as the fact that Hicks had command of the brigade over him. In fact, Worthington suggested that Sherman had "a purpose of his own" in subordinating the 46th Ohio and its commander under a man like Hicks—a man "at war ... with all regular officers and with strict discipline." So Worthington gave up his efforts to reform Hicks' military discipline and forbade his own men "on pain of imminent death or disgrace ... from indulging on picket duty in such agreeable but dangerous and most unmilitary practices." In a prophetic comment, he suggested that troops suffering under such lack of discipline as Hicks' demonstrated were easily "surprised ... [their] posts lost, and ... killed and captured in the early period of the war" (Worthington *Report* 12). While Worthington and his men dutifully endured the mundane drudgery of daily camp life, the Union high command was conceiving a major offensive movement against the Confederacy. And if Worthington's life had, as he claimed, "been a blank" for the past ten years, that emptiness was about to be filled in.

At Paducah where Worthington's men awaited their next orders, Major General William Tecumseh Sherman was running what in modern terms would be called a "movement control center." In his own words, he was "busy sending boats in every direction" in answer to orders from General Halleck in St. Louis, General Grant at Fort Henry, and General Buell in Nashville. But Sherman was also "organizing out of the new troops arriving at Paducah a division" for himself—a division he had been promised by General Halleck—in the event that he got the opportunity to "take the field" (Sherman 253). That Halleck would even promise Sherman a division to command demonstrates the patronage of Major General Ulysses S. Grant.[11] For "Sherman's life up to 1861," writes T. Harry Williams in *McClellan, Sherman and Grant*, "was a record of small successes, large failures, and frustrated ambitions" (45). Since Sherman is the man with whom Worthington would enter into a bitter military association and a lifelong battle for his honor, an important part of comprehending Worthington's personal war with Sherman rests in understanding Sherman himself, particularly the events leading up to his command at the Battle of Shiloh.

"CERTAINLY SHERMAN ... ACTED INSANE"

By the time Sherman surfaced in Paducah, Kentucky, in February 1862, both his civilian and military careers had already shown failure and self-doubt.[12] Born in Ohio on February 8, 1820, William Tecumseh Sherman had been raised by Senator Thomas Ewing after the boy's father died at age nine. Like Tom Worthington, Sherman leveraged his family influence to gain an appointment to West Point, where, in 1840, he graduated sixth in his class. Like Worthington, he served in the Mexican War and then returned to civilian life, where he struggled for success before the outbreak of the Civil War. Trying his hand at banking and law, Sherman drifted to California and Kansas during the 1850s, but he failed at both enterprises (*Civil War Homepage*; Marszalek 4). At the time the war began, he had found some limited success as superintendent of a military academy, which would later become Louisiana State University. Leaving the South upon Louisiana's secession, Sherman, nicknamed "Cump" by his friends, went to St. Louis and took the position of head of a streetcar company. That position would not last long, for Sherman, like Worthington, answered the clarion call and joined the Union Army. He was appointed colonel of the 13th Infantry on May 14, 1861.

Sherman's first exposure to battle came in July 1861 when the 2nd and 3rd divisions of the Union Army at Bull Run had been staggered by the Confederates and were streaming from the battlefield in a near rout. Having been given command of a brigade of volunteer troops, he led them against the enemy at Bull Run. Already a critic of volunteer troops, their hesitancy and disorder in battle at Bull Run reinforced his disdain for the citizen-soldier. Following the Union debacle at Bull Run, then–Colonel Sherman, who had personally fought well in the engagement, came to believe the Union Army was on the brink of destruction. Witnessing the Federals "degenerate into an armed mob" frightened him and further undermined his confidence in volunteer units recruited to oppose secession. In Washington briefly, Sherman was promoted to brigadier general by mid–August and ordered to serve as deputy commander of the

Photograph 4.1 Major General William Tecumseh Sherman, Tom Worthington's commander at Shiloh and his bitter enemy throughout the remainder of his life (Library of Congress).

Department of the Cumberland in Kentucky and Tennessee. He would be second in command to the man to whom Tom Worthington had dedicated his *Volunteer's Manual*— Robert Anderson, the hero of Fort Sumter. "Sherman was happy to leave the chaos of Washington," writes John F. Marszalek in his biography, *Sherman: A Soldier's Passion for Order*, "but when [Sherman] and Anderson later met with Lincoln, he [Sherman] exacted a promise that he would never be asked to command again" (156).

While in Kentucky in the fall of 1861, Sherman gained a reputation for being (a) an alarmist who constantly overestimated the enemy threat, and (b) a pessimist without peer with regard to the fate of the Union Army stationed there. Constantly afraid that spies were running rampant within his camps and suspicious (not without cause) of newspaper reporters, Sherman worked himself into a near frenzy with dire predictions of massive Confederate invasions and the inevitability of his small force being overwhelmed. Sherman's nervousness and pessimism only increased when, on October 8, Robert Anderson resigned, forcing Sherman to take command against his stated wishes. He clamored for more troops to defend Kentucky, claimed "inaccurately that he was outnumbered three to one," and worried himself to "the verge of nervous exhaustion" (Marszalek 162).

> Sherman's eccentric behavior, long whispered about, now became a major topic of open conversation. Sherman stayed up until 3 a.m. most nights at the telegraph office waiting for dispatches, and when it closed, he paced the corridor leading to his hotel room until dawn. He would tell anyone who would listen his catalog of worries.... Tennessee Senator Andrew Johnson thought Sherman was "much of the time incapacitated for command." The assistant secretary of war, Thomas W. Scott, bluntly pronounced what many others had been thinking for some time: "Sherman's gone in the head, he's luny [sic]" [Marszalek 163].

Part of Sherman's seeming paranoia about Confederate troop strength, his nervousness, and his self-admitted "gloomy view of affairs" within the Union Army came from what was not a totally inaccurate assessment of the poor condition of training and equipment present in many of the volunteer units. While still in Kentucky he wrote in a letter to his brother, Senator John Sherman, in November 1861:

> Troops come here from Wisconsin and Minnesota without arms and receive such as we have here for the first time, and I cannot but look upon it as absolutely sacrificing them. I see no hope for them in their present raw and undisciplined condition, and some terrible disaster is inevitable [Thorndike 135].

PHOTOGRAPH *4.2* Major General Henry Halleck gave Sherman another chance at military success (Library of Congress).

That disaster would come at Pittsburg Landing in April of the following year, and Sherman, who in the same letter quoted above declared that he would "never allow [himself] to be in command" until the readiness issue was resolved, would, indeed, be in command.

On November 13, Don Carlos Buell was named to replace Sherman in Kentucky, and Sherman was ordered to report to General Halleck in St. Louis. But under Halleck, Sherman fared little better. Sent by Halleck to inspect troop dispositions in Missouri, he ended up being recalled by his commander for overstepping his authority and for what Halleck considered serious behavioral problems.[13] Before long the newspapers had picked up the story of Sherman's erratic behavior and had begun circulating the charge that he was insane. "Mad Billy" they called him, suggesting in no uncertain terms that soldiers under his command might have been in more danger from their commander than from the enemy. During his command in Kentucky and his work for Halleck in Missouri, Sherman's behavior had disturbed not only his commander but also his peers, his wife, his brother, and Sherman himself. The physician who examined him diagnosed his condition as "one of such nervousness that he was unfit for command" (Welsh 301). Despite considerable evidence to the contrary, many historians continue to claim, as does Marszalek, that Sherman "was far from crazy" (163).

In a clinical sense, it would be extremely difficult for a twentieth-century historian, not privy to substantiating medical records, to diagnose a nineteenth-century man as "insane." The word *insane* denotes a "consistent mental disorder or derangement," and while Sherman might have demonstrated symptoms of insanity during periods of his life, the symptoms did not appear consistently throughout his life (*American Heritage Dictionary* 664). Perhaps more descriptive of Sherman's behavior might be the term *lunacy*, a word that denotes derangement relieved intermittently by periods of clearmindedness. Yet even that term is a bit strong, for it suggests that Sherman's behavior was erratic and disturbing more often than it was not. He did not demonstrate *periods* of clearmindedness; rather, he exhibited *periods* of aberrant, melancholic, militarily inadequate behavior. Whether the fruit of a family history replete with mental disturbance or the result of Sherman's own particular physical and mental makeup, his behavior demonstrates that he was, on various occasions, at a minimum, impaired in his military judgment. If, however, Sherman was not technically and medically insane, he was sometimes not far from it. Historians who show in Sherman's behavior all manner of mental instability, yet stubbornly and incredibly refuse to conclude that he was possibly insane, demonstrate a healthy capacity to ignore the elephant in the living room.

Perhaps they are afraid to admit he lost his mind, even temporarily, for fear of undermining his combat accomplishments later in the war. But if a man can lose control of his reasoning and judgment, then regain it and succeed as a combat leader, is he not all the more to be admired? Another factor influencing those who would continue to argue that Sherman was not mad is the fact that Sherman was, for most of his career, quite successful. Thus, the conclusion that, if he were successful, he must not have been insane prevails. History is replete with characters who were both quite successful and quite insane. It is only when a military leader loses, or fails in his mission, that history seems willing to label him insane.

So Sherman was assigned to what amounted to a logistics position in charge of marshaling Union troops arriving at Paducah, Kentucky. And when he came under the command of Ulysses S. Grant, his currency within the Union Army command structure began to regain some of its value. In Grant's *Personal Memoirs*, he commends Sherman for keeping him readily supplied during this time and for constantly encouraging him. As the relationship between the two men grew, it only seemed natural that Sherman's newly organized division would be assigned to Grant. And though it was Halleck who sent Sherman to Paducah, it was Grant who ignored the reports of Sherman's madness and allowed him the chance at command — a debt Sherman would repay many times through his unwavering loyalty. "General Grant," Sherman once said, "is a great general. I know him well. He stood by me when I was crazy and I stood by him when he was drunk; and now, sir, we stand by each other always" (Williams 46). Sherman's loyalty, Worthington would later claim, transcended telling the truth.

Movement up the Tennessee River

By February 1862, Major General Grant had won two important victories, at Fort Henry and Fort Donelson, which opened a causeway into the heart of Tennessee, Mississippi, and Alabama via the Tennessee River. Anxious that those victories be rapidly followed up with an offensive movement up the Tennessee River, General Halleck determined that the forces gathering at Paducah, among them Worthington and the 46th Ohio, should provide the invasion force for Grant's operation. "The main object of this expedition," Halleck wrote on March 1, 1862, "will be to destroy the railroad-bridge over Bear Creek, near Eastport, Mississippi; and also the railroad connections at Corinth, Jackson, and Humboldt" (Sherman 252). Halleck expressly told Grant to "avoid any general engagements with strong forces" and stated that "it will be better to retreat than to risk a general battle" (Sherman 252). He also suggested that Major General C. F. Smith "or some very discreet officer" should command the expedition. Three days later, Halleck did more than suggest. He chastised Grant for not responding to his earlier messages, ordered him to place Major General Smith in command of the expedition up the Tennessee, and told Grant to remain at Fort Henry.

The difficulties between Colonel Tom Worthington and his division commander, Sherman, began before the first steamer loaded with troops ever left Paducah. In his memoirs, Sherman wrote:

> Among my colonels I had a strange character — Thomas Worthington, colonel of the Forty-sixth Ohio. He was a graduate of West Point, of the class of 1827; was, therefore, older than General Halleck, General Grant, or myself, and claimed to know more of war than all of us put together [254].

Within days of being marshaled into Sherman's division at Paducah, Worthington was already questioning and second-guessing some of the military decisions of the officers in the theater before him. Tom was "surprised to hear that Florence [Alabama], at the foot of the muscle shoals ... had not been occupied immediately after the capture of Fort Henry" (Worthington *Report* 4). He suggested to General Sherman that he and the 46th be sent there to "hold the place" and prevent the anticipated junction of General Albert Sidney Johnston's and General Leonidas K. Polk's Confederate forces. Sherman nixed the colonel's idea, but clearly sensing friction already occurring in their relationship, he offered to reassign Worthington's regiment to the Army of the Mississippi under General John Pope. Worthington declined the offer, as he wrote after the war, so as not to miss what he expected to be "the main battle-ground in the Southwest" (Worthington *Report* 4). As further evidence of the immediate friction between the two men, Worthington suggested to Sherman that his regiment be attached to General Ormsby M. Mitchell,[14] then operating near Nashville on the Cumberland River. Mitchell was "an old West Point school-mate" with whom Worthington had "a previous arrangement," and it was Mitchell to whom he had asked to be assigned in his letter to Halleck. Worthington's arrangement, or gentleman's agreement with Mitchell, carried no weight with Sherman, who refused the request. Instead, Sherman suggested that Worthington might like to remain in Paducah and assume command of Fort Anderson on the river. Worthington refused that offer for fear of being "kept ... out of the coming campaign," thus sealing the uneasy union between Tom Worthington and William T. Sherman.

Orders finally arrived on March 6 for the army at Paducah to begin the journey up the Tennessee River toward the objectives General Halleck had outlined. Special Order Number 74 from General Sherman's headquarters, District of Cairo, Paducah, Kentucky, read as follows:

> The following regiments will embark to-day for Savannah, Tennessee River, and there report to Major-General Smith.
>
> The commanding officers will see that their regiments have eight hundred rounds of ammunition and all the means of transportation on hand. Baggage must be reduced to the minimum, and the quartermaster, Captain Pearse, will obtain a house in which to deposit all baggage left behind.
>
> Ohio 46th, Colonel Worthington; Ohio 48th, Colonel Sullivan; Illinois 40th, Colonel Hicks; Ohio 53rd, Colonel Appler; Ohio 72nd, Colonel Buckland.
>
> The quartermaster will at once provide the transportation necessary.
>
> By order of Brigadier-General W. T. Sherman.
>
> F. H. Hammond, A.A.G. [Worthington *Report* 5].

Worthington, ever in search of flaws in his leaders' actions and decisions, found one in this order. He was disturbed by the fact that Sherman had made no provision to leave the "hundreds" of sick men behind at Paducah. With hospitals and proper care available at Paducah, Worthington believed:

> There was no possible excuse for the extravagance, impolicy, and inhumanity of hauling sick men to crowded boats, where to properly care for them was impossible.... All weak and ailing men should ... have been left behind [Worthington *Report* 5].

Since disease was the constant companion of every Civil War unit, it does seem rather odd that Sherman did not make some provision for garrisoning the sick men from various units and then transporting them to join the advancing body upon their recovery. One of the young captains in Colonel Crofts Wright's 13th Missouri Volunteers, Sherman's division, indicated in a letter to his colonel that as late as January he "found a large proportion [of his men] complaining of sickness and few capable of doing severe duty." Soon after departing Missouri for Paducah the unit had "[left] several behind in [the] hospital which numbers had been constantly increased" (Richards 2). Leaving troops who were too incapacitated for duty behind in the hospital seems to have been a common approach when marshaling for movement to the field, but Sherman chose to do otherwise.

Several boats loaded with troops had left on March 6. Worthington managed to gather ten days' additional stores and some shelled corn for his mules and horses, but he found only 30 rounds of ammunition per man for his .54-caliber muskets, and he didn't scare that up until 11:00 P.M. on the night of the 6th. Worthington was not alone in his armament difficulties, for the commander of the 48th Ohio also complained of having an insufficient supply of "worthless muskets." They had received Austrian rifles on March 5 (Bering and Montgomery 1).

The 53rd Ohio, under command of Colonel Jesse J. Appler, did not receive its arms at Paducah until March 7, the day they left for Savannah. The regiment had not had so much as a battalion drill when it went to the field (Dawes 1).

Sometime around midnight on March 6, Worthington had a run-in with Sherman. It seems that Sherman chastised Worthington for "being slack in his departure from Paducah" (Worthington *Report* 5). Worthington protested that he had to take extra time looking for provisions and ammunition, which his division commander had failed to supply. But find them he did, and his boat, the steamer *Adams*, finally left at 3:00 A.M. on the morning of March 7 (Zook 11).

The full convoy, including those that left on the 6th, consisted of 82 steamers and must have presented an imposing sight to the southern citizens who observed them steaming upriver (Bering and Montgomery 2). The convoy of steamers, in which the *Adams* was near the end, moved up the high river toward Fort Henry in what Division Commander Sherman called "splendid order." Private Zook of the 46th offered a wide-eyed, young man's view of the movement. "There were a good many sights to see as we came up the river, we all ways laid low over night [and] ... we passed Fort Henry the first day" (14). Near Fort Henry, Sherman reported in person to General C. F. Smith, commander of the expedition per General Halleck's orders. Smith then ordered Sherman's division to continue upriver to "the remains of the burned railroad bridge to await the rendezvous of the rest of Smith's army" (Sherman 254).[15]

When Worthington and the 46th Ohio, aboard the *Adams*, reached Fort Henry the next day about noon, they found clustered along the bank many of the boats that had left the previous day. They were waiting to rendezvous per Smith's instruction. But at this point in the mission, scarcely a day out of Paducah, Worthington had other ideas as to how this river operation should be run, and never bashful about declaring those ideas, he took action. He discovered that Colonel Taylor's 5th Ohio Cavalry had been there a week awaiting orders, and he learned that one gunboat and a single transport (carrying about half the 40th Illinois) had continued upriver. While at Paducah Tom had heard rumors about mistreatment of Union sympathizers at Savannah, Tennessee, and also stories that the Confederates were contemplating a general draft "of all men fit to bear arms." It seemed an obvious conclusion to Worthington that he should proceed upriver to Savannah, perhaps gain some forage before the rest of the army arrived, and maybe even interdict the enemy efforts to conscript the good citizens of Savannah. With a gunboat already ahead of him and at least one troop transport already en route, Worthington must have felt his route upriver was reasonably secure. Thus, the *Adams* pressed upriver in advance of the rest of the division and the entire army. Tom would, in fact, have had the pilot continue the voyage even during darkness were the latter not worried about the enemy's masked batteries along the shore.

According to Sherman, Worthington became impatient at the delays en route and "did not keep his place in the column, but pushed on and reached Savannah a day before the rest of my division" (Sherman 254). What must the division commander, then aboard the steamer *Continental*, have thought, let alone uttered, when he saw the *Adams* continue upriver with the 46th Ohio while the remainder of his division docked at the remnants of the Danville Bridge waiting to join up with the rest of Smith's army? It is easy to envision the audacious Worthington taking the captain of the *Adams* aside and very directly ordering him "full steam ahead" as Sherman and the remainder of his troops halted along the shore. And it is equally easy to understand why Sherman would have been put out with Worthington for bolting from the convoy of steamers and presumptuously taking the lead of his division.

Worthington offered his own interpretation of his actions. "One of five regiments ordered to report to Gen. C. F. Smith at Savannah, Tennessee," Worthington wrote, "the 46th Ohio was the only regiment that promptly executed the order" (Worthington *Brief History* 2).

After halting for the night, the *Adams* continued about sunrise, stopped at Britt's Landing and took on oats for the stock, stopped at Clifton and some other small landings, and eventually reached Savannah at sunset on March 8. At Savannah, Worthington found that the steamer that had preceded him upriver had deposited about half the 40th Illinois under the command of Lieutenant Colonel James W. Booth. Ever the West Pointer, Worthington wrote after the war that he "took command, and threw out 120 men as pickets—also a patrol, which took up 40 to 50 stragglers of the 40th who, having imbibed while onboard their transport, were now liberating many of the local houses of valuables" (Worthington *Report* 3).[16] Worthington's quick action to protect the property of Savannah citizens was admirable, but his stunt of reaching Savannah a full day before Sherman and the remainder of the division and, for that matter, Smith's entire army, smacks of insubordination. At a minimum it would serve to embarrass Sherman — a man fighting the skeletons of his own previous bizarre behavior.

At some point in the days following Worthington's arrival at Savannah, a story circulated in the Ohio newspapers that the 46th had been captured at Savannah for "ignorantly going ahead of the fleet." Worthington in his writings after the war indicated that not only was the 46th not captured, but he cites his anticipatory action as having protected the 40th Illinois from just such a fate.

On Sunday, March 9, Worthington conducted a dress parade and during the afternoon even sent some of his officers upriver on the gunboat *Lexington* for the thrill of firing gunboat artillery inland in the vicinity of Pittsburg Landing. Worthington had an extremely convenient arrangement. He was commander in chief of the village of Savannah, host to a military parade, and protector of the Unionist citizens — all without having to answer to Sherman or C. F. Smith or any of the other officers who outranked him. He was an independent operator, and he clearly enjoyed himself in that role. He also indicated that upon learning from a local citizen named William H. Cherry that the Confederate Army would attempt to conscript able-bodied men in the vicinity, Worthington received the would-be conscripts to the safety of his troops, managing to enlist "forty or fifty" recruits into the 46th Ohio.

On Monday the 10th of March it rained. Lieutenant Colonel Booth had run out of supplies and requested that Worthington allow him to forage from the citizens of Savannah until the remainder of the army arrived. Worthington refused his request — an act later considered an insult by the 40th Illinois regimental commander, Colonel Hicks, who Worthington had already noted as martially incompetent while in Paducah. On the 11th, the steamer *Golden Gate* arrived as the lead of the army flotilla of troop transports, with the remainder of the boats landing about 2:00 P.M. Worthington had the 46th lined up along the bluff in parade formation to greet the arrivals. But if Worthington thought he would receive any praise for his initiative in reaching Savannah in advance of the army, he was deceiving himself. His early arrival was "anything but agreeable to General C. F. Smith and the general officers of the Army of the Tennessee" (Worthington *Report* 10). Sherman was livid:

> When I reached that place, I found that Worthington had landed his regiment, and was flying about giving orders, as though he

were commander-in-chief. I made him get back to his boat, and gave him to understand that he must thereafter keep his place [Sherman 254].

General C. F. Smith was furious with Worthington for the "presumption and insubordination of a Colonel of Volunteers" to precede the expedition "in command of a *regular officer* [emphasis added] of the Army of the United States" and a "Major General of volunteers" (Worthington *Report* 11). Worthington by no accident attributes Smith's ire to the volunteer-regular dichotomy, yet Worthington's advance arrival seems to have been a rather insubordinate act regardless of the officers' source of commission. Smith was so angry he would not even receive Worthington's report; instead, he chastised him for not going through the chain of command — brigade and division — in rendering his report. Worthington believed he had obeyed the spirit of Sherman's Special Order Number 74, which stated that the various regiments should proceed to Savannah and there "report to Major-General Smith." While he had obeyed the letter of the order, he had clearly chosen to ignore the intent of the order, specifically that the entire brigade would travel together to Savannah. That Worthington would find a loophole in Sherman's order and exploit it for the benefit of independent operation is not surprising, particularly given the fact that Worthington believed Sherman had "snubbed" him by chastising him for tardy departure from Paducah on the 6th.

On the 12th, Worthington attempted to respond to General Smith's rebuke and tender his report to Colonel Hicks, his brigade commander. Despite the fact that half of Hicks' 40th Illinois was in Savannah, Hicks had landed the other half of his regiment on the west side of the Tennessee River. Worthington, unable to obtain a boat to cross the river that morning and provide Hicks with his report, put the report in the hands of Sherman's adjutant, Captain Hammond, and went about his business of the day (i.e., gathering more corn aboard the *Adams* for his anticipated movement on Florence, Alabama). When his report had not arrived to Hicks by 1:00 P.M., Hicks had Worthington arrested. Perhaps Hicks held a grudge toward Worthington over Tom's refusal to allow the 40th Illinois to forage in Savannah prior to Hicks' arrival. Perhaps he, too, was angry at Worthington for beating the rest of the brigade and division up the river. Perhaps he was motivated by both issues. At any rate, Worthington was held under arrest until he pleaded his case to Sherman and obtained a release at 5:00 P.M. that afternoon. Hicks claimed in a letter that he only arrested Worthington with Sherman's approval, indicating that Sherman might have been playing the two men against each other. In his writings after the war, Worthington indicated that this incident, coupled with his advance arrival at Savannah, prompted reports back in Ohio that Worthington had been "degraded for misconduct and neglect of duty in preceeding the army without orders" (Worthington *Report* 12–13). One must wonder why, given the fact that half of Colonel Hicks' 40th Illinois reached Savannah even *before* Worthington, does neither Sherman's memoirs nor Grant's memoirs nor any official correspondence even hint at chastising Colonel Hicks or the men of the 40th Illinois for arriving in advance of the division.

Worthington says Sherman not only reprimanded him personally for his impetuous early arrival at Savannah, but he also "vented his rage" upon the "sick men" of the 46th Ohio. Claiming that Sherman was negligent and inhumane to have brought sick men on the deployment from Paducah, Worthington described yet another run-in with his division commander. Worthington had arranged for the sick men of the 46th to be housed in the home of a Confederate officer named Martin, gaining permission of the officer's brother to do so. But when the officer's wife complained to Sherman, the general confronted Worthington.

"Being in a room above the stairs about sunset" on the 12th of March, Worthington wrote, he heard the officer's wife loudly complaining outside about the men's presence in her home. Worthington ordered the sick men out of the house and back to the boat and went outside to find the woman berating Sherman for the presence of the men of the 46th Ohio. Reconstructing the conversation from Worthington's diary account, the encounter offers insight into the tone and demeanor of many confrontations between Worthington and Sherman.

> "What are those men doing in this house?" Sherman demanded.
> "They're sick men," Worthington replied. "I got permission from the owner's brother and I brought them here while the boat is being cleaned."
> "It is an outrage to put men in a house where there is a parcel of women." Sherman turned to some soldiers of a nearby Missouri regiment. "I want you to turn those men out of that house immediately!"
> "I've already ordered them out," Worthington countered. "They're going as fast they can." He clutched Sherman's arm. "Please be quiet. You can see for yourself that they're leaving."
> Ignoring Worthington, Sherman shouted to the Missourians. "Clear them out *now!*"

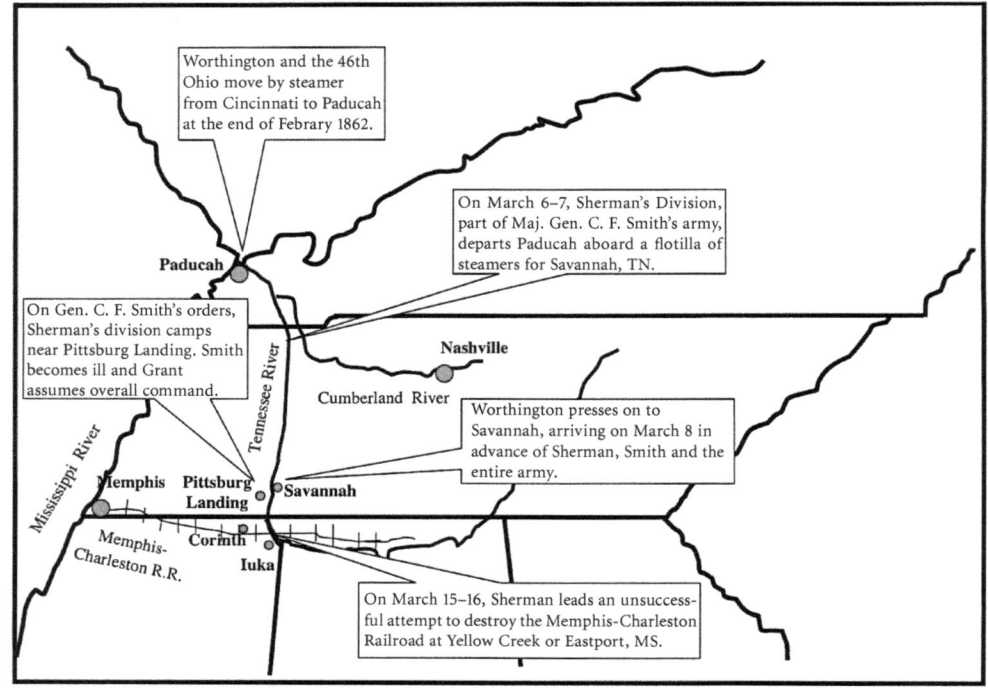

Map 4.2 The Federals' Tennessee campaign.

Worthington indicated in his diary that the Missouri men were slow to respond to Sherman's order to "commit violence upon sick men," a response that likely angered Sherman all the more. Again, Worthington had, at least in Sherman's mind, usurped his authority.

Worthington's claim of having prevented "perhaps one thousand citizens" from joining the Confederate Army cannot be substantiated, nor can it be disproved. This claim, offered well after the war, might have been Worthington's attempt to mitigate his own arrogant usurping of Sherman's command position. Private Zook indicated that the gunboats that preceded the troop ships to Savannah had "scared all the rebel troops away," except for perhaps two companies, which Zook indicated "took to their heels ... leaving everything behind, even their arms, so badly were they frightened" (17).

While remaining in Savannah for the next six days, the 46th had its first encounter with a living, breathing enemy. The troops captured "7 secesh [sic] cavalry, with their horses, equipment and all; their arms were double shot guns" (Zook 17).

YELLOW CREEK EXPEDITION

One of the principal targets of the Federal invasion into the Tennessee River valley was the east-west supply link formed by the Memphis-Charleston Railroad. Running across northern Mississippi, it provided the Confederacy with a means to consolidate men and materiel for an anticipated defense of Corinth, Mississippi. On March 14, Smith ordered Sherman to take his division upriver, land in the vicinity of the mouth of Yellow Creek, and strike to destroy the Memphis-Charleston Railroad in the vicinity of Burnsville, Mississippi. Sherman left Savannah at midnight on March 14 with a convoy of 19 steamboats under the escort of the gunboat *Tyler*. When the force reached the mouth of Yellow Creek, Sherman sent his cavalry late that night under Major Elbridge G. Ricker, 5th Ohio Cavalry, down the Red Sulphur Springs Road in the direction of Burnsville. The creeks were swollen from the incessant rain of the previous day, and while the cavalry departed during a lull in the storm, the rain began again with a vengeance. Sherman attempted to follow his cavalry with his first brigade, Colonel Hicks', in the lead and his other brigades in numerical order behind Hicks. The cavalry made it almost to Burnsville, but as the rains became even more intense, the infantry only made it four and a half miles from the steamboats before they found themselves unable to proceed. The water was rising "at the rate of 6 inches per hour," the mission was clearly a bust, and Sherman was faced with the difficult business of recalling his division to the steamers. "The rain was still falling and the slough to our rear was rising rapidly. I saw no other alternative but to return to our boats," Sherman wrote in his official report (*War of the Rebellion*, Vol. 10, 23). Sherman was fortunate to get his men back to the boat given the speed with which the streams and creeks were rising; but for disassembling one of his field pieces, he might have had to abandon the cannon on the far side of one of the most swollen and swift-running of the streams that laced the northern Mississippi backwoods.

Sherman personally conducted a reconnaissance farther upriver to attempt another landing at a site short of Chickasaw, but the conditions of the landing there (it was basically underwater) were equally prohibitive of any kind of dismounted operation. Sherman chose in this—his first expedition against the enemy—to lead his division with Hicks' brigade. The privilege of leading the division did not likely go to Hicks' brigade simply because of numerical sequence. Commanders generally lead a movement of their forces with the element that they trust above other subordinate units. (He would again use the 1st Brigade as the lead element in a brief reconnaissance effort to assess the enemy situation in the vicinity of Pittsburg Landing a little more than a week later.) Sherman must have seen something in the brigade to commend it as his lead element. Worthington and the 46th Ohio, well-drilled and disciplined, offered a counterpoint to Hicks' rather undisciplined outfit, and while we do not know the order of march for the movement, it is likely that Sherman was satisfied to have a fellow West Pointer in the lead as opposed to a volunteer officer, even though Sherman had not seen fit to enforce discipline on Hicks or his men at Paducah.

Sherman abandoned his efforts to break the Memphis-Charleston Railroad, but during this attempt he had gained some important information about enemy strength in the area:

> The main force is quartered at Iuka and Corinth. They are shifted from one to the other and back again, but the accounts of the actual force vary so widely that I do not pretend to form an opinion, but knowing the importance of them to the safety of the Charleston and Memphis Railroad, no one can doubt that between those two points will be gathered all the force they can command [*War of the Rebellion*, Vol. 10, 23].

Despite Sherman's obvious conclusion that the enemy would be consolidating forces in northern Mississippi near the Tennessee border, his inability, or unwillingness, to "form an opinion" as to the enemy's intentions would leave his division unprepared for an attack that would take place within one month. From the unsuccessful Yellow Creek expedition, Sherman's division returned to their steamers that Saturday afternoon exhausted, hungry, and with wet feet. "We changed socks, and dried and warmed our feet well," Private Christian Zook of the 46th Ohio wrote home. But they would not be afforded long to rest. At midnight on Saturday, March 15, Worthington and the 46th Ohio steamed north to Pittsburg Landing, some eight miles upriver from Savannah. From the landing Sherman again went ashore in an attempt to reach the Memphis-Charleston Railroad but again he was unsuccessful, as enemy cavalry shadowed the roads and harassed his every movement. Because the weather had rendered all but one road muddy and slow-going terrain, Sherman did not feel secure about moving his entire division along the road, and he called off the effort. Sherman wrote on March 17, "[Cutting the railroad] without a general or serious engagement ... is impossible from here, because the ground is well watched and dash cannot be made" (*War of the Rebellion*, Vol. 10, 26). Upon their return from this second effort against the railroad, most of Sherman's division, including Worthington's 46th Ohio, remained on their boats for several days before returning ashore.

Once they did return ashore, Zook noted that the quiet Pittsburg Landing boasted only a storehouse, a grocery, and one dwelling. His desire for action, however, would soon be met as the army's subsequent movement inland would bring it the long-awaited meeting with the enemy.

CHAPTER FIVE

"In Virtue Worthy"

Worthington at the Battle of Shiloh

*Camp Shiloe [sic], Harding Co. Tennessee
March the 23d 1862
I do not think we will have much of a fight for they hardly ever fight fare [sic], if they fight at all, they cannot stand us an open fight no time.* — Private Christian Zook, 46th Ohio Infantry

QUIET CAMP IN THE TENNESSEE WOODS

When Private Zook wrote home to his family in Fairfield County, Ohio, he had been camped in the wooded Tennessee countryside five days. On the previous Sunday morning, March 22, he and the men of the 46th Ohio had disembarked from their river transport, spent the day building a corduroy road up the bluff from the river, and over the next two days moved gradually inland approximately three miles from the Tennessee River.

The 46th Ohio was now part of Col. John Adair McDowell's brigade under General Sherman; the brigade comprised the right-most element of the division and occupied a campsite along the road that led between the villages of Hamburg and Purdy.[1] The 6th Iowa Infantry (McDowell's own

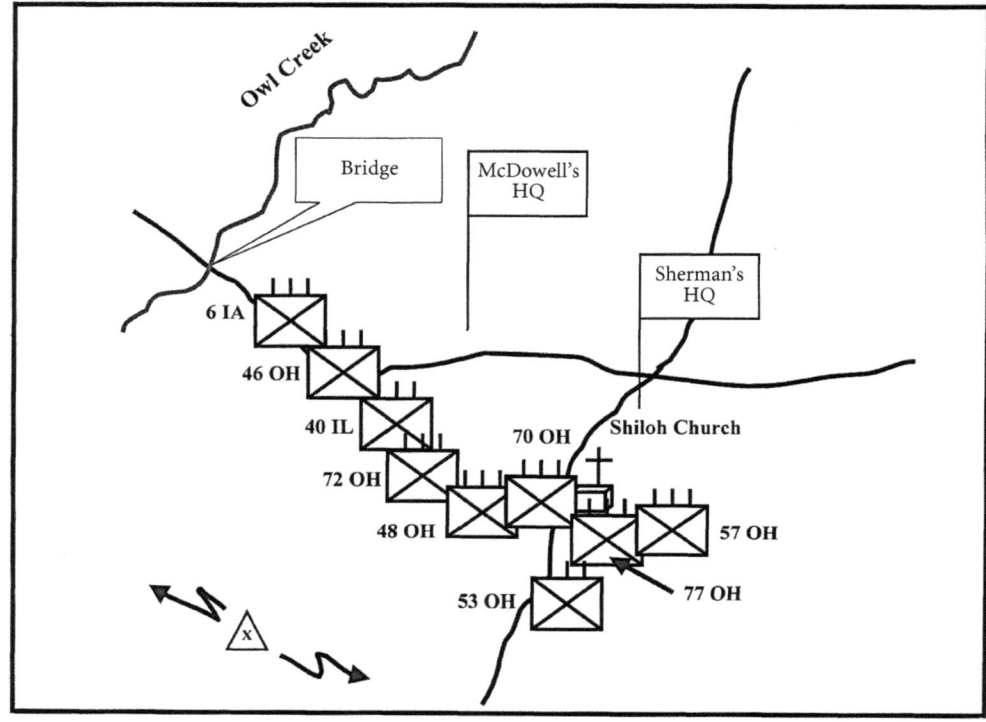

Map 5.1 Campsite of Sherman's division.

regiment), under the command of Captain John Williams, occupied a campsite 400–500 yards southwest of the Hamburg-Purdy Road and about 900 yards southeast and uphill from Owl Creek. To the left of the 6th Iowa, perhaps 200 yards and roughly parallel to the Hamburg-Purdy Road, the 46th Ohio camped. Behr's battery of the 6th Indiana Light Artillery was positioned with five guns about 150 yards to the left of the 46th. The last element of McDowell's brigade, the 40th Illinois Infantry under Col. Stephen Hicks (the militia officer who Worthington chastised for lax discipline at Paducah), was encamped about 300 yards across a deep ravine from the remainder of the brigade. As Map 5.1 indicates, the entire brigade's sector of defense was oriented south-southeast.

Worthington's men erected their tents in an old, open field of wild sage grass standing a foot and a half high. Fruit trees were in bloom, and blackberries were abundant. In the days after arriving at their appointed bivouac site, many of the men were impressed by the quantity of game available in the area. Unfortunately, they were forced to only gaze at deer and wild turkeys while their "very mouths watered," as they were under strict rules not to fire their weapons unless ordered to do so. Neither were they allowed to venture outside the picket line that Colonel Worthington established some quarter of a mile southwest of camp (Zook 20).

The remainder of Sherman's division camped on similar terrain. Buckland's brigade, consisting of the 72nd Ohio, the 48th Ohio, and the 70th Ohio, was adjacent to the 40th Illinois in the order stated. The 70th Ohio, under the command of Col. Joseph Cockerill, had its left resting beside a small log Methodist Episcopal church called Shiloh, which in Hebrew means "peace" (Daniel 131). Next came Hildebrand's brigade, comprised of the 77th Ohio, the 57th Ohio, and the 53rd Ohio. This latter regiment, under the command of Col. Jesse J. Appler, made its campsite well south of the general line of the remainder of the division on the Rea Farm, one half mile south of Shiloh Church. His camp was separated from the 77th Ohio by "some two hundred yards" (Dawes 2). "The nearest troops on our [the 53rd's] left, or rather in our rear, were Prentiss' division, just one-half mile away" (Dawes 2). His position formed something of a salient, extending south beyond the general line formed by Sherman's division. Unfortunately, the 53rd might have been the worst possible regiment to be placed in such a position. The 50-year-old Appler's most recent military experience appears to have been some limited service aboard a sloop of war, the *Hornet*, prior to the outbreak of hostilities.[2]

Appler had been a probate court judge in the mid-1850s, and he narrowly lost an election as the Democratic candidate for state treasurer shortly before the war. At the beginning of the war he had raised Company D of the 22nd Ohio Volunteer Infantry and was later appointed colonel of the 53rd Ohio (Evans 221). Unfortunately, neither Appler nor his executive officer, Lt. Col. R. A. Fulton, had any knowledge of drill procedures or army regulations, and the only man capable of actually training the troops, Major H. S. Cox, succumbed to illness and was unable to conduct drill during the weeks preceding the battle (Dawes 1).

General McLernand's division was encamped on the left of and slightly behind Sherman's division and Prentiss' division, extending to within a half mile of the river. General Prentiss' division was the southernmost Union force encamped at Pittsburg Landing, its forces astride the Eastern Corinth Road and advanced more than two miles south-southwest of the landing. General Hurlburt's Division occupied a position nearer Pittsburg Landing and in the rear of the remainder of the forces described above. General Don Carlos Buell was marching with 50,000 troops through middle Tennessee to join Grant's army at Pittsburg Landing, but he was not expected to arrive until the 7th or 8th of April.

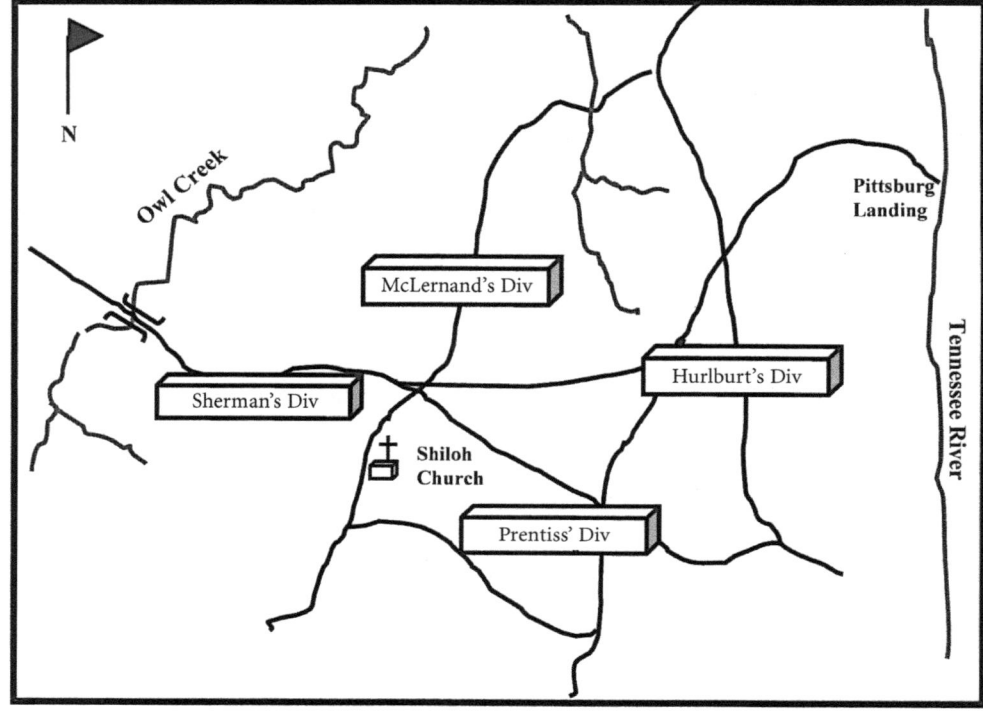

MAP 5.2 Overview of Shiloh Battlefield.

Table 5.1 reflects the order of battle for Sherman's division encamped in the vicinity of Shiloh Church on April 6, 1862. Some changes in the organization and command structure had occurred since the division's departure from Paducah, Kentucky.

Table 5.1
Order of Battle for Sherman's Division at Shiloh

Brigade	Units	Commander
McDowell's	40th Illinois Inf.	Col. Stephen D. Hicks
	6th Iowa	Capt. John Williams
	46th Ohio Inf.	Col. Thomas Worthington
Stuart's	55th Illinois Inf.	Lt. Col. Oscar Malmborg
	71st Ohio Inf.	Col. Rodney Mason
	54th Ohio Inf.	Col. T. Kilby Smith
Hildebrand's	77th Ohio Inf.	Lt. Col. Wills De Hass

Brigade	Units	Commander
(Hildebrand's)	57th Ohio Inf.	Lt. Col. Americus Rice
	53rd Ohio Inf.	Col. Jesse J. Appler
Buckland's	72nd Ohio Inf.	Lt. Col. Herman Canfield
	48th Ohio Inf.	Col. Peter Sullivan
	70th Ohio Inf.	Col. Joseph Cockerill
Maj. Ezra Taylor's	Batt B, 1st Illinois Light	Capt. Allen C. Waterhouse
	Batt E, 1st Illinois Light	Capt. Samuel E. Barrett
	Morton's Batt, 6th Indiana	Capt. Frederick Behr

GENERAL STRATEGIC SITUATION

The Federal campsite near Shiloh Church and Pittsburg Landing constituted the point of a dagger aimed at the heart of the Confederacy. With the destruction of the South's northern line of defense, which had reached from Columbus, Kentucky, through now-occupied Fort Donelson and into eastern Tennessee, a massive Union Army was poised to strike deep into the South. Perhaps more important, that Army had severed one of the Confederacy's primary east-west rail arteries, which linked Nashville and Memphis. Realizing that southerners needed a counterstrike that was fast and decisive, Gen. Albert Sidney Johnston decided to leave his base of operations in northern Mississippi and conduct a surprise attack on Grant's Union troops near Pittsburg Landing. If he acted quickly, Johnston reasoned, he could defeat the Federal invasion by striking Grant before General Buell could reinforce him with the 50,000 men en route from Nashville. With Grant defeated, the momentum of the Federal thrust down the Tennessee River would be halted, and Johnston and a victorious southern army could then turn its attention to either defeating or containing further progress by Buell's army.

The initial concept of the operation had Johnston's army, now assembled at Corinth, Mississippi, conducting a forced march some 20–30 miles northward and striking Grant's forces on Saturday, April 5. They would cover the ground in two days and fall upon the unsuspecting Federals. But inexperienced troops and neophyte leadership created just enough delays along the march to prevent the Army from reaching assigned attack positions until late Saturday — the day the attack was supposed to have commenced. This march toward a deliberate attack by the inexperienced Confederate troops had been "a frolicking affair." Noise discipline was nonexistent, for as soon as the rain that had plagued the two-day march

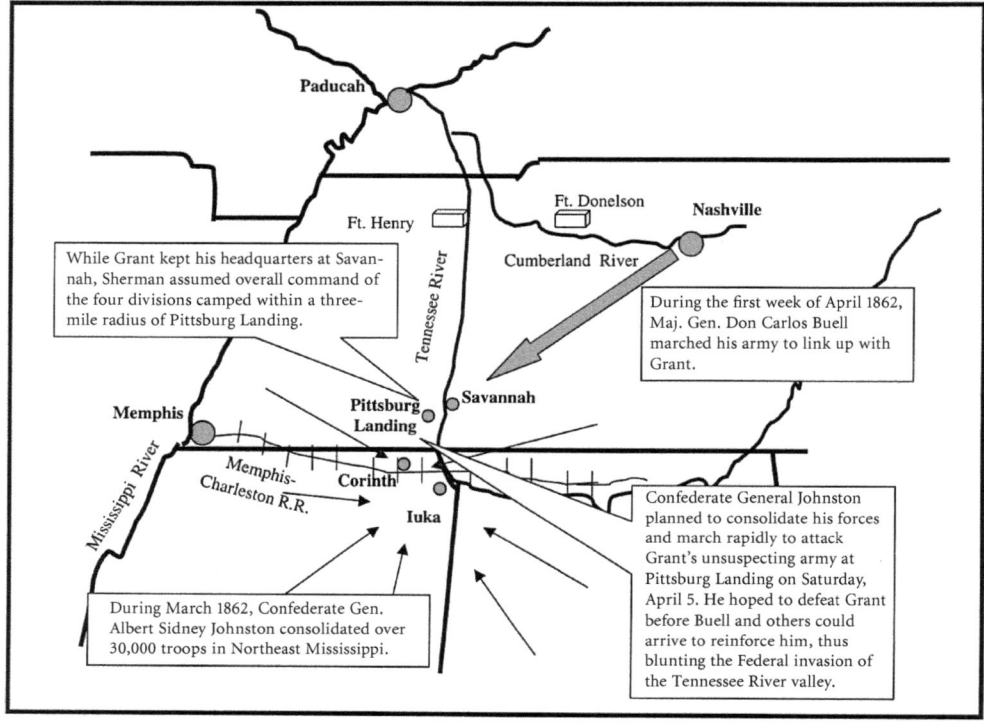

MAP 5.3 Tennessee campaign and the Confederate strategic plan.

ended on Saturday, soldiers began to test-fire their weapons, some companies even firing in volley. Units beat drums on the march, sounded bugle calls, and even cheered General Johnston as he rode along the column. All of this occurred on the afternoon and evening of April 5, within a mile and a half of Prentiss' and Sherman's divisions' campsites (Daniel 129).

The delay in the timetable, coupled with the Army's undisciplined approach, caused General Johnston to have second thoughts about going through with the attack. On the evening of Saturday, April 5, a frustrated Johnston held his now-famous council of war with his corps commanders:

> As soon as it had become evident that the day was too far advanced for a decisive engagement, General Johnston called ... an informal council, in the roadway, near his temporary headquarters *within less than two miles* [emphasis added] of those of General Sherman, at the Shiloh meeting-house [Roman 277].

Maj. Gen. Leonidas K. Polk informed Johnston that he had exhausted his rations during the march. With the transportation wagons several miles to the rear and still attempting to close to the front over muddy roads, Johnston knew the food supply for his entire Army was anything but certain. P. G. T. Beauregard argued against proceeding with the attack and in favor of conducting a reconnaissance-in-force. Certain that the enemy knew of their presence and convinced that Buell's march to support Grant would "be hastened" upon such knowledge, Beauregard presented his view to Johnston: "Now they will be entrenched up to their eyes," he declared. But Johnston was steadfast in his desire to attack, and though he appeared "shaken" by Beauregard's recommendation, he nevertheless stood by his decision. Johnston told his officers:

> Gentlemen, we shall attack at daylight tomorrow. I would fight them if they were a million. They can present no greater front between these two creeks [Lick Creek and Owl Creek] than we can; and the more men they crowd in there, the worse we can make it for them [Roman 278; Daniel 128].

The Confederacy planned to provide an early morning surprise for General Sherman's and General Prentiss' divisions, which lay unsuspecting in their camps. At least some were unsuspecting, but others, like Worthington's 46th Ohio, were on alert, sensing the danger signs, and some units, like Appler's 53rd Ohio, were just plain jittery.

SHILOH TIMELINE

From his arrival in Paducah through the Battle of Shiloh, Tom Worthington maintained a diary. In it he noted his requests for supplies, his general observations about the competence of his leadership, and his misgivings about ongoing operations. Worthington not only used the diary entries after the battle to develop his charges against Sherman and Grant, but he used the material after the war to produce scathing publications impugning the leadership and competence of both men. The diary entries chronologically present some of Worthington's primary complaints and offer some insights into what he believed went wrong at Shiloh. However, to fully understand the role of the 46th Ohio Infantry during that first day of the Battle of Shiloh and Worthington's subsequent charges against Sherman, it is necessary to view the 46th Ohio Volunteer Infantry's actions in terms of the overall flow of the battle. Such a study has as its by-product a thorough examination as to the truth and accuracy of Worthington's claims regarding his own conduct and the conduct of the 46th Ohio. The following general timeline, rather than a straight narrative, offers a method of defining Worthington's actions and the role of the 46th Ohio. The timeline allows the reader to conceptualize exactly what Worthington knew and when he knew it in relationship to evolving events in the days leading up to the battle and during the battle itself. The timeline also provides insight into the significance of the battlefield movements of the 46th Ohio in relationship to Sherman's division and the entire Federal Army encamped at Pittsburg Landing. Both of these issues relate directly to charges levied or claims made by Worthington after the Battle of Shiloh: (a) that Sherman had more than adequate early warning of a Confederate attack and should have been better prepared to meet an attack, and (b) that quick, decisive action by the 46th Ohio Infantry saved the Federal right during the first day of the battle.

Since Worthington's more than 20-year war with W. T. Sherman centered upon the events leading up to and including the first day's fighting at Shiloh, this book's emphasis and detailed analysis will cover only that time period. Events of the second day at Shiloh, while important in the overall outcome, do not significantly inform the discussion of Worthington's claims.

Tuesday, April 1, 1862

Worthington made the following diary entry:

> Have now over one hundred rounds of ammunition for all available men, and feel easy on that point. Ordered the Captains to send in accounts of clothing, etc., wanted which the Quartermaster is very careless about getting. Still no axes, which now he cannot get if he would, and which are worth more than guns at present [*Court-Martial Record* Exhibit A].

Wednesday, April 2, 1862

The troops of Sherman's division were occupied by company and battalion drill, fatigue duty, and other tasks.

Thursday, April 3, 1862

0800—The 5th Ohio Cavalry, under Col. W. H. H. Taylor, moved about six miles down the Corinth Road, where from the 1st Alabama Cavalry they captured a prisoner and discovered that the enemy had three regiments of infantry, one regiment of cavalry, and a battery of artillery at Monterey, scarcely five miles from the Federal camp at Pittsburg Landing. Colonel Taylor reported this information to General Sherman later that morning (*War of the Rebellion*, Vol. 22, 86).

During the day, Worthington made the following diary entry:

> Rode to Pittsburg Landing. The place is crowded and in disorder below, with noise and gambling on the bank above, across the road from the post office. Hunted up and down for clothing and axes,[3] and found that Sherman had forbidden his Quartermaster from receiving anything. That General Smith's Quartermaster will answer no requisitions outside of his immediate command, and the Post Quartermaster, Baxter (Grant's), will only answer the requisitions of the Division Quartermasters. The reason that Sherman's Quartermaster will not receive any stores is that he had no place to put them. There are now at least six boats hired by the day at the landing (as I hear) at not less than two thousand ($2,000) a day, when two thousand dollars with that many men could in ten days, or less, put up storehouses sufficient for an army of one hundred thousand men.[4] And so the government will pay on this expedition so far not less than twenty thousand dollars, and perhaps ten times that before the war is over, and lose not less than one to ten million dollars in quartermaster and commissary stores, occasioned by the improvidence and neglect of its Major-General here, to say nothing of the disorder and danger growing out of such a state of things [*Court-Martial Record* Exhibit A].

Just as Worthington had claimed during his Mexican War service, he felt he was poorly utilized and misplaced within the military hierarchy at Shiloh. In his diary entry for the 3rd of April, he noted the anniversary of his appointment as a cadet to West Point, and he lamented that the only benefit he had from that experience was his "present position as one of the lowest Colonels in this war." He accused his superiors of incompetence, improvidence, and negligence, and he believed himself endangered by the "want of capacity or integrity amidst the many above and the masses below" him.[5]

Afternoon—The 48th Ohio Infantry conducted a reconnaissance "about five miles on the road to Corinth." Two companies advanced as skirmishers and were soon engaged with the rebel cavalry, but as the orders were "not to be drawn into battle" (a classic reconnaissance axiom — avoid decisive engagement), the skirmishers fell back and "returned to camp, arriving a little before dark" (Bering and Mongomery 5).

Worthington continued to fear an attack, warning McDowell of such and urging that he obtain "at least six batteries and two regiments of cavalry" within their brigade. He claimed the pickets were only advanced a mile out and suggested that the undergrowth would allow little opportunity for early warning of an enemy approach. He indicated a belief that the brigade was covering too much ground and expressed a concern that the number of sick men in camp would hamper their ability to withstand an attack.

Friday, April 4, 1862

During the morning, E. C. Dawes of the 53rd Ohio reported "a considerable skirmish about one mile in front of [his] camp" (3). The enemy prisoners from this skirmish were housed in Shiloh Church where Dawes said they "claimed to be the advance of a great army that would drive us into the river the next day" (Dawes 3).

1400— The left of the 48th Ohio's picket line was attacked by enemy cavalry, and eight men of the 70th Ohio were captured, along with Lieutenant Greer of the 48th, who was on Buckland's staff. Upon hearing the news, Sherman sent Major Ricker and the 5th Ohio Cavalry to investigate. Buckland, quite concerned at this point, sent three more companies forward to ascertain the situation. When these companies of the 48th deployed, the enemy cavalry retreated, losing several killed and wounded and giving up a few prisoners. In the pursuit, Major Ricker's cavalry crested a hill and discovered a Confederate infantry battle line in waiting, supported by three artillery pieces. The enemy opened fire, and Ricker's men retreated, reporting immediately back to Buckland. When Buckland and Ricker returned from the engagement, they were met by Sherman. Buckland could tell "he [Sherman] was not pleased" (Sword 124). When Buckland tried to explain his foray, Sherman angrily chastised him for possibly drawing the whole Army into a battle, then sent him back to his camp.[6] When Ricker explained that he had found "at least two regiments of infantry and a large cavalry force," Sherman mocked him: "Oh!— tut, tut. You militia officers get scared too easily." Sherman in his report later that night dismissed the enemy presence as a reconnaissance-in-force (Sword 124).

Saturday, April 5, 1862

Grant reported to Halleck regarding Buckland's encounter the previous day with enemy cavalry "in considerable force." "They had with them three pieces of artillery and cavalry and infantry. How much cannot of course be estimated. I have scarcely the faintest idea of an attack (general one) being made upon us" (*War of the Rebellion*, Vol. 22, 89).

Five. "In Virtue Worthy" 87

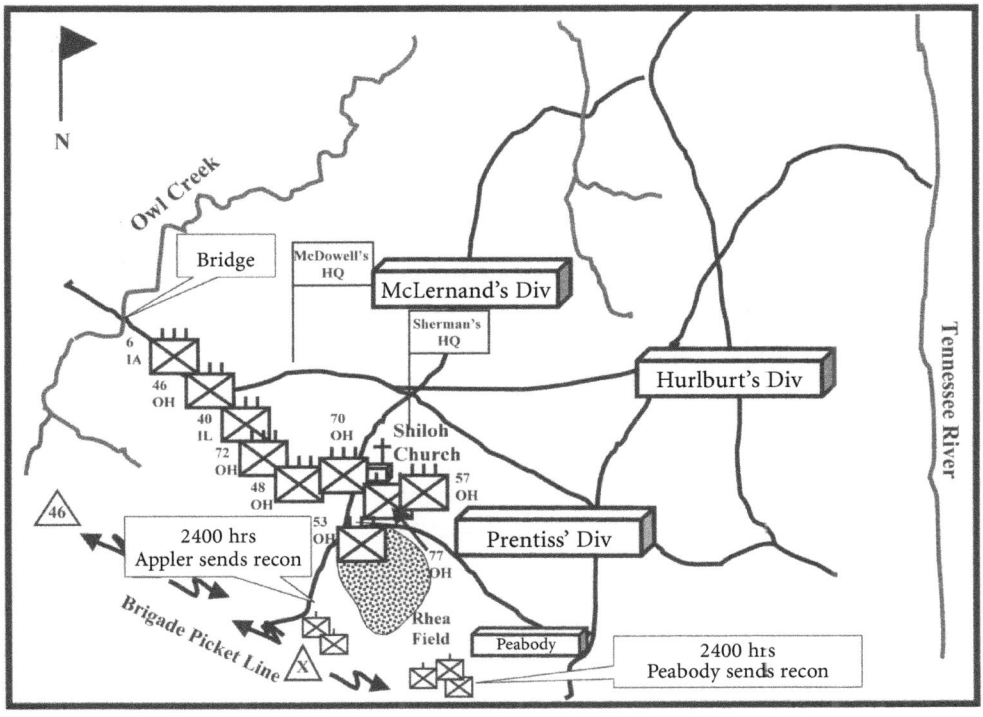

MAP 5.4 Action in the vicinity of Pittsburg Landing on April 5, 1862.

That morning, Sherman lost Ricker's 5th Ohio Cavalry and two batteries to an ill-timed reorganization of the Federal forces at Pittsburg Landing. Grant had decided several days prior to consolidate the artillery at the division level (forming what in modern terms would be called DIVARTY). The action was not seriously attempted until Saturday, but once begun, it effectively stripped Sherman of all available cavalry, leaving him blind in terms of reconnaissance except for using his infantry regiments as extended pickets (Daniel 138).

1400 — Col. Everett Peabody, a Harvard graduate and a successful railroad engineer before the war, reviewed his 1st Brigade of Prentiss' division in Spain Field. This review was observed from a distance by some 200 Confederate cavalry. Wrote one soldier:

> To show how complete and successful was the advance of the enemy, their advance guard lay in the woods on the 5th, witnessing our parades and reviews. One of our returned paroled prisoners, a

mule-driver, who was captured two days before the battle, had told me that he was taken through their whole army, which was camped three miles from ours, the night before the attack [More 108].

Peabody notified Prentiss that his review was being watched (Daniel 141).

Sherman, accompanied by colonels (?) McPherson and David Stuart, conducted a personal reconnaissance of the ford over Lick Creek in front of Stuart's position and the Federal left. The water in the creek had dropped three feet and Sherman was concerned that the 100-foot ford might provide the enemy an easy route into what he had heretofore believed was a virtually unassailable position (*Court-Martial Record* 10).

In the early afternoon, pickets of Hicks' 40th Illinois reported a glimmer off what they believed to be three brass field guns located southeast of the Widow Howell's house. Although Colonel Buckland personally rode forward to confirm this, he saw no guns.

1600— Appler in his extended position in front of the division had been "very uneasy" all day. When mounted men were observed at the end of the field south of the 53rd Ohio's camp, a platoon went forward and found "a picket line of men in butternut clothes" (Dawes 4). Meanwhile, on Appler's left, Peabody sent a patrol of two companies of the 25th Missouri toward enemy cavalry, which had been seen forward of his position. One of the troops reported, "we could hear the enemy moving in every direction" (Daniel 141). General Prentiss, when informed of this, indicated there was nothing to be alarmed about.

1630— Appler ordered the 53rd Ohio into line and sent his quartermaster, Lieutenant Fulton, to report the situation to Sherman. Sherman sent Fulton back. Fulton said, within hearing of the forming regiment, "Colonel Appler, General Sherman says, 'Take your damned regiment to Ohio. There is no enemy nearer than Corinth.'" The regiment laughed at Appler and broke ranks without awaiting orders to do so—an act indicative of the lack of drill and discipline that Worthington so despised.

1700— The 48th Ohio heard the long roll and formed a battle line. They listened to firing in the distance for about an hour, and then they were dismissed. The cavalry behavior and the attacks on the picket line "convince[d] [them] that [the Rebel] army was in force in [their] immediate front" (Bering and Montgomery 5).

Capt. A. G. Sharpe of the 46th Ohio located an enemy cannon at the Widow Howell's at 5:00 P.M. When he reported this information directly to Sherman, the division commander told him he would have the artillery in readiness for counterbattery fire if required.

1900—Hildebrand informed Appler that Sherman had come to his tent and told him the enemy before him consisted of two regiments of cavalry, two regiments of infantry, and one battery of artillery.[7] Sherman ordered Hildebrand to prepare to send the 77th Ohio out at 6:30 Sunday to the Seay House on the Corinth Road (about one and a half miles from Shiloh Church) to support a movement of cavalry to drive away or capture the enemy (Dawes 4).

2000—Appler was "not entirely satisfied" with Hildebrand's report of Sherman's response, so he sent forward a picket of 16 men to the southern end of Rhea Field with orders to report any enemy movements to their front and to return to camp at daybreak, but the men were ordered not to fire unless attacked. Still stinging from Sherman's rebuke, Appler did not inform Sherman of this action.

2400—Colonel Peabody was equally concerned by all the indications of enemy movement to his front, and he was not satisfied with General Prentiss' assurances that all was well. Without Prentiss' approval, Peabody went out on a limb and sent forward three companies of the 25th Missouri and two companies of the 12th Michigan to find out what was going on south of his camp (Daniel 142). Meanwhile, Buckland was so apprehensive of a possible attack upon his brigade that he had a drummer boy sleep with him in his tent just in case he might have to awaken in the night and sound the long roll (Daniel 138).

Sounding the long roll and calling troops into battle formation is only effective if they are competent in drill and tactics, and, unfortunately, many of Sherman's units were well trained in neither subject. But if Worthington and Sherman agreed on any aspect of prosecuting a war, it was the need for drill and instruction. In the monotonous days of camp life during the first week of April, the men in Sherman's division had found themselves in near-constant drill and ceremony. Sherman had seen what happened to unprepared soldiers at Bull Run, and he seemed determined to not suffer the same fate again. In this concern he found an ally in fellow West Pointer Worthington, whose experience in the Mexican War and whose knowledge of drill and tactics reinforced in him the same concerns as Sherman. Many units remained poorly disciplined despite the division-ordered drill practice, but the 46th Ohio was one of the regiments that had stood tall back on April 2, when General Grant conducted a field inspection and "seemed favorably impressed" with Sherman's division (Sword 119).

But for all the marching, parade, and drill, there was among the encampment of Sherman's division a distinct lack of one critical commodity—intelligence as to the enemy disposition and intention. That is not to say there was no information about the enemy's whereabouts and plans; rather, the information that existed was not processed into intelligence. Intelligence is the distillation of information from various sources into a systematic view of the enemy's location, strength, and likely course of action. So it is fair to say that, for all the marching, all the "right shoulder arms," and all the regimental band music, Grant and his "informal" camp commander, Sherman,[8] could say with no certainty that they knew what to expect from the Confederate Army. In fact, General Halleck in St. Louis had previously prodded Grant on March 31 insisting that Grant give him "more information about the enemy's numbers and position." Halleck appeared concerned that Grant's "scouts and spies" had not discovered any significant information as yet (Sword 118). The simple truth was that neither Grant nor Sherman had any spies, and the information produced by their scouts had yet to be turned into intelligence. Less than 30 miles from their camp on April 2, an enemy force of 30,000 men had gathered from every direction. Indicators of this fact appeared in the form of isolated southern soldiers and deserters, who were either captured or who made their way to Pittsburg Landing, as well as from observations of reinforced cavalry excursions feeling out the Federal position. Yet neither Sherman nor Grant seems to have realized the situation:

> The Sherman at Shiloh was a rejuvenated and foolish Sherman who kept telling himself nothing was wrong. Clearly, he was not the Sherman of Louisville, who had ceaselessly warned about enemy attacks. The new Sherman suspected nothing [Hirshson 113].

"Sick Men and Lingerers, Leave the Camp!"

Worthington's days of nervousness and his sense of an impending attack were about to be justified. For two or three days prior to that fateful Sunday, he had ordered two of his companies to sleep on their arms in anticipation of an attack, and as recently as Saturday morning his pickets had been driven in by the enemy at about 7:00 A.M. (Worthington *Report* 2). Now the firing he heard in the distance exceeded the intermittent patter of the previous day, and it had been growing in intensity since daylight. Worthington had already deployed the 46th Ohio in line of battle on the military crest of the hill south of his camp, overlooking a branch of Owl Creek that opened out into the creek proper. His skirmishers, reaching as far as the Widow Howell's field, were extended more than a half mile to the front (south-southwest) over ground that the enemy's reconnais-

Five. "In Virtue Worthy" 91

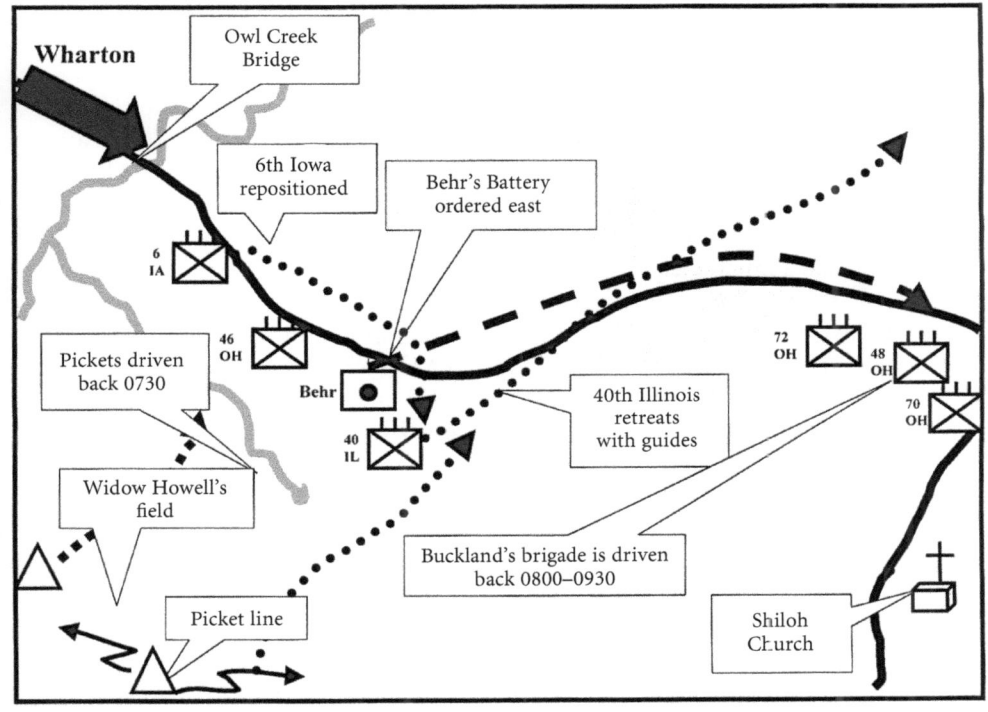

MAP 5.5 Early action on April 6, 1862.

sance had contested with Union forces just the previous day. Worthington had ridden out to his picket line in the B.M.N.T (before morning nautical twilight), and while somewhere near the Widow Howell's field at sunrise, he "observed the enemy by the glitter of their arms, marching to attack the centre at Shiloh Church" (Worthington *Report* 2).[9]

Sunday, April 6, 1862

0400— Col. Jesse Appler awakened Adjutant Dawes in his tent. "Adjutant, get up, quick!" Appler had "been up all night" and indicated he had heard constant firing (more likely sporadic but steady) beyond the 53rd Ohio's pickets.

0430— The 53rd Ohio's 16-man picket returned "sure that there was a large force in [their] front" (Dawes 5). Appler's lack of knowledge in military drill and his general sense of nervousness began to betray him. First, he ordered Adjutant Dawes to form the regiment, then quickly countermanded the order and ordered Dawes to go find Colonel Hildebrand. But before Dawes could leave to find Hildebrand and "ascertain the facts," Appler called him back again and sent one of his soldiers to the brigade picket line to find out what was happening (Dawes 5).

0445— A soldier from the 25th Missouri, who had been shot in the arm, rushed into Appler's camp shouting, "Get into line. The rebels are coming!" (Dawes 5). Appler formed his regiment in line of battle. Meanwhile, Colonel Peabody's men conducted a reconnaissance-in-force, encountering the picket post of the 57th Ohio and boasting "we're going to catch some Rebels for breakfast" (Daniel 143).

0450— Appler dispatched the only two mounted men in his regiment: his executive officer to warn Hildebrand and his quartermaster to provide a situation report to Sherman. Meanwhile, Peabody's reconnaissance force cautiously crossed Fraley Field and encountered the outposts of the skirmish line of S. A. M. Wood's brigade of Hardee's corps. The skirmish line consisted of Maj. Aaron B. Hardcastle's 280-man 3rd Mississippi Battalion.

0515— Sherman had listened to Appler's quartermaster report the situation from the 53rd Ohio's salient position in advance of the division, and he had summarily dismissed its importance. The quartermaster returned to Appler and spoke to him in a lowered voice: "General Sherman says, 'You must be badly scared over there'" (Dawes 6).

At approximately the same time, Confederate General Albert Sidney Johnston was having breakfast around a small fire with Generals Braxton Bragg, William J. Hardee, and P. G. T. Beauregard. The group heard sharp volleys of musketry, which would have been Peabody's reconnaissance force coming upon Hardcastle's skirmish line. "The battle has opened, Gentlemen," Johnston said. "It is too late to change our dispositions" (Daniel 144).

0515–0630— Powell's men of Peabody's reconnaissance force fought Wood's brigade and then withdrew.

0520— Appler's executive officer returned with orders from Hildebrand to send two companies to reinforce the picket (presumably, the brigade picket).

0530— The 53rd Ohio sent two companies out to the brigade picket line. Near this same time, Confederate General Johnston mounted up to ride to the front and, speaking rhetorically to Beauregard said, "Can it be possible they are not aware of our presence?" (Daniel 145).

0600 Sunrise— Adjutant Dawes marched the 53rd Ohio to face south to deploy against any enemy crossing Rhea Field. The captain from one of the two companies thrown forward in picket support came running back, exclaiming, "The rebels are out there thicker than fleas on a dog's back" (Dawes 6). Just east of that position, General Prentiss chastised

Colonel Peabody for bringing on an attack by sending out an unauthorized reconnaissance party.

0630 — The 48th Ohio of Buckland's brigade was having breakfast after an "unusually still" night. But when the occasional picket firing they had heard since daylight increased to volleys, the long roll sounded, and the regiment formed on the color line. On the Confederate side, orders had finally filtered down the chain of command, and the attack began in earnest.

Appler, with his 53rd Ohio, saw that he was flanked and declared, "This is no place for us." He commanded, "Battalion, about face; right wheel!" (Dawes 6).

0645 — Appler ordered, "Sick men to the rear!" The 53rd Ohio marched through camp, halted along a ridge line in the rear of the officers' tents, and lay down in the brush. Two pieces of artillery from Waterhouse's battery arrived and were positioned to the regiment's right.

0700 — Pickets of the 46th were driven in by the enemy. "The entire Brigade [Hildebrand's] line was visible from Shiloh Church" (Daniel 157). Sherman and his staff rode into Rhea Field several hundred yards in front of the 53rd (Daniel 158). Sherman was standing on the high ground in front of the 53rd Ohio's Company A, peering through a looking glass at the Confederate line emerging from the woods at the far end of Rhea Field. He had not yet noticed another line of enemy troops emerging from the brush on his right. These Confederates, men of Hardee's corps, halted, raised their rifles, and took dead aim at Sherman and his staff. A lieutenant ran toward the general to warn him. "General, look to your right!" the lieutenant shouted. Sherman lowered his eyeglass and, seeing the enemy about to fire upon him, threw up his hand as if to protect himself. "My God," Sherman shouted, "we are attacked!" (Dawes 8).

Sherman escaped the volley fire, but his orderly did not. He fell dead beside the general. Galloping past Appler's position, Sherman ordered him to hold the line and indicated he would support him. About that time the first Federal cannons of Waterhouse's battery went into action, answering an enemy battery firing on the 53rd Ohio.

The Confederate attack had now fully commenced on Hildebrand's and Buckland's brigades, and Colonel Buckland ordered the 48th to support their pickets. Near Owl Creek they saw enemy bayonets glistening on *their* side of the creek. The 48th fell back on line with the 72nd Ohio color line.

> Jesse Nelson, our [48th Ohio] drummer-boy, who was but a stripling youth, when the battle began threw down his drum and stepped into the ranks, with a rifle. He was shot through the head

PHOTOGRAPH 5.1 Monument to the opposing forces in the vicinity of Hildebrand's brigade, Sherman's division (photograph by author).

by a musket-ball, early in the engagement, while on his knees, in the act of firing [Bering and Montgomery 7].

0715— The 53rd Ohio and the supporting Waterhouse artillery devastated the attacking 6th Mississippi Infantry and the 23rd Tennessee Infantry under Col. Pat Cleburne.

0730— Worthington remained out with the pickets west of Mrs. Howell's Field, where he observed the enemy approaching Shiloh Church (Worthington *Report* 2). Peabody fought the Confederate units of Shaver and Wood southeast of Rhea Field.

Just after the 53rd Ohio's volley fire had devastated the enemy pressing their position on the ridge line, Appler cried out to his men, "Retreat, and save yourselves." The 53rd Ohio began a disorganized retreat.

0740— The 53rd Ohio rallied behind some of McLernand's men, who had rushed forward toward the sound of the guns, and they were subsequently positioned in front of Sherman's headquarters.

Five. "In Virtue Worthy"

PHOTOGRAPH 5.2 Confederate attack at Shiloh Church (courtesy Shiloh National Military Park).

0750— Under the leadership of Lt. Col. A. V. Rice, the 57th Ohio fell back through its camp, its ranks broken by tents. About this time Adjutant E. C. Dawes of the 53rd Ohio found his colonel lying on the ground behind a tree, "his face ... like ashes ... reflecting the awful fear of death" (Dawes 7). Dawes urged him to order the regiment to support the 57th Ohio's withdrawal, but the confused and frightened Appler hesitated.

> Our miserable position flashed upon me. We were in the front of a great battle. Our regiment never had a battalion drill. *Some men in it had never fired a gun.* Our lieutenant colonel had become lost in the confusion of the first retreat, the major was in the hospital, and our colonel was a coward [Dawes 9].

Colonel Appler jumped to his feet and "literally ran away."

To the left and east of Hildebrand's brigade and the disorganized 53rd Ohio, Colonel Peabody searched in vain for General Prentiss. At this point

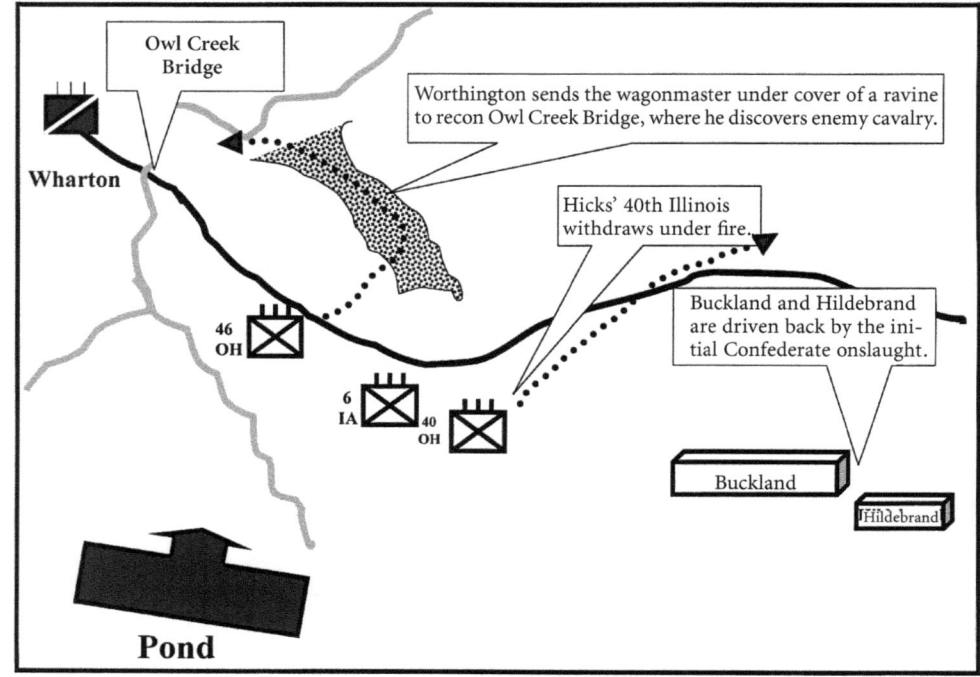

MAP 5.6 Worthington sends recon to Owl Creek Bridge.

in the fight, Sherman said that he "became satisfied *for the first time* [emphasis added] that the enemy designed a determined attack on our whole camp" (*War of the Rebellion*, Vol. 10, 249).

0800— The fight now spread in the direction of McDowell's brigade as Hicks' 40th Illinois formed a line of battle on a hilltop. Meanwhile, on the Union left, Peabody retreated through his camp.

0830— Concerned that the Confederates might attempt to flank the Federal right, Worthington ordered the acting wagonmaster on a reconnaissance of Owl Creek via the ravine behind the Hamburg-Purdy Road (Worthington *Report* 4). Meanwhile, the Confederates rolled up Peabody's camp and continued their attack.

0900— Sherman realized that he must attempt to keep his division in some semblance of a line that would be mutually supporting, so he ordered McDowell's brigade (including the 46th) to fall back northwest through the center of its camp.

Sherman indicated in his report that at this time Appler's unit broke in disorder, but, in fact, the disintegration of the 53rd Ohio had occurred

PHOTOGRAPH 5.3 The view from Worthington's camp west toward Owl Creek Bridge (photograph by author).

30 minutes or more before. Sherman also recognized that Prentiss was decisively engaged and falling back, exposing the Federal left (*War of the Rebellion*, Vol. 10, 250).

Sherman quickly changed his previous order to McDowell's brigade to retreat by the center and ordered them now to retreat by the left flank to join McLernand's right.

0915 — Worthington attracted enemy fire while crossing "an old field," and several men in Company C under Captain Wiseman were wounded as the Confederate attack spread toward McDowell's brigade and the 46th Ohio (Worthington *Report* 5).

0920 — Wharton's cavalry (Terry's Texas Rangers), the extreme left unit of the Confederate attacking force, reached Owl Creek Bridge.

0930 — Worthington returned to the Brigade Headquarters (posted 400 yards northeast of the 46th Ohio's camp) to determine McDowell's intent.

Meanwhile, the acting wagonmaster of the 46th Ohio returned with a report of enemy cavalry (Wharton) at Owl Creek Bridge (Worthington *Report* 5).

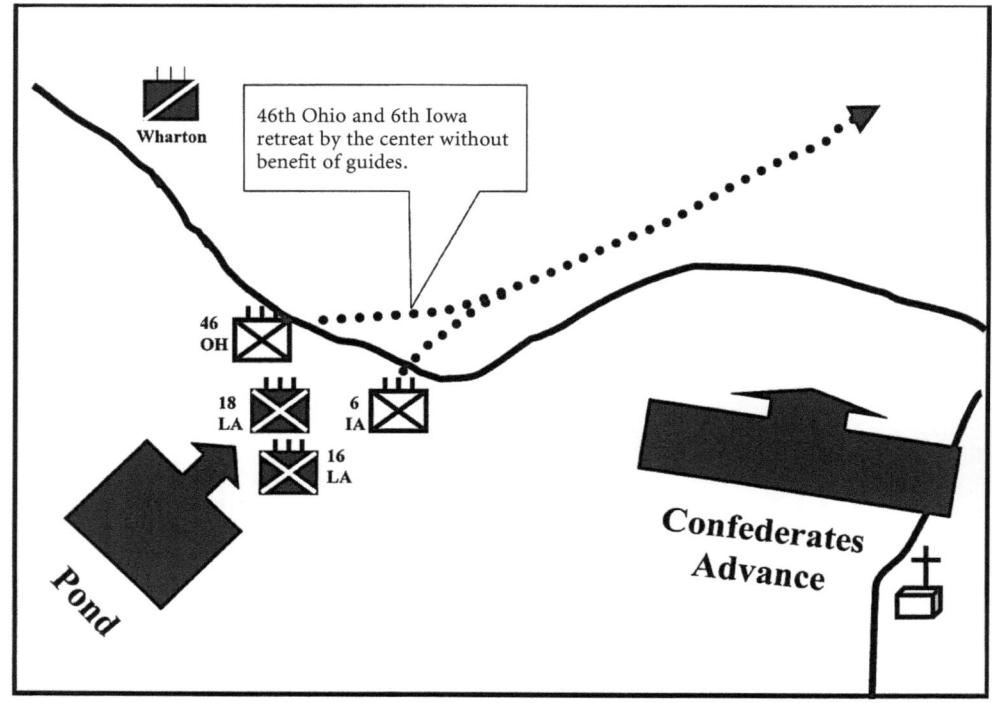

MAP 5.7 46th Ohio and 6th Iowa reposition without the benefit of guides.

0935—Fugitives from the 70th Ohio and Buckland's brigade, dispersed by the undergrowth and the confusion of battle, streamed through the 46th Ohio's camp with warnings of a massive attack.

Worthington rode along the regimental front and held a council with his company commanders, calling Captain Heath of Company A aside, Worthington warned him to watch for a flank attack by the enemy cavalry approaching Owl Creek Bridge.

0940–1000—Worthington conducted a personal reconnaissance forward across a "wooded ravine" near the position of Hicks' 40th Illinois (Worthington *Report* 6).

1000—Hicks' 40th Illinois withdrew to the west side of Crescent Field. The 48th Ohio, Buckland's brigade, was ordered to withdraw to the Hamburg-Purdy Road, and Behr's battery withdrew on orders from General Sherman.

Worthington returned to the 46th Ohio to find the 40th Illinois and McDowell's staff retreating about one mile northeast to Crescent Field.

PHOTOGRAPH 5.4 Position of Behr's battery upon redeployment from control of McDowell's brigade (photograph by author).

On the Confederate side, Pond's 3rd Brigade of Ruggles' 1st Division in Bragg's corps moved through McDowell's camps. The 18th Louisiana Orleans Guard and the 16th Louisiana moved up the ravine between the 46th Ohio's camp and the original position of Behr's battery. Elements of Colonel Robert P. Trabue's Kentucky Orphan Brigade approached the south end of "a long, crescent-shaped field," thereby beginning a gradual swing to the west, which would later threaten the Federal right and bring them into direct combat with Colonel Worthington's men.[10]

1030— Behr's battery of the 6th Indiana Light Artillery reached the crossroad north of Shiloh Church and received the order "action right" from Behr (see Photograph 5.4). Immediately upon issuing the command, Behr was shot from his horse and killed instantly. Drivers and gunners fled in disorder with their caissons, abandoning five guns without firing a shot (*War of the Rebellion*, Vol. 10, 250).

Sherman said that "about 10:30" his aides "conducted" McDowell's brigade to join McClernand's right in preparation for a limited counter-

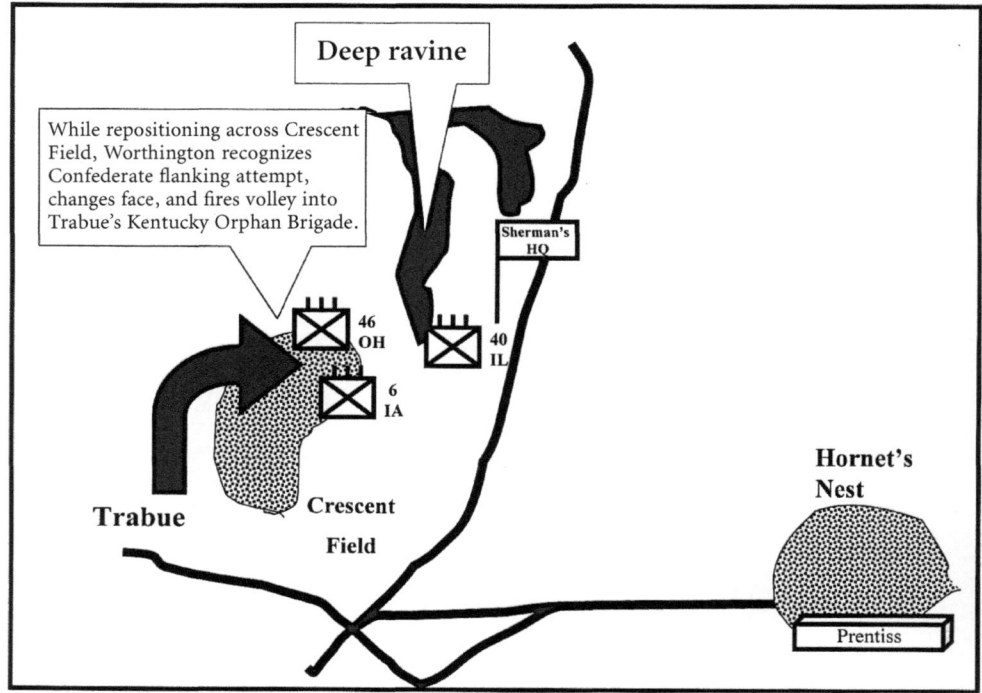

Map 5.8 Meeting engagement with Trabue.

attack (*War of the Rebellion*, Vol. 10, 250).[11] But the 46th was not with the 40th Illinois, and apparently only the 40th and McDowell's staff were "conducted."

1100— The 13th Missouri/22nd Ohio, Crofts Wright's unit, was attached to Sherman's division. Wright's unit had originally been assigned to McArthur's brigade of W. H. L. Wallace's division.

1130— Hicks' 40th Illinois, with McDowell's staff and the division staff accompanying them, had now moved northeast, leaving the 46th Ohio and the 6th Iowa to fend for themselves.

1135— A gap formed between the two regiments as the 46th Ohio and the 6th Iowa moved without the benefit of guides in the direction where McDowell and the 40th Illinois had withdrawn (toward the northeast side of Crescent Field).

1200— Hicks' 40th Illinois, with McDowell and staff nearby, occupied a secondary position beside troops from Raith's brigade of McLernand's division.

A brigade of Confederates under Colonel Trabue advanced across the

Five. "In Virtue Worthy" 101

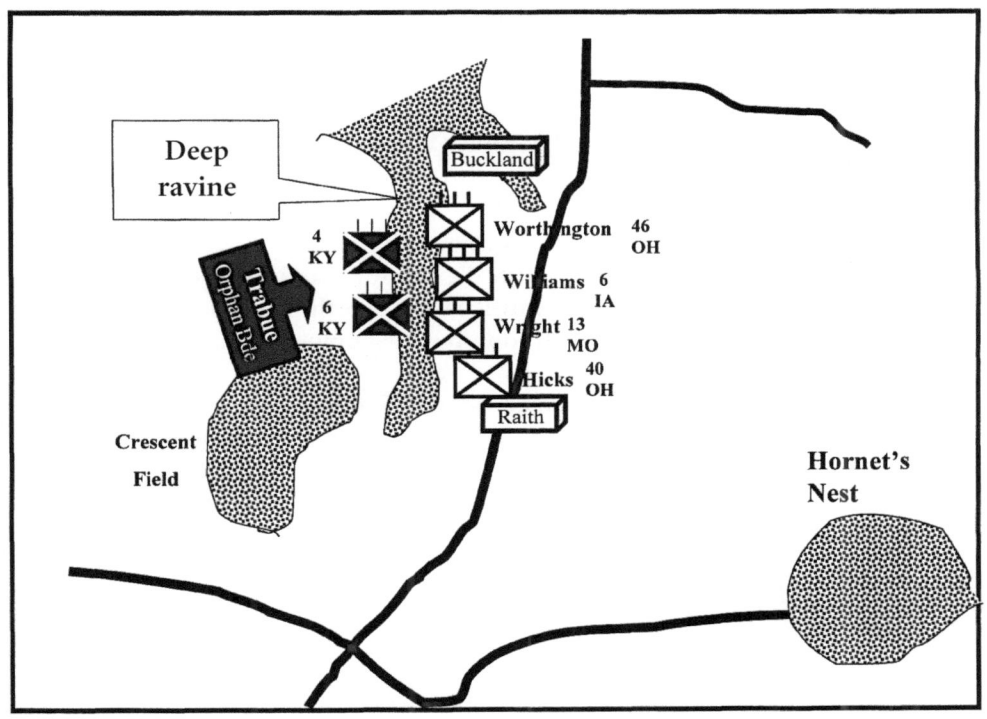

MAP 5.9 Defense of McDowell's brigade.

west edge of Crescent Field where they observed the 46th Ohio and the 6th Iowa "in the woods across the field." Trabue wrote that he "immediately moved by the left flank to the left, and confronted [the 46th Ohio]" as they marched to occupy the forward slope of a hill across a sharp ravine. "I had scarcely taken my new position, in fact, was changing the front of the left wing when [the enemy] deployed before me" (Thompson 84). But Trabue's attempt to flank the 46th had been discovered by Captain Heath, commander of Company A, who warned Colonel Worthington. Worthington immediately ordered the regiment to "change face and engage."[12] Simultaneously, Maj. Thomas B. Monroe of the 4th Kentucky ordered a change of front to engage Worthington's men. The 46th fired first, but their volley went over the heads of most of the Kentuckians. The return fire of the 4th Kentucky's brand-new Enfield rifles took a heavy toll on Worthington's line, but to their credit they did not break and run (Walden 2).

1210–1300— The 46th Ohio continued to engage Trabue's brigade northeast of Crescent Field and the ravine beyond. First Sergeant Burr of

Captain Pinney's company was killed here. "The combat here was a severe one," according to Colonel Trabue, as the 46th Ohio and 6th Iowa closed the gap between them and continued to defend across the ravine against the 4th Kentucky, the 6th Kentucky, and the 9th Kentucky of the Orphan Brigade. Lieutenant Colonel Walcut, Worthington's executive officer, received a wound in the upper left arm, as did Jack Neal, the 46th Ohio's adjutant.

1300–1400— The 46th Ohio continued its heaviest fighting of the day, as Worthington's men, along with the 6th Iowa and the 13th Missouri, struggled to hold off the Orphan Brigade. Worthington had begun the day's fighting with about 700 troops, but his numbers were being rapidly depleted.

While the 46th was resisting from the hillside shown on map 5.9, the main effort of the Confederate attack had become fixated on destroying General Prentiss' division, which now held a stubborn line of defense along a sunken road surrounded by woods, less than a half mile west-southwest of Worthington's position. Prentiss' men, fighting shoulder to shoulder and supported by massed artillery, began to fight off charge after charge, blasting the Confederates rushing across Duncan Field with both small arms and concentrated artillery fire.[13]

In front of Worthington's position, Colonel Trabue and his Kentuckians continued to press the Ohioans. Trabue indicated that he

> kill[ed] and wound[ed] four or five hundred of the Forty-sixth Ohio Infantry alone, as well as many of another Ohio regiment, a Missouri regiment [Col. Crofts Wright], some Iowa troops [the 6th], from all of whom we eventually took prisoners [Thompson 85].

During this fight with Worthington, Trabue admits that he lost "many men and several officers," yet he was about to press the offensive.[14] "The enemy appeared to outnumber us greatly," Trabue wrote. "I was for a while reluctant to charge; as he was in the woods, too, with some advantage of position" (Thompson 85). But eventually Trabue "gave the order to fix bayonets and move forward in double-quick time at a charge." Down the slope and across the ravine the Kentuckians came and, with "a shrill Rebel Yell," succeeded in dislodging McDowell's brigade from the defensive position they had held for nearly two hours (Walden 2). "The enemy, unwilling and unable to stand this charge, ran through their camps into the woods in their rear," Trabue indicated in his report.

1400— Col. Tom Worthington would not have characterized the 46th

PHOTOGRAPH 5.5 Shiloh National Battlefield Park monument recognizing the sacrifice of the men of the 46th Ohio Volunteer Infantry at their 2:00 P.M. position on Sunday, April 6, 1862 (photograph by author).

Ohio's retirement from the fight with the Kentuckians as anything less than an orderly retreat. The 6th Iowa and 46th Ohio withdrew to Jones Field. As they retreated, Captain Geary of Company B and Lieutenant Wilson were killed. The regiment rallied in the rear of the 11th Iowa near the center of McLernand's original camp.

    1430— The 6th Iowa moved to support Webster's line of artillery near the river. General Johnston died near the peach orchard as a result of a wound in his leg, which had gone unnoticed and untreated for almost an hour. With the loss of their commander in chief, the Confederate attack began to lose focus (Sword 272).

    1500— Worthington left the regiment and found Grant on the *Tigress*, where he offered a situation report.

    1545— Worthington left Grant and, having noticed the arrival of initial elements of Buell's forces, informed McLernand that reinforcements were coming.

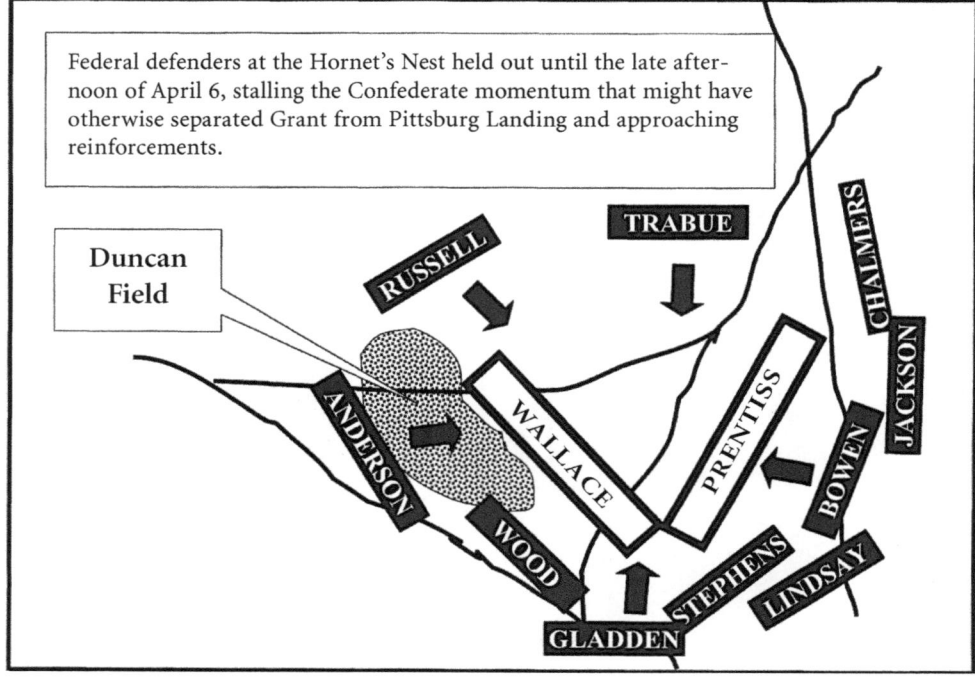

MAP 5.10 Surrender of the Hornet's Nest.

1600— While in the rear, Worthington assisted McAllister's battery in identifying an impending attack upon it and in responding to the attack (Worthington *Report* 11–12).

1700— General William Nelson's and General Jacob Ammen's divisions began arriving.

1715— Still moving about in the vicinity of Pittsburg Landing, Worthington was ordered by General Grant to return to the battle line with the 46th Ohio. Grant might have viewed Worthington's presence as interfering in the disposition and operation of other commands, as well as meddling in Grant's handling of the placement of the coming reinforcements.

1730— The "most prominent salient in the fast-retreating Union lines" during that fateful Sunday had been General Prentiss' division at the Hornet's Nest. At last, after withstanding numerous bloody assaults, Prentiss, now surrounded and out of ammunition, surrendered his division along the sunken road. His determined resistance had, however, caused the momentum of the Confederate attack to stall. In retrospect, many have suggested that by isolating and bypassing Prentiss, the Confederates could

Five. "In Virtue Worthy" 105

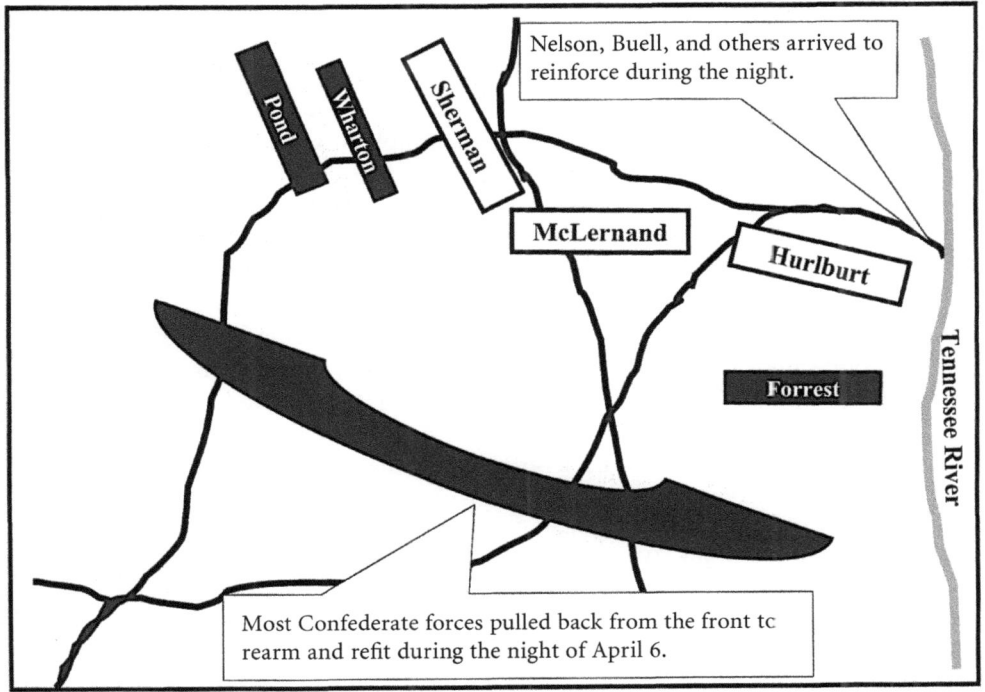

MAP 5.11 Last Federal position, nightfall, April 6, 1862.

have pressed the primary attack toward Pittsburg Landing and perhaps prevented Buell from reinforcing Grant. By interposing a force between Grant and the landing itself, the Confederates might have surrounded Grant and forced him to surrender before Buell's troops could arrive.

Night fell and General Beauregard, who had succeeded Johnston in command of the Army, called off the attack. Communications being less than precise, Major General Bragg did conduct one final bayonet assault after Beauregard's order to cease attack, but the assault was unsuccessful in dislodging the Federals. The Union forces had been driven back some three miles from their initial campsites and had lost thousands of men killed and captured in the process. But they had finished the day without surrender (except for Prentiss' surrounded division), they still held a solid line anchored on Snake Creek on the left (northern) flank and on Pittsburg Landing on the Tennessee on the right (southern or eastern) flank. Perhaps most important, they held the road to Crump's Landing and Savannah over which Buell's men would march to reinforce them during the night. They held the advantage of interior lines, occupying a shorter, more compact position than the Confederates—a position that was supported by artillery, commanded the high ground, and loaned itself to only being taken by a frontal assault (Hicks and Shultz 53).

Stretching out before them in the darkness for more than three miles and now occupied by exhausted yet triumphant Confederate troops was a mangled, body-strewn, horror-filled expanse of death, suffering, and destruction. The cacophony of sounds that reached the Federal lines that night must have been gut-wrenching. The pitiful voices of men from both sides crying out for help in the night bombarded the soldiers' ears. A heavy rain began to fall, and the air was thick with the smell of death. The cool night air chilled them as they huddled behind their last line of defense, wondering whether or not Buell would arrive in time to spare them from certain death or capture once the Confederates renewed their attack at daylight.

Worthington, now back with his regiment, took stock of his losses, cross-leveled ammunition, urged the men to remain calm, and tried to prepare them for the next day. But along with his attention to his troops that Sunday night, Worthington also nurtured a burning resentment of Sherman for his lack of preparedness. Already he held his division commander responsible for much of the death and destruction he had witnessed that day. His growing lack of confidence in Sherman's ability festered, and he must certainly have wondered what new horrors awaited him the following morning.

Trabue's brigade, which had fought so hard against Worthington and the 46th northeast of Crescent Field, had during the afternoon effectively closed off the only escape route of Prentiss' division and had been thus instrumental in its capture. That evening, after being forced out of a position near the river by Federal gunboat artillery fire, Trabue's brigade marched back along the Hamburg-Purdy Road and occupied the camps of the 46th Ohio and the 6th Iowa near Owl Creek Bridge. Though the assault and resulting ransacking of the camp during the day's attack had left it disheveled, the Kentuckians managed to find enough food and supplies to cut the chill and give them some comfort during the rainy night. Sergeant Henry "Unk" Cowling of the 5th/9th Kentucky Infantry discovered a large round of cheese, property of one of Worthington's men, "which he carried stuck on his bayonet until his colonel made him throw it away" (Walden 2).

During the darkness, however, Buell's 50,000 men began arriving and ferrying across the Tennessee River to replenish Grant's decimated army. Confederate Colonel Nathan Bedford Forrest's scouts observed the reinforcement and he warned the Confederate commander, General Beauregard, but his warnings went largely ignored.

Five. *"In Virtue Worthy"* 107

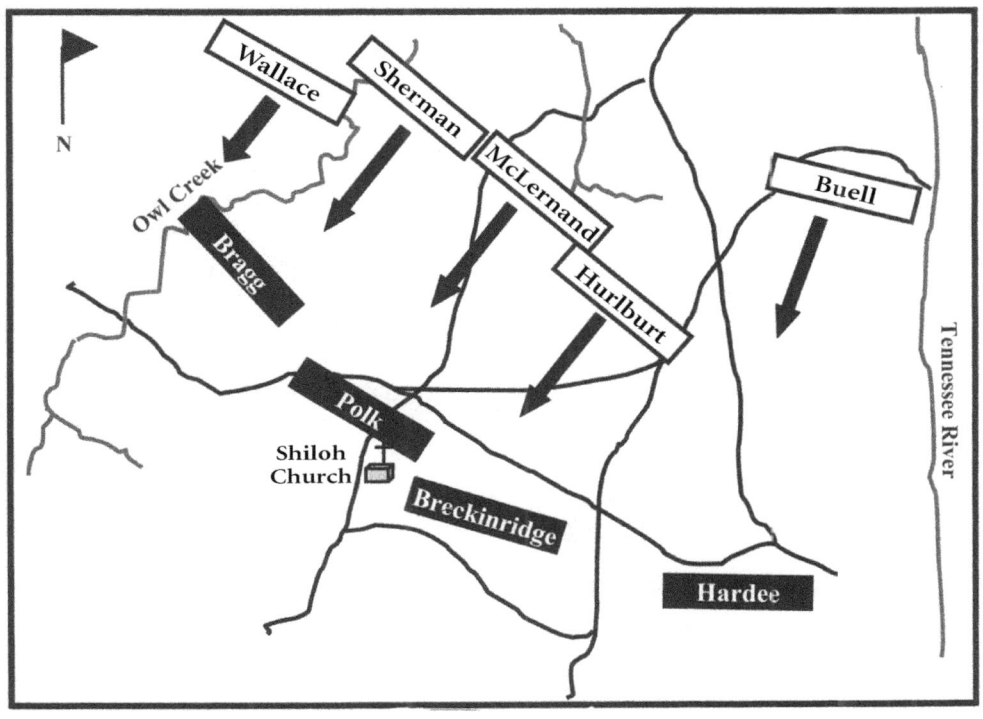

MAP 5.12 Federal counterattack, second day at Shiloh.

Second Day of Shiloh

Even with the arrival of Buell's troops during the night, General Grant was still senior commander on the scene. Yet because of Halleck's open disapproval of how he had handled the movement and actions along the Tennessee River, Grant refused to assume overall command of the forces now combining for a counteroffensive on Monday morning. With the rising sun that morning came a new opportunity for the Federals to regain the ground they had lost the previous day and to put an end to the Confederate offensive. So, at 5:00 A.M., having significantly superior numbers, the Union forces attacked from their positions along the river. But since Grant did not assume overall command, he and Buell launched independent, uncoordinated attacks. Despite this lack of unity, they were successful in pushing the Confederates back, and by noon it became apparent to General Beauregard that Grant had been strongly reinforced by "at least twenty-thousand fresh troops in addition to [General] Lew Wallace's command" (Roman 381). Continuing the fight would only result in more casualties than the Confederate Army could sustain and still remain a viable force to prevent further penetration of the South by the Union Army. Thus, according to Beauregard:

> The only plan left was, in appearance, to fight a[n] *outrance*, so as to deceive the enemy as to his real intentions, and, so deceiving him, to effect, at the proper time, an orderly, safe, and honorable retreat [Roman 318].

So Worthington's 46th Ohio and Sherman's division joined the new troops under Buell in pressing the Confederates back, although their decimated ranks were considerably less engaged than the previous day. It was "slow, bloody work" for Buell and Grant. The roads were muddy from a heavy rain during the night, and the Confederates maintained a bold front, stubbornly giving up the ground for which they had paid so dearly the previous morning (Hicks and Shultz 54).

By late afternoon, the Federals had retaken most all of their original camps, even those of Prentiss' and Appler's regiments well to the southwest. In a halfhearted pursuit, elements of Sherman's division engaged Col. Nathan Bedford Forrest and Capt. John Hunt Morgan's cavalry fighting a rearguard action at Fallen Timbers just south and west of Widow Howell's house. In the final moments of this exchange, in which Sherman's troops were stung and halted by Forrest's sudden attack, Tom Worthington appeared on horseback, armed with a musket. Sherman was less than pleased to see him and immediately ordered him back to rejoin his regiment. So ended the Battle of Shiloh — a battle that had begun with Sherman and Worthington at odds and that ended the same way. But the fight between these two men was to escalate over the following days, months, and years.

REST AMID THE CARNAGE

"That night [Monday], hungry and weary, we slept once more in our old camp," wrote a member of the 48th Ohio Infantry. His camp, like most of the others, had been rifled by the Confederates, who had occupied it the previous night, carrying away anything of value. As they cooked their supper Monday evening, the Federal troops found themselves surrounded by dead horses, wrecked wagons, caissons, guns, and all kinds of war implements strewn over the field. "The dead were lying in every conceivable shape. Some had fallen with their guns fast in their hands, others ... had sought the shelter of logs and trees, and laid down to die" (Bering and Montgomery 9). A soldier wrote home in a letter:

> I found ... a rebel, covered with clotted blood, pillowing his head on the dead body of a comrade. Both were red from head to foot. The dead man's brains had gushed out in a reddish and grayish mass over his face. The live one had lain across him all that horrible long night [Sunday] in the storm. The first thing he said to me was, "Give me some water. Send me a Surgeon — won't you! O God! What made you come down here to fight us? We never would have come up there." And then he affectionately put one arm over the form, and laid his bloody face against the cold, clammy, bloody face of his dead friend [More 106–107].

Such were the conditions throughout the camps, although since McDowell's brigade was engaged late in the morning and rapidly repositioned, the camp of the 46th did not contain the mass of dead and dying troops found elsewhere. The camp had not, however, avoided being ransacked by the Confederates.

Worthington and his men, along with those of the other Federal units, saw anger and hatred on both sides. "I saw one of our dead soldiers," an anonymous Union soldier wrote home, "with his mouth crammed full of cartridges until his cheeks were bulged out. Several protruded from his mouth. This was done by the rebels" (More 107).

On Tuesday, the morbid business of burying the dead and taking inventory of losses in both men and materiel began in earnest. Digging shallow pits, the Federals tossed in bodies, which landed with a splash and a thump against the bottom. "Many a hopeful, promising youth thus indecently ended his career" in such a manner (More 107).

> Some of our boys were disposed to kick the secesh into these pits. One fell in with a heavy thump on his face. The more humane proposed to turn him over. "O, that'll do," said a Union Missourian, "for when he scratches, he'll scratch nearer hell" [More 108].

Amid all of this, Tom Worthington steadily recorded the events that had transpired during the last three horrific days, and the record he kept would soon jeopardize his Army career.

Chapter Six

Fallout from Shiloh

In the Aftermath: Charges and Claims

The controversy over Shiloh had begun even before the last Federal soldier fired the final parting shot at Confederate General Nathan Bedford Forrest's cavalry rearguard at Fallen Timbers, just south and west of the battlefield. And until the last Shiloh veteran went to his grave in the twentieth century, these war-weary men debated in speech and in print the actions of Union and Confederate officers on that fateful April Sunday in 1862. Taking up the guidon of controversy, historians, scholars, and military leaders teaching history and tactics have argued for more than a century whether or not the Federal Army was surprised at Shiloh. And it is precisely this charge of surprise, or "lack of preparedness," as Union General Benjamin Prentiss, defender of the Hornet's Nest, kindly termed it, which forms the crux of Tom Worthington's charges against General Sherman.

The kindling for the controversy first began to smolder within hours of the battle. Initial reports reaching the northern newspapers described a desperate Federal Army fighting against overwhelming odds and prevailing in a great victory. But in addition to tolling the victory bell, the papers also carried what claimed to be eyewitness stories of how U.S. soldiers, particularly those of General Sherman's division, were completely surprised by the Confederate attack. Many stories filed by newspaper reporters either at the battle or near it told of Federal soldiers being bayoneted in their tents by frenzied rebels driving hard toward the river with blood in their eyes and the taste of imminent victory on their lips.

Cincinnati Gazette newspaper reporter Whitelaw Reid left Shiloh after the battle and within ten days had published a story of the fight. Where previous newspaper accounts had been generally laudatory of the Federal troops, Reid's account was harshly critical of Sherman and Grant, blaming them for being ill prepared to receive an attack. The story made sensational claims about "Union officers being bayoneted in their beds and being left 'gasping in their agony for two days'" (Hirshson 121). Much of Reid's story was correct, but much of it was erroneous as well, as he based some of his reporting on information gathered from stragglers and terrorized men of Sherman's brigade, who had bolted from the front and hid by the river landing for a large part of Sunday, April 6. Their skewed view of the battle, while fundamentally true in the lack of preparedness of the Federal forces initially, reflected an army caught *completely* off-guard. Perhaps realizing that he had blundered by not taking reconnaissance reports seriously and not getting more information on the enemy, Sherman sought to repair the damage by attacking Reid and those he believed were purveyors of falsehoods about the battle:

> The hue and cry against Grant about surprise is wrong. I was not surprised and I was in advance. Prentiss was not covered by me, and I don't believe he was surprised, although he is now a prisoner and cannot be heard. It is outrageous for the cowardly newsmongers, thus to defame men whose lives are exposed. The real truth is the private soldiers in battle leave their Ranks, run away and then raise these false issues. The political leaders dare not lay blame where it belongs.... In the 302 dead, and 1200 wounded of my Division, there was not a bayonet or knife wound, and the story of men being bayoneted in their tents is a pure lie.... It is all a lie got up by the cowards who ran to the River & reported we were surprised and all killed [Thorndike 143].

Sherman craftily combined the false reports about men bayoneted in their tents with the reports of "surprise" and hoped that the falsity of one would rub-off on the other. But the newspaper-reading public, at least initially, and the historians who came after them were smart enough to recognize a difference. It was to this audience that Colonel Tom Worthington would appeal in the months after the battle and in the years after the war. But during the weeks following Shiloh, Sherman was desperate to blame somebody other than himself for the bad press he was receiving at home. Alfred Andreas points out that so intermixed were the units and so dense the vegetation that the soldiers who fought at Shiloh had to wait until "the newspapers from the North" arrived to "learn what [they] had done"

(116). Sherman must have believed that his bravery on April 6 and his ability as a general would not go unrecognized. Some newspaper reports were exaggerations. Some contained blatantly false information. But many did not. And as much as Sherman tried to claim that the newspaper reports about Shiloh reflected the ravings of cowardly newspapermen who only talked to refugees and shirkers, the truth about Shiloh was arriving home in the letters of the soldiers themselves.

Among those writing was Tom Worthington who, as soon after the battle as April 15, wrote a letter detailing what he believed was the incompetent leadership of Federal forces during the Battle of Shiloh[1]:

Camp Shiloh Tenn Apr 15th 1862

Dear Sir

... The terrible battle of the 6th grows more terrible in the distance as time is given to reflect on what might have been the consequence of our   loss of tens of thousands of lives, hundreds of millions of money, perhaps the extinction of the govt. The danger was created ...[by] imprudence — mismanagement [and] *neglect*. I am now carrying out an order for defensive measures which I urged over a month ago and which if carried out before the bloody 6th would have either prevented the attack or made it easy to repel it. Sherman ... permitted [the enemy's] pickets to fire almost into our camp — knew a week before that an attack was imminent, knew that a   of artillery and half a dozen reg[imen]t[s] were a mile off at 2 p.m. of the 5th and yet allowed them to march up to the encampment while men of the reg[imen]t were at breakfast. His troops were too scattered and were beaten in detail as was the whole Army. He had no cavalry and   artillery in the reg[imen]t and no use was made of what he had. There was no supports, no concert of action. There was no contingent arrangement made — no rallying points in a country covered with timber and underbrush — nothing to indicate there was a general in the [command]. Grant (a man of [little] capacity and much pretense) shares the blame as being a Major General in chief command, and at Savannah when the attack was made.... the attack was desperate, but they had marched two nights before the battle and Friday night were exhausted. Under the circumstances — so far as the 46th is concerned it ... was the last reg[imen]t of the division to leave its original line of battle, and it was the first of its brigade to attack the rebels at noon or near 3:00. The unit found that it did so effectively and it did not retreat till ordered by Gen. Sherman to do so ... losing 270 men in all [Worthington Letter 15 Apr. 1862].[2]

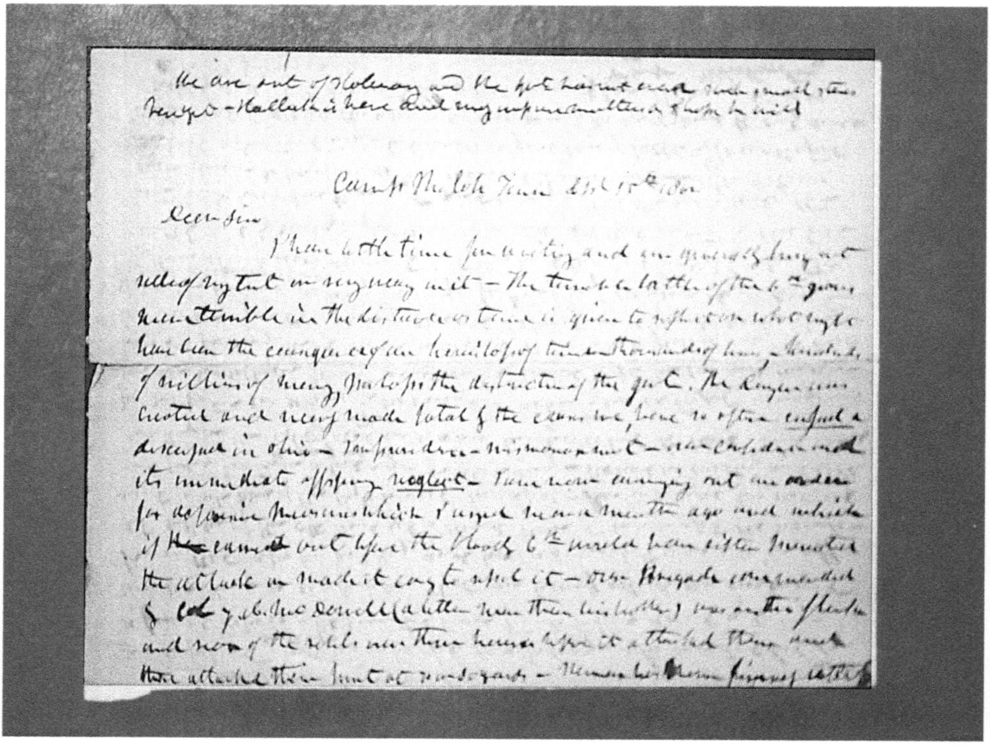

Photograph 6.1 Tom Worthington's hastily written letter denouncing Sherman shortly after the Battle of Shiloh (courtesy Ross County Historical Society).

Colonel Worthington made serious allegations in this letter, but he was by no means the only soldier documenting in letters home the circumstances surrounding the battle. When Major John H. Foster, 3rd Ohio Volunteer Cavalry, wrote home to his son about the battle, he neither hedged the facts as he knew them, nor did he paint a more positive picture than warranted:

> Savannah — April 17, 1862
>
> ... Strange as it may appear on Sunday morning about six o'clock a.m. *our line was surprised* [emphasis added]. Some Regts [had] no pickets out and some Regts [were] attacked in their tents and literally cut to pieces or taken prisoner. Such was the rout of our Army at first it was about impossible to form line of battle. Our forces under Genl Grant extended a line about four miles and were attacked at several points at the same time [Foster 1].

Six. Fallout from Shiloh

Foster indicates how on the first day they fought "from about seven o'clock a.m. until 5 o'clock p.m. being awfully whipped up to that time." He credits Nelson's arrival as making the difference, describing panicked Federals who ran from the front, hugging the landing for cover. "Such was the terror of our troops that they rushed for the boats and Genl. Nelson had to charge bayonets to keep them from sinking the boat." He continued:

> I suppose you will read of the so called Great Victory of the Federal forces at the Battle of Shiloh, Tenn, but here let me say it is no victory for us. 1st we have lost 2400 men prisoners; 2nd about 40 pieces of cannon more than we took back   the transportation wagons, mules, and horses of at least two regiments and I think many more. We have only 500 prisoners. We have lost 2000 killed. ... I am sorry to say we got the worst of it having more killed than they do. Our soldiers are too careless about their duty and would seem as if they never would learn [Foster 2].

An anonymous soldier at Shiloh declared:

> To show how complete and successful was the advance of the enemy, their advance guard lay in the woods on the 5th, witnessing our parades and reviews. One of our returned paroled prisoners, a mule-driver, who was captured two days before the battle, had told me that he was taken through their whole army, which was camped three miles from ours, the night before the attack [More 108].

Yet on the details of Shiloh, Grant and Sherman closed ranks in an alliance that would last for years. The newspaper reports contained just enough mistakes to undermine the truths they presented, thus casting doubts on the motives of the reporters. At that point in the war, the nation needed generals it could believe in far more than it needed reporters. Since "the nation was looking for a hero" (Andreas 121), Grant and Sherman rose in stature and rank rather than sitting before a court-martial, where, as many argued, they deserved to be. When the secretary of War read Grant's report of the battle, he sent Sherman's name to the president for promotion. As soon as President Lincoln received General Halleck's recommendation for Sherman's promotion, he made it happen. Thus, in early May, William Tecumseh Sherman received his promotion to major general.

But promotion or no promotion, the controversy about Shiloh simply would not go away. And newspaper reporters were not the only source of the criticism. No less than the lieutenant governor of Ohio, Benjamin Stanton, levied charges against Sherman and Grant for their behavior. Dispatched on a fact-finding and humanitarian mission after the battle, Stanton reported to Governor Tod on April 28 that "the disasters of Sunday, April 6th, were the result of surprise, which is justly chargeable on the commanding officers." Stanton charged "blundering" and "incompetence" against some of the officers in the battle, and he wrote to the governor that "our lines were so carelessly and negligently guarded that the enemy were absolutely on us, in our very tents, before the officers in command were aware of their approach" (Ewing 3). Sherman and those who supported him (e.g., his brother, the senator) were so concerned that no criticism of his performance at Shiloh should stand the light of scrutiny, that Thomas Ewing wrote an extensive letter to Stanton in which he tried to refute virtually all of Stanton's findings.[3] Ewing impugned, without credibility in many cases, the witnesses Stanton relied upon for his information, questioned Stanton's motives, and suggested in Stanton a lack of patriotism for trying to "prevent enlistments and induce insubordination and desertion." Ewing said Stanton's criticisms were published to "demoralize" the Army. Ewing is strangely eloquent in what amounts to an ad hominem argument that purports to exonerate Sherman but in reality reeks of partisanship.

Indeed, Tom Worthington was far from alone in his desire that Sherman be held accountable for his actions at Shiloh. Stanton challenged Sherman to take the matter before a court-martial "composed of independent and intelligent army officers" where Stanton fully expected to convict Grant, Prentiss, and Sherman of gross negligence (Marszalek, "William T. Sherman," 83). But other leaders and newspaper writers came to Sherman's defense, describing him as "proudly among the world's heroes," and Stanton ultimately lost his war of words before the jury of public and political opinion (Marszalek, "William T. Sherman," 81). Other writers who remained critical of Sherman were shouted down and accused of being out to get him or portrayed as untrustworthy. People's interests eventually, and perhaps rightfully, turned to the next critical movements and battles of the war. In their many letters and orations, Sherman's heavy hitters, including Ewing, John Sherman, and a host of others, hammered anyone who attempted to talk about the oversights and mistakes of Shiloh, labeling them as partisans simply passing on rumor and innuendo. By the end of May, Sherman was promoted, the move against Corinth was underway, the carping about Shiloh and who was responsible had dwindled to a murmur, and the only person still demanding answers was Tom Worthington:

> Sherman emerged victorious in this [Stanton's charges] and all his Shiloh controversies. He who had been pushed to the brink of military and personal disaster by an Ohio newspaper in 1861 [charges of insanity], had, in 1862, as a result of Shiloh debates, vanquished all his Ohio opponents.... In the meantime the war went on, and the Shiloh controversy was lost in the mire of new military and verbal battlefields [Marszalek, "William T. Sherman," 84].

Lost, perhaps, to everyone except Tom Worthington.

Sherman would later state under oath that he believed much of the adverse press about the Union forces at Shiloh came from reporters and other noncombatants talking to Tom Worthington and examining extracts from his personal diary. It is true that within days of the Battle of Shiloh Worthington was approaching his fellow officers with his inflammatory allegations of Sherman's incompetence.

Strangely, on April 21, William Sherman's brother John, a senator from Ohio, wrote to Adjutant General Lorenzo Thomas praising Worthington's "great ability at the battle of Shiloh" and describing him as a man "believed to be far superior to several officers, who, by filling their regiments sooner, outrank him." These words sound more like something Worthington would have written about himself rather than the words of General Sherman's brother. Sherman had commended Worthington in his official report, indicating that Worthington had "displayed great personal courage," and now, Sherman's brother was declaring, "It is the desire, I am informed, of *all* [emphasis added] his superior officers that he rank from the date of his appointment, August 1861. Cannot that order be made?" (*War of the Rebellion*, Vol. 10, 252; McCormick 35).

Presumably, *all* his superior officers must have included General Sherman. Eighteen days later, Senator Sherman stated on the floor of the Senate that Worthington's actions at Shiloh were worthy of "the highest credit ... for courage and good conduct." McCormick argues that these actions were a combination of "honest appraisal, partisan support of an Ohio officer," and "an attempt to quiet Worthington's criticism of General Sherman's actions" (McCormick 35).

THE CAMPAIGN CONTINUES

Even while the horrors of Shiloh kept Worthington awake at night, and his distrust and dislike of Sherman gnawed away at him, the Ohio colonel knew he must soldier on. In the months following the battle,

Worthington returned to the business of commanding the 46th Ohio, but he did not let up in his criticism of Sherman. On May 5, Sherman issued a circular from his headquarters urging conservation of food due to the poor condition of the roads and the subsequent effect upon resupply. He directed that horses eat "bushes, such as elm, cotton-wood, and sassafras" and that the men use "every axe and spade" on improving "our roads and defenses."

> In front of the whole line, underbrush must be cut to a distance of three hundred yards, and heavy logs felled as a breastwork along the front of the artillery and camps. Picket guards and sentinels must be visited often, and the utmost vigilance maintained [Worthington *Blunders* 12].

These words reflect the tactics of a new William Tecumseh Sherman — a Sherman stung by his lack of preparedness at Shiloh and determined not to be taken again by surprise and overrun. What Sherman would never admit in his later life and career is betrayed by his own orders issued less than a month after the Battle of Shiloh. But Worthington took issue even with this circular, which contained enough references to improving the defensive position that it might have been extracted from Worthington's diary prior to Shiloh. From his camp near Monterey (about ten miles south of the Shiloh battlefield), Worthington fired off a letter to General Halleck, citing as his duty the need to call Halleck's attention to the circular. Worthington proceeded to attack Sherman's ration conservation by saying:

> If we are to be put upon half rations and chance forage at thirteen miles from our base of operations by a few hours rain, how can the army hope within any reasonable time to effect the object of its organization and put an end to the war? [Worthington *Blunders* 12].

Worthington also enclosed a copy of Sherman's April 25th Order No. 21, issued in an attempt to tighten up the regiments' laxity toward drill. Sherman wanted "no officer or soldier to be absent" from drill, indicating that an officer must be excused to the hospital or by the division surgeon. A soldier was to be excused from drill only if he were in the hospital or serving as a picket or a sentinel on post. The part of this order that angered Worthington was Sherman's removal of the authority of a regimental commander to excuse his soldiers from drill. "If the men are unable to bear arms, they will form on the left of the company, unarmed," Sherman ordered. He further stated that if men were not in the hospital, "but suffering from diarrhea, they can be hauled to the drill-ground by the colonel's order, and there they must be silent and observe the movements of the division" (Worthington *Blunders* 13). If soldiers were too ill to drill, Sherman wanted them watching the division drill at a minimum. Recalling Worthington's frequent protestations about Sherman's handling of the sick prior to Shiloh, it is not surprising that the colonel took issue with his commander's plan to "haul" soldiers to drill who were suffering from diarrhea. In his letter to Halleck, Worthington noted that Sherman's order exhibited "far more zeal than discretion," stating that men with "the usual camp diseases above all things require quiet, and whatever their disposition, are not in a condition to study brigade drill." Worthington continued, "The object of such orders is obviously to produce discontent and demoralization, of which there is an ample amount existing." Worthington then suggested that if Sherman paid more attention to supplying the troops with "fresh bread and better hospitals," they would improve much more rapidly than through the kind of orders his division commander was issuing (Worthington *Blunders* 12).

Tom's sister Sarah arrived at Pittsburg Landing on May 15 with her Catholic relief organization to attend to the wounded from Shiloh and to prepare hospital boats for the casualties anticipated as a result of a battle near Corinth, Mississippi. She managed an occasional "hurried visit with Tom" but spent most of her time caring for the wounded on board various hospital ships. Fully a month after the battle, reminders of the carnage remained painfully present as Sarah wrote to her son, Rufus, on May 18th:

> The high bank is covered with dirty tents and wagons and horses and dirtier looking men. The trench is still stifling from the dead bodies of horses and mules — and of men buried 6 inches under the surface [Sarah Worthington, 18 May 1862].

One day not long after writing that letter, having not had a chance to see Worthington for several days, Sarah encountered a grim-looking doctor. He solemnly informed her that Tom had been "killed by a sentry shot and his body was on one of the boats at the wharf ready to be shipped home." Sarah wrote to her son on May 24 that she rushed to the boat that she might pay last respects to Tom and upon arriving, asked to have the wooden casket opened. Before the box was opened, a young officer appeared and announced that he was the funeral escort to return the body to the soldier's "widow and children." "Judge then of my happiness," Sarah

PHOTOGRAPH 6.2 A burial trench at Shiloh (photograph by author).

wrote, "to find that the unfortunate gentleman was Colonel Worthington of Iowa, and not my brother, Tom!" (McAllister 317).

FEDERAL OFFENSIVE CONTINUES—AT A CRAWL

In the aftermath of Shiloh, the Federal campaign through the heart of Tennessee and into northern Mississippi slowed to a crawl. Even though the Federals had succeeded in defending their camp at Pittsburg Landing and in ultimately regaining the ground they lost on the first day, the Union troops there had suffered a blow that staggered them. The primary Confederate accomplishment at Shiloh had been to stop the Union juggernaut that had overrun Fort Henry and Fort Donelson, to remind the Union rank and file that they were not invincible, and to instill a heavy dose of caution in its leadership. General Halleck, nicknamed "Old Brains," had resumed full control of Federal forces after Shiloh, and being a cautious man he determined to "at all costs avoid mistakes" (Catton, *Grant Moves South* 265):

Six. Fallout from Shiloh

PHOTOGRAPH 6.3 Burial trench display (photograph by author).

> This army which was beginning a new offensive would think constantly about its own defense, and every camp would be deeply entrenched, down to the position of the last platoon. The army would go south with gelatinous majesty, as if it were conducting a moving siege, burrowing its way with a ripple of earthworks always going on ahead [Catton, *Grant Moves South* 265].

For what would turn out to be a crawl toward Corinth, Halleck had assembled at Pittsburg Landing the largest force ever gathered on the continent. Halleck divided his 125,000-man army into three elements: the Army of the Ohio under Maj. Gen. Don Carlos Buell (the man many believed to have been the true savior of Shiloh), the Army of West Tennessee under Maj. Gen. Ulysses S. Grant, and the Army of the Mississippi under Maj. Gen. John Pope. Grant, who Halleck still did not estimate to be a particularly capable commander, was relegated to the position of commanding the right wing and the reserve. Halleck proceeded to bypass Grant with his orders for the right wing, making Grant "little more than an observer" (Cozzens 17). Grant protested but to little avail.

Corinth, Mississippi, was the primary objective of the Federal advance because it hosted the junction of the Memphis and Charleston Railroad and the Mobile and Ohio Railroad. Loss of Corinth would mean the Confederacy's east-west primary supply connection between the Atlantic coast and the Mississippi River would be crippled. Thus the Army crept southward while General Beauregard used various deceptions to maintain the illusion that the southerners were ready to fight at any moment in defense of the town and the railroad junction. Still reeling from the spanking they had received at Shiloh, the Federals were ready to believe any number of exaggerated enemy strength and movement reports.

Tom Worthington and the men of the 46th Ohio, still under Sherman's command, pressed south in this laborious advance. In many ways they were just glad to be escaping the putrid, overcrowded campsite on the battlefield of Shiloh. Men of the 46th had suffered in the aftermath of the battle from diarrhea as well as other illnesses due to lack of sanitation. The situation must have reminded Worthington of Matamoros and Camargo in the Mexican War. The sutlers, gamblers, prostitutes, reporters, and curious onlookers had descended on the Shiloh encampment in the days following the battle, bringing with them the usual distractions. Worthington and his men were relieved to be actually doing something even if it was a slow, deliberate advance. Bruce Catton in his book *Grant Moves South*, describes what the men of the 46th and other regiments faced:

> Corduroying roads through the endless swamps was hard work, with parties of six or eight men, lugging ten-foot logs, hour after hour; the roads that were built in this way were bumpy and slippery, and loaded wagons often slid off and were hopeless[ly] mired, the horses sometimes sinking entirely out of sight [270].

Many units less disciplined than the 46th and, indeed, possibly even some of Worthington's men resorted to looting property from the southern citizens in their path. One landowner complained that he had "been robbed of everything but my hope of eternal salvation." In addition, the Ohio units suffered from an infestation of chiggers. Some of them claimed that "for twenty-eight days they were not able to get their clothes off" (Catton, *Grant Moves South* 270).

Worthington and his men met with little more than an occasional skirmish while pressing slowly southward, although the Confederates had managed to keep up the illusion of their readiness and willingness to strike at any moment. Of course Worthington indicated in his postwar writing that he knew all along that the enemy strength was overreported and that

Six. Fallout from Shiloh

they might have been defeated by some bold maneuvering. But being an engineer officer by commission, he seems to have found plenty to do orchestrating the road building and hasty breastworks that were an everyday chore. Historians have second-guessed Halleck's tedious advance against Corinth, calling it one of the slowest uncontested advances ever recorded of any army and suggesting that if Halleck had been more aggressive, Beauregard's army might have been surrounded and captured.

As the Army approached Corinth toward the end of May, Grant showed signs of depression about his relegation to the status of an onlooker in the process. Having made some suggestions about how to defeat Beauregard that were dismissed out of hand by Halleck, Grant was ready to leave. Worthington's nemesis, Sherman, appeared at Grant's camp one day and found his trunks and boxes packed up and ready to be loaded. Explaining to Sherman that he was going home on leave, Grant indicated that he felt useless in Halleck's army and stated that he could not take it anymore. Along with Grant being sidetracked in the chain of command, newspaper reports had charged him with incompetence at Shiloh, and the accusations of drunkenness plagued him as they would for most of his military career. Sherman argued with Grant, insisting that he should reconsider and stick it out. He pointed out that he, himself, had only months before been called a lunatic by the newspapers and had been relegated to inspecting troops in Missouri. Accounts of the details of this encounter differ, with one version having Sherman extract from Grant a promise not to leave until he again talked it over, and another version depicting Sherman as tearing up Grant's letter of resignation and asking him to wait three weeks before making a decision. Sherman reminded Grant that he, too, once considered leaving amid all the lunacy accusations, but he had stuck it out and after Shiloh found himself "in ... high feather" (Hirshson 127; Catton, *Grant Moves South*, 274). Whatever the nature of the exchange between Grant and Sherman, it seems to have convinced Grant to remain, and it, without doubt, sealed the bond of mutual support between the two officers.

A few days after this meeting, Beauregard successfully evacuated his 33,000-man army from Corinth right under the nose of the Federal Army, and while he gave up the city without a fight (much to the consternation of Confederate President Jefferson Davis), he did escape with his command intact. He had completely fooled Halleck, Grant, Sherman, and the entire Federal leadership as to his intentions, bringing forth more criticism from northern newspapers about what many considered dawdling and incompetence among the Union high command.

Following the Federal occupation of Corinth, Mississippi, Sherman's division received orders to move into western Tennessee with the ultimate target of occupying Memphis. Thus, Worthington and the men of the 46th Ohio began a month-long march to Memphis via La Grange, Tennessee (later a major Federal supply depot and troop staging point); Grand Junction, Tennessee (a critical railroad intersection); and Holly Springs, Mississippi. Worthington's regiment pulled guard duty along the Memphis and Charleston Railroad during this period, skirmishing with enemy cavalry, building a redoubt at Lafayette, Tennessee, and conducting rather mild security duties. In a letter to West Point after the war, Worthington described some of the action:

> June 25, 1862 — being left on detached service with his regiment of about 300 men to defend the depot and the railroad at Lafayette, Tennessee under an order declaring an attack imminent he immediately constructed the first redoubt built in the campaign thus protecting his troops from probable attack or capture by a superior rebel force [Worthington 14 Jan 1866].

Worthington commanded at Lafayette in late June and early July, and nearby Col. Ralph Buckland (72nd Ohio) commanded the railroad guard at Moscow, Tennessee. The two Ohioans, both still under the command of Sherman, who headed up the military district containing Lafayette and Moscow, cooperated in maintaining the security of the rail line. Little significant confrontation with the enemy occurred during this time, and their duties seem to have been primarily making sure the trains had escorts through their area to protect them from marauding Confederate cavalry. Representative of their duties is Buckland's telegram to Grant on July 1:

> Genl Sherman left for Holly Springs at two P.M. yesterday under orders from Genl. Halleck to act in concert with Genl. Rosecrans going from Corinth via Ripley [Mississippi]. One Regiment left here. Train of sixty wagons with one Regiment of Infantry left for Memphis at 4 A.M. heard nothing from it. Suppose it safe as Oakland is only five miles from the road ... rebel cavalry attacked Col. Worthington at Lafayette last evening all quiet this morning [Simon 189].

By the end of July, Worthington and the 46th Ohio had assumed provost duty at Fort Pickering in Memphis. Sherman had assumed, in addition to his regular military duties, supreme command of the city of Memphis. Not only was he responsible for battling guerrillas operating near the town and along the river, but he was also daily facing a "barrage of complaining civilians" (Marszalek 197). Memphis had been virtually shut down upon the Federal approach, but once he arrived, Sherman restored the city's mayor to office and tried, with limited success, to control the sale of contraband food and weapons to Confederate agents. The policies he established in Memphis encouraged prostitution and drinking, with the number of liquor establishments increasing significantly during late July and August. "He considered prostitution and liquor private matters not within his jurisdiction," according to Marszalek (197). Hirshson in *The White Tecumseh* quotes a reporter as saying that a person was likely within some ten feet of alcohol sales at any location within Memphis during these days, and in an observation of particular importance given Tom Worthington's behavior during this period, Hirshson writes:

> Inebriated soldiers were everywhere. When stopped for being drunk, they merely took their apprehenders out for a drink. The gin sold in most places was cut with turpentine, the wine with camphene. For this "refined and devilish species of torture," concluded the reporter, "we must thank General Sherman, whose ingenuity is certainly only equaled by his versatility" [130].

It was here, amid this atmosphere of widespread alcohol abuse and not only toleration of such by Sherman but encouragement by his policies, that Tom Worthington committed the acts that would drive Sherman to bring the old colonel's military career crashing down around him.

CHARGES AGAINST SHERMAN

Every time General Sherman thought he had the skeletons of Shiloh safely buried, Tom Worthington would thrust a bony hand from the grave of ignominy and grab Cump by the ankle. From his command in Lafayette, Worthington wrote a letter to General Halleck on July 11, reminding him of their first meeting back on April 17. In the letter he indicated that had he known then that Halleck would later claim that Sherman had "saved the day" on the 6th of April at Shiloh, he would have "at once dissented from that opinion." He said he would have back in late April sent "through the regular channel" extracts of his diary, which he now had included in his letter. Worthington reminded Halleck that he had refused Worthington's charges at their April 17 meeting, and he also reminded him that later, at a meeting in Monterey (about eight miles south of Shiloh), Halleck had told Worthington that he expected "to see something *spicy*" when Worthington sent his charges through "the regular channel." Of course Halleck knew that "the regular channel" meant passing the charges through Sherman himself, thus Halleck would not likely have ever had to deal with the information. Sherman was, apparently, still Halleck's anointed one, and Halleck seemed more interested in silencing Worthington than in examining the truth of his accusations. But Worthington would not be deterred:

> Having a little leisure here, I have had the extracts [of my diary] copied, and you now have them, with such crude remarks as I can hastily throw together, referring you to a report of the proceedings of my regiment & others, for their proper understanding. I hold General W. T. Sherman responsible for the condition of the army at Shiloh up to the 7th of April, and besides what occurred in his own division, for everything arising out of that condition, directly or indirectly. And this for the reason that to him was confided the advance of the expedition of Tennessee. He is, or is supposed to be, a man of more intellect than any general officer engaged in that battle. There was a general disposition to give him every opportunity to develop his military abilities before and especially on the second day of the battle, and the chiefs of the army have concurred, without dissent, and equally without investigation, according to your statement, in giving him the most favorable and prominent position in the result of those about equally disastrous days. Far more disastrous in their immediate results, as they will doubtless prove in their ultimate consequence, than the writer of *diary* anticipated. General Sherman was entirely aware of everything occurring or likely to occur, which is expressed or implied or supposed probable, in the above extracts [Worthington *Blunders* 9].

Then, perhaps in an appeal to Old Brains' own vanity, Worthington detailed how Sherman violated numerous tenets contained in Halleck's own book, *Elements of Military Art and Science*. In summation, Worthington argued:

> First, [Sherman displayed] utter disregard of the immediate and obvious indications of an attack after Friday noon, as shown by his leaving all things as they were; second, his utter disregard of his artillery, with respect more especially to its ammunition; third, his failing to make any provision for his own wounded and sick men; fourth, his fatuity in leaving useless his right brigade, to

say nothing of his left, either of which might, if thrown on either rebel flank, have driven back the first attack even as late as 8 a.m.; fifth, his unaccountable sacrifice of five guns of Behr's battery, when the whole might have been, as one gun was, preserved with the first brigade; sixth, his useless and reckless waste of life in the charge by Colonel Hick's [sic] 50th Illinois regiment; seventh, his so hastily leaving the weakest and most exposed part of his line, where his presence would seem most needed; and eighth, the fact of his leaving such a point so exposed [Worthington *Blunders* 11].

Worthington concluded his letter to Halleck by declaring:

> General W. T. Sherman did more to prepare the army of Tennessee for a defeat on the 6th of April, and more to accomplish that defeat in the course of the battle, than any officer on either side, on the bloody field of Shiloh.
>
> Very Respectfully, yours,
>
> T. Worthington
> Colonel, 46th Ohio Volunteer Infantry
> [Worthington *Blunders* 12]

Colonel Tom Worthington had now bypassed the chain of command to levy serious allegations against his division commander. Up to this point, Sherman might have been able to tolerate the second-guessing of his leadership, and he might have been able to withstand Worthington's not-so-subtle suggestions that he knew more about warfare than Sherman. But once Worthington wrote directly to Halleck and basically said that Sherman was responsible for the deaths of thousands of Union soldiers at Shiloh, Sherman was compelled to take action. Worthington knew this all too well and fully understood the ramifications of this communication to his military future. Still, his hatred of Sherman was strong enough to drive him ahead with his letter to Halleck.

What made Worthington angry enough at Sherman to risk his commission and his Army career? The answer is both simple and complex. Worthington was furious over what he believed to be the needless loss of life, money, and military momentum caused by Sherman's lack of preparedness at the Battle of Shiloh. The 46th Ohio Volunteer Infantry and dozens of other volunteer units had suffered horrific casualties at the Battle of Shiloh. The roster in table 6.1 crystallizes, at least for the 46th Ohio, the cost in lives and capability for which Worthington held Sherman responsible.

Table 6.1
Casualties of the 46th Ohio Volunteer Infantry at Shiloh

Name & Company	KIA at the Battle of Shiloh	WIA at the Battle of Shiloh	Died of wounds from the Battle of Shiloh	Died in camp at Shiloh before the battle	MIA at the Battle of Shiloh	Total casualties from the Battle of Shiloh
Field & Staff						
John B. Foster						
John B. Neil		X				
Charles C. Walcutt		X				
Company A						
William Agler		X				
John Boroff		X				
Alexander B. Brown		X				
Aquilla Crogan		X				
David P. Dunathan		X				
George Dunathan		X				
John M. Harper, Jr.		X				
Henry Hauts		X				
Sheldon Hays				X		
John Heppard		X				
William H. King						
William M. Lytle						
Thomas McGlothin		X				
Joseph Mortimore			X			
Enoch Thomas			X			
David Truby				X		
James M. Tullis		X				
Aliers Williams		X				
Daniel Wollets		X				
Total for Field & Staff and Company A		15	2	2		19
Company B						
George M. Carter		X				
George W. Finks	X					
Henry Heller			X			
Elias McKinney		X				
Owen R. Mansfield		X				

Six. Fallout from Shiloh

Name & Company	KIA at the Battle of Shiloh	WIA at the Battle of Shiloh	Died of wounds from the Battle of Shiloh	Died in camp at Shiloh before the battle	MIA at the Battle of Shiloh	Total casualties from the Battle of Shiloh
(Company B)						
William Shirey		X				
Henry Stiles	X					
John A. Swank		X				
Charles Wallace		X				
Eli Williams		X				
John P. Williams		X				
Total for Company B	2	8	1			11
Company C						
William Beady				X		
William Gye	X					
John W. Hanson					X	
Jacob Hare		X				
Albert L. Morton						
David M. Noe			X			
David R. Noe	X					
Martin V. B. Odell		X				
George Parkinson			X			
John Rowles	X					
Otto Shane	X					
Franklin Smith		X				
John Stewart	X					
David Taylor	X					
James A. Thompson		X				
Lewis Walmire	X					
George H. Wise	X					
Andrew S. Wise					X	
Rezin Yontz		X				
Williams Yontz		X				
Total for Company C	8	6	2	1	2	19
Company D						
Adrian Banecroft					X	
George Bear	X					

Name & Company	KIA at the Battle of Shiloh	WIA at the Battle of Shiloh	Died of wounds from the Battle of Shiloh	Died in camp at Shiloh before the battle	MIA at the Battle of Shiloh	Total casualties from the Battle of Shiloh
(Company D)						
James Blair					X	
William C. Dalton		X				
George Frankenburg		X				
Harding C. Geary	X					
William H. Hempy		X				
Anthony McGill		X				
Andrew Sheridan					X	
Jacob Shilling			X			
Daniel O. Smith		X				
James White	X					
Total for Company D	3	5	1		3	12
Company E						
Eli Barker	X					
John Brentinger		X				
Henry C. Burr	X					
Charles S. Comstock					X	
Alexander Coon						
Henry Fellows		X				
James Heller	X					
William Jones		X				
John Merlin		X				
Edward Sebring		X				
Henry Shuttie		X				
Joel Stutler	X					
Total for Company E	4	6			1	11
Company F						
John Broyles		X				
John Carran		X				
Joseph M. Cherry		X				
Jerome W. Fields	X					
George Griesley		X				
Benjamin F. Hasson	X					
James Kyner		X				

Name & Company	KIA at the Battle of Shiloh	WIA at the Battle of Shiloh	Died of wounds from the Battle of Shiloh	Died in camp at Shiloh before the battle	MIA at the Battle of Shiloh	Total casualties from the Battle of Shiloh
(Company F)						
Richard H. Lee				X		
Thomas McKiernan		X				
Nicholas Naw						
John O'Rilely		X				
John Ritter		X				
Silas Roby	X					
Daniel Shetter		X				
John M. Stevenson		X				
Eli Swartz	X					
Christian Zook		X				
Total for Company F	4	11		1		16
Company G						
Howard G. Afleck		X				
Neley Alexander		X				
Jefferson Bicket		X				
Bruce W. Brown	X					
Joseph Campbell		X				
James M. Church	X					
James Clawson		X				
Mankin Gibbins	X					
Michael Hamm		X				
John Hays		X				
Alfred Kock		X				
Benedict Levy		X				
Martin Myers		X				
William H. Newland		X				
John D. Reed		X				
Martin Regner	X					
Samuel Richards		X				
William Sayne		X				
William P. Smith		X				
Tansy Thomas						
Hiram B. Wilson	X					
Total for Company G	5	15				20

Name & Company	KIA at the Battle of Shiloh	WIA at the Battle of Shiloh	Died of wounds from the Battle of Shiloh	Died in camp at Shiloh before the battle	MIA at the Battle of Shiloh	Total casualties from the Battle of Shiloh
Company I						
John S. Atwater		X				
John Brown	X					
Joseph Fisher		X				
Jethro Hall		X				
Alexander Jeremiah	X					
Adam Moore		X				
John Staley		X				
Total for Company I	2	5				7
Company K						
Jackson Balding		X				
William Bodle		X				
Patrick Conlon		X				
Abram Delong		X				
Isaac Dilborne		X				
Nathaniel Dunafon		X				
John Geertler		X				
Phillip Glen	X					
John Greaves		X				
Daniel Hipshire		X				
William Ireland		X				
Tillman Lewis				X		
John McCullough		X				
John Miller		X				
Caleb Roberts		X				
James Watson		X				
William Zimmerman		X				
Total for Company K	1	15		1		17

In Table 6.1, the figures for total casualties resulting from the Battle of Shiloh do *not* include more than 35 men who died days or weeks afterwards of wounds sustained at Shiloh nor men who were discharged for disability resulting from their wounds. Worthington had been a party to the deadliest battle in the history of American warfare. The 23,000 com-

PHOTOGRAPH 6.4 Shiloh Cemetery (photograph by author).

bined Confederate and Union casualties nearly doubled the losses from Manassas, Wilson's Creek, Fort Donelson, and Pea Ridge combined (Daniel 305). Considering that the Union Army lost some 17,000 men killed, wounded, or captured (Catton, *Grant Moves South* 243), the price was high indeed for the lack of preparedness Worthington charged.

WORTHINGTON ARRESTED AND CHARGED

Tom Worthington's righteous indignation over the cost in human lives at Shiloh had now taken the form of open criticism of his commanding officer. In Memphis during July and August, Worthington began openly talking to fellow officers, his own soldiers, the citizens of Memphis, and anyone else who would listen to his story about Sherman's failure as a leader. In addition, Sherman received reports and even claimed to observe himself on one or two occasions, Worthington taking advantage of the free and open consumption of liquor, consumption that Sherman would charge was to excess and constituted interference with Worthington's duty as an officer. Worthington's behavior had grown so disturbing to Sherman that something had to be done. So, in late July of 1862, Sherman placed Col. Thomas Worthington under arrest in his quarters, preferred charges against him, and called a court-martial to try him and — if successful — remove him from the service.

PART III

Chapter Seven

Court-Martial of Thomas Worthington

In Memphis, Tennessee, during August, the humid summer air sits heavily upon a person, and sweat beads emerge on the skin when one is simply sitting still. Tom Worthington would have been sweating not only from the oppressive heat but from the realization that his military career and his family name stood on the threshold of destruction. Worthington had finally gone too far or, if you believe his explanation of the circumstances, just far enough, and he had gotten himself court-martialed. The order convening the court-martial read:

> Headquarters, Memphis
> August 12, 1862.
> General Order No 69
> A General court Martial to be comprised of nine members (a greater number of proper rank   approved without manifest injury to the service) will assemble at Fort Pickering in Genl. Denver's Headquarters at 10 o'clock a.m. of Thursday August 14th 1862 for the trial of Col. Worthington, 46th Ohio Volunteer Infantry, and said prisoners as may come properly before the court.
> Detail of the Court.
> Brig. Genl. S. A. Hurlburt, 4th Division[1]
> Brig. Genl. J. W. Denver, 3rd Brigade, 5th Division[2]
> Brig. Genl. J. C. Veatch, 2nd Brigade, 4th Division[3]

[PRIVATE AND CONFIDENTIAL.]

EXTRACTS FROM A DIARY

OF THE

TENNESSEE EXPEDITION, 1862.

BY

T. WORTHINGTON, Col. 46th Reg't Ohio Vol. Infantry.

WEDNESDAY, March 26, 1862.—At Camp Shiloh, three miles from Pittsburg Landing. A company being called for for picket duty to-day, detailed Captain Sharp's Company B. Indications of an attack, if the country people are to be believed. Their pickets are around and *too near us*, showing a strong effective force.

THURSDAY, March 27, 1862.—This afternoon two of Sharp's pickets were fired on by the rebel horse about 4½ P. M., not a mile from camp. A disgrace to the army that such should be the case and an indication that they are covering some forward movement, yet Sherman is improvident as ever, and takes no defensive, and scarce any precautionary measures.

FRIDAY, March 28, 1862.—Having suggested to McDowell the sending out of a stronger picket, he ordered thirty more men, which were immediately volunteered. If Beauregard does not attack us he and the chivalry are disgraced forever, *if for noth-*

[SATUR]DAY, March 29, 1862.—Sherman has refused to sign a requisition for seventy-[ax]es for my regiment, making it twenty-two; and while a slight abattis might prevent or avert an attack, there are no axes to make it, nor is there a sledge or crowbar in his Division and scarce a set of tools out of his regiment.

MONDAY, March 31, 1862.—Further indications through the pickets that an attack is imminent, and though I do not fear the result, a sudden attack, if violently made, *as it will be*, may throw us back for months. The men are discouraged at our delay here and the close vicinity of the rebel pickets, which should be driven off. Sherman is inviting an attack, which I hope may occur, but for which we are unprepared.

TUESDAY, April 1, 1862.—Have over one hundred rounds of ammunition for all available men, and feel easy on this point. Ordered the Captains to send in accounts of clothing, &c., wanted, which the Quartermaster is very careless about getting. Still no axes, which now he cannot get if he would, and which are worth more than guns at present.

WEDNESDAY, April 2, 1862.—Rode to Pittsburg Landing. The place is crowded and in disorder below, with noise and gambling on the bank above, across the road from the post office. Hunted up and down for clothing and axes, and found that Sherman had forbidden his Quartermaster from receiving anything. That Gen. Smith's Quartermaster will answer no requisitions outside of his immediate command, and the Post Quartermaster, Baxter, (Grant's,) only answer the requisitions of the Division Quartermasters. The reason that Sherman's Quartermaster will not receive any stores is that he had no place to put them. There are now at least six boats hired by the day at the Landing (as I hear) at not less than two thousand ($2,000) a day, when two thousand dollars with that many men could in ten days, or less, put up store houses sufficient for an army of one hundred thousand men. And so the Government will pay on this expedition so far not less than twenty thousand dollars, and perhaps ten times that before the war is over, and lose not less than one to ten million dollars in Quartermaster and Commissary stores, occasioned by the improvidence and neglect of its Major-Generals here, to say nothing of the disorder and danger growing out of such a state of things.

Thirty-nine years ago this day, April 3d, 1823, when a boy of sixteen, I received my appointment as cadet. Its only result, besides, &c., is my present position as one of the lowest Colonels in this war, controlled by incompetent, improvident and negligent Generals, and now in danger of death or disgrace from the want of capacity or integrity amidst the many above and the masses below me.

The indications are (still) of an attack, which I have also indicated to McDowell; we should now have on our right at least six batteries and two regiments of cavalry to warn the rear. With thick woods before us and our pickets scarce a mile out, we have no defences whatever and no means of giving an alarm but by the sound of musketry. The troops cover too much ground and cannot support each other, and a violent attack which we may expect, may drive them back in detail. God help us with so many sick men in camp, if we are attacked, there being over five thousand unfit for duty.

FRIDAY, April 4, 1862.—One of McDowell's pickets was shot in the hand about noon. A detail of Taylor's cavalry was sent out three or four miles; found four to six hundred rebel cavalry, and fell back, returning about 2 P. M.

Everything is carried on in a very negligent way, and nothing but the same conduct on the other side will save us from disaster. They can concentrate one hundred thousand men from the heart of rebeldom, and with three or four railroads have far greater facilities for handling troops than we have.

Have Brigade orders to stack arms at daylight till further orders. Keep two companies lying on their arms, and though as quiet as possible, look for an attack every hour.

SATURDAY, April 5, 1862.—Rode out to Sharp's pickets at sunrise, and found two more (rebel pickets) wounded yesterday, who died last night at the Widow Howell's. About 7 o'clock A. M., the rebels drove in Lieut. Crary from the Widow Howell's, getting possession of their dead men. Heard in the evening that the rebels had established three guns (six pounders) opposite Hildebrand's Brigade, on our left, across the valley. Hear of fires of their regiments arriving to-day.

APRIL 26, 1862.

The undersigned hereby certify that most of the facts above set forth are correct from their own knowledge and that Col. Worthington's remarks and anticipations are in correspondence with his general conversation for ten days before the battle of the 6th of April, 1862.

WILLIAM SMITH, Major, 46th Reg. O. V. I.
J. W. HEATH, Captain Co. A, " " "
A. G. SHARP, " " B, " " "
JNO. WISEMAN, " " C, " " "
ED. N. UPTON, Lt. Cg. " D, " " "
M. C. LILLY, Captain " H, " " "
C. C. LYMAND, " " L, " " "

Col. John Williams, 3rd Iowa Infantry
Col. John Logan, 32nd Illinois Infantry
Col. William Mungen, 57th Ohio Infantry
Col. W. Q. Gresham, 53rd Indiana Infantry[4]
Col. Peter Sullivan, 48th Ohio Infantry
Col. B. H. Grierson, 6th Illinois Cavalry
Captain McCoy, Judge Advocate [*Court Martial Record*, 1–2]

TUESDAY, AUGUST 12, 1862

The court met pursuant to General Order No. 69 with all above listed as present on August 12, 1862. The major events of the first day included the reading of the charges against Worthington and General Sherman's testimony against him. Worthington was charged with drunkenness on the streets of Memphis on August 6, 1862, and at his own quarters within Fort Pickering "in such condition"; habitual drunkenness; making false and libelous statements; and conduct unbecoming an officer. Worthington was asked if he objected to any of the members named in the order, and he replied that he did not. What he did object to was what he knew to be Sherman's dual role as both the man who preferred the charges and the man who named the court that tried Worthington. This legal proceeding becomes even more mired in irregularity when one considers that Sherman was also the primary witness against Worthington. When Tom objected to Sherman's duplicitous role, only one member of the body of officers hearing the case sustained his objection: Colonel Walter Q. Gresham, commander of the 53rd Indiana. Gresham wrote after the war:

> It seemed to me then, and has ever since, contrary to our institutions to allow the accuser to name the court to try the accused. Other members of the court were lawyers by profession and must have known better than to vote to override the challenge [Gresham 184].

Next, the persons who would testify withdrew until called for, and Colonel Worthington applied for leave to have counsel. Capt. J. W. Alexander appeared as his counsel. Next the court read Worthington's Diary of

Opposite: PHOTOGRAPH 7.1 Worthington's "personal and confidential" diary extract, Exhibit A from the court-martial record of Thomas Worthington (photograph by author).

the Tennessee Expedition openly in court as evidence of the third specification, third charge (false and libelous statements) and marked it as "Exhibit A." Worthington's counsel objected but was overruled.

Testimony of Sherman

Tom Worthington would argue both during the ongoing court-martial and for 20 years afterward that the ultimate goal of his behavior — publishing the diary extract, sending the circular to Sherman, engaging in constant diatribes about the battle and Sherman's culpability to anyone who would listen — was to lead to this singular moment. At long last Worthington had his opportunity. General Sherman was on the stand and under oath.

The court-martial transcript reads that Sherman, a "witness for the prosecution," made the following sworn statement.[5]

> Col. Worthington commanded 46th Ohio in Col. McDowell's Brigade, 5th Division, on July 18th, 1862, he commanded a redoubt built by himself or his command at Lafayette — with orders to protect the railroad and bridges — about 10 A.M. of that day I reached the station and saw Col. Worthington in a condition of disgraceful drunkenness, I saw standing around him men of his own Regiment, many officers of my Division, and he was seen by all of my staff who noticed his condition and spoke of it in unqualified terms.
>
> Of the 2nd Specification 1st Charge I know nothing.
>
> 2nd Charge 1st Specification. Habitual drunkenness, I can testify as to [the] 18th and 19th July, cannot trust my memory as to other dates—
>
> Of the facts set forth in 1st Specification, 3rd Charge, I know nothing of my own personal knowledge, it came by Official Report.
>
> 3rd Charge, 2nd Specification — as to these facts I testify that about the 10th Inst [Aug.], one of my staff brought a sheet of printed matter which was left for me by Capt. Geisey of 46th Ohio, that sheet contains matter false and libelous — which can be proven so, by contemporaneous and official documents (paper A shown and identified) though marked "private and confidential," bears on its face evidence of its intent for circulation — under date of March 29th, 1862, by this paper he uses the "Sherman has refused to sign a requisition for 72 axes for my Regiment, making it 22." I did so rightfully, I knew what axes were on hand and expected, and

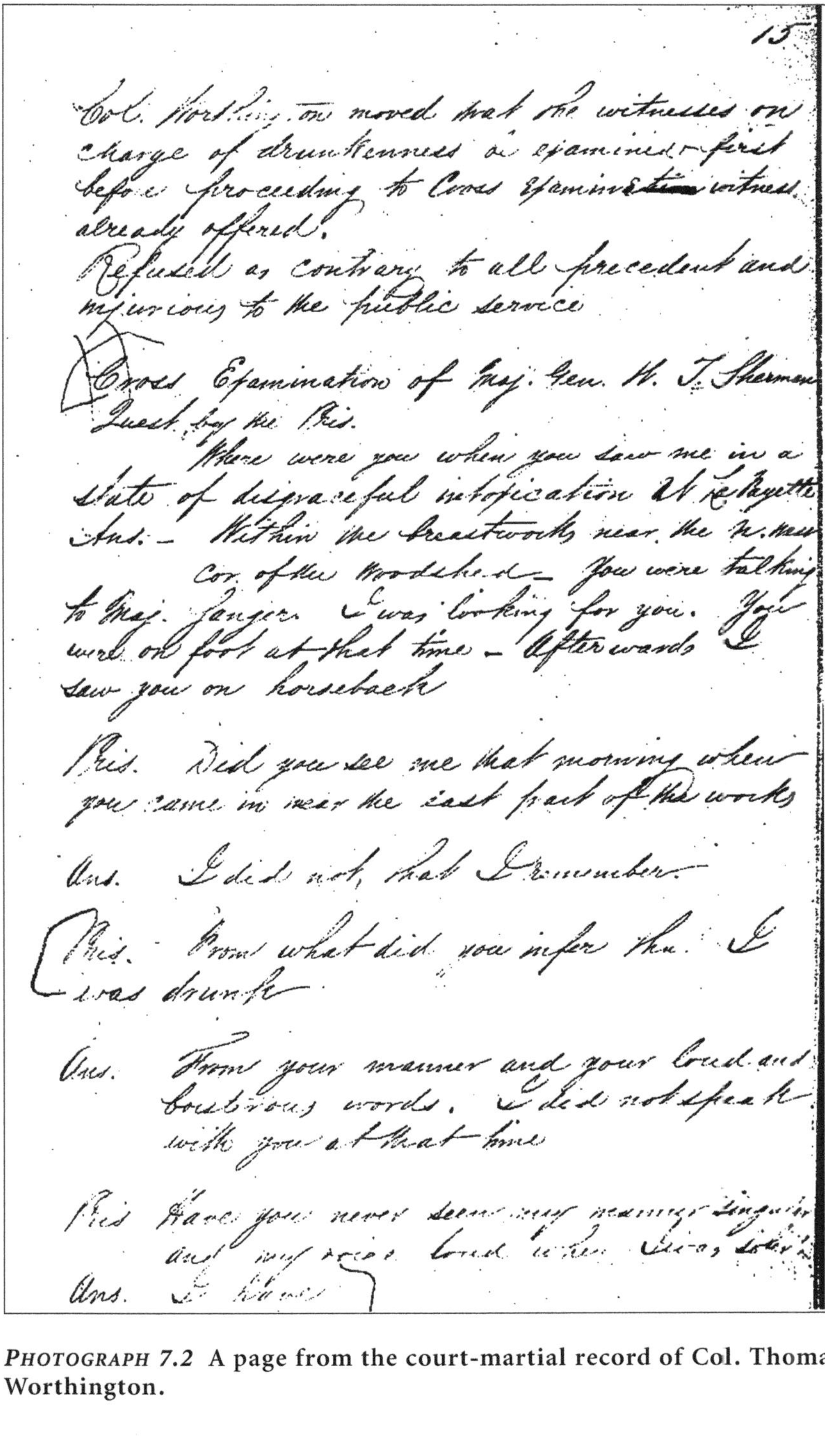

Col. Worthington moved that the witnesses on charge of drunkenness be examined first before proceeding to Cross Examination witness already offered.

Refused as contrary to all precedent and injurious to the public service

Cross Examination of Maj. Gen. W. T. Sherman
Quest. by the Pris.
Where were you when you saw me in a state of disgraceful intoxication at LaFayette
Ans. — Within the breastworks near the N. West Cor. of the Woodshed — You were talking to Maj. Sanger. I was looking for you. You were on foot at that time — Afterwards I saw you on horseback

Pris. Did you see me that morning when you came in near the east part of the works

Ans. I did not, that I remember.

Pris. From what did you infer that I was drunk

Ans. From your manner and your loud and boisterous words. I did not speak with you at that time

Pris. Have you never seen my manner singular and my voice loud when I was sober
Ans. I have

PHOTOGRAPH 7.2 A page from the court-martial record of Col. Thomas Worthington.

was the judge not Col. Worthington of their distribution — He says there was "no sledges or crowbars in the Division," he had no knowledge on the subject. He says a "slight abatis might have prevented an attack," *what business was it of his whether his Superior Officer invited an attack or not?*[6] [emphasis added]. The Army Regulations will show him that no fortifications can be made except under order of the Commanding General — *to have erected fortifications would have been evidence of weakness and therefore would have invited an attack* [emphasis added].

The entry of March 31, 1862 must have been fabricated after the date, for squadrons, regiments, and brigades were on the ground five days after this entry was made — Col. Worthington may have thought an attack imminent — because for weeks he was predicting the worst and hoping it might happen —

The entry of Thursday April 3, 1862 is false and libelous. Troops were arriving from every quarter by water, wagons were coming to the landing from camps in the interior, high water contracted the levee to a very small space, and many other causes well known to Col. Worthington produced confusion which no General could have prevented, and which no one could charge to Gen. Grant.

Why the Government Agents preferred to keep their stores afloat was none of his business, but the reasons were that we might be prepared to shift our base to Crumps Landing, Hamburg, or Eastport, should circumstances make it advisable. I admit that Col. Worthington was meandering up and down the river hunting for clothing and axes, but his assertion that "Sherman had forbidden his Quartermaster to receive anything" is an absurdity. Now in this connection, while Col. Worthington was wandering up and down after axes, I will show what the men in front were doing.

On the 3rd of April the whole of Buckland's Brigade moved directly to the front 6 miles and deployed skirmishers to the right and left from Owl Creek to Lick Creek, covering the whole peninsula. They encountered squads of the enemy's cavalry known to be there but saw no infantry, artillery, or other concomitants of an army, this was in obedience to my orders of April 3rd (which was here read, a copy of which is marked B).

On the 2nd April I ordered Col. Stuart in the night to send the 54th Ohio along up Lick Creek to Jack Greers to be in ambush at daylight of the 3rd — at the same time I ordered Col. Taylor's Cavalry to start every man he could mount (at midnight) out on the Corinth Road, to make a circuit and drive in any cavalry in my front (here copy of order to Cols. Stuart and Taylor was read which is marked C). Thus on both night and day of April 3rd my force covered the entire peninsula, over which the attacking army had to come. And here I mention for future history that our right flank was well guarded by Owl and Snake Creeks, our left by Lick Creek—leaving us simply to guard our front. No stronger position was ever held by an army. Therefore on Thursday two days before the battle when Col. Worthington was apprehensive I knew there was no hostile party within six miles, though there was reason to expect an attack, I suppose Col. McDowell like myself had become tired of his [Worthington's] constant prognostications, and paid no attention to him, especially when we were positively informed by men like Buckland, Kirby Smith, and Maj. Ricker, who went to the front to look for enemies, instead of going to the Landing.

And here I will state that Pittsburg Landing was not chosen by Gen. Grant, but by Maj. Gen. Smith—I received orders from Gen. Smith and took post accordingly, so did Gen. Hurlburt, so did his own Division—The line of McClernand [*sic*] and Prentiss was selected by Colonel, now Genl. McPherson. I will not insult Genl. Smith's memory by criticizing his selection of a field. It was not looked to so much for defense as for ground on which an army could be organized for offense. We did not occupy too much ground. Gen. Buell's forces had been expected rightfully for two weeks and a place was left for his forces, although Genl. Grant afterward had determined to send Buell to Hamburg as a separate command. But even as we were on the 6th April, you might search the world over and not find a more advantageous field of battle—flanks well protected and never threatened—troops in easy support, timber and broken ground giving good points to rally, and the proof is that 43,000 men of whom at least 10,000 ran away, held their ground against 60,000 chosen troops of the South with their best leaders, *on Friday no officer nor soldier not even Col. Worthington looked for an attack* [emphasis added] as I can prove.[7]

On Friday April 4th, our pickets were disposed as follows: McDowell's Brigade embracing Worthington's Regiment looked to Owl Creek Bridge, and had nothing to do with any other Buckland and Hildebrand covered our line to the Main Corinth Road. Pickets one company to a regiment were thrown forward a mile further making a chain of sentinels. About noon of that day Buckland's Adjt. came to my tent and reported that a Lieut. and seven men of his guard had left their post and were missing, probably picked up by a small cavalry force which had hovered around for some days and which I had failed to bag. I immediately dispatched Maj. Ricker with all my cavalry in a tremendous rain to the front. Soon after I heard distant musketry, and finally three cannon shot which I knew must be the enemy's as we had none there.

This was the first positive information any intelligent mind on that field had of any approaching force; before that no scout, no officer, no responsible man had seen any infantry or artillery soldier nearer than Monterey; for weeks and months we had heard all sorts of reports, just as we do now this week. Old women had reported Beauregard was coming with sometimes 10,000 sometimes 300,000, when in fact he did not leave Corinth until after even Col. Worthington had been alarmed for safety — as soon as I heard the cannon, I and my staff were in the saddle and off for the front. We overtook a part of Buckland's and Hildebrand's Brigades going forward to the relief of the Pickets. On reaching a position in advance of the Guard House a mile and a half from Shiloh, they deployed into line of battle and I awaited the return of my cavalry and infantry still to our front. Col. Buckland and Major Ricker soon returned and reported encountering infantry, artillery, and cavalry near the fallen timbers six miles in front of our camp. We then knew we had the elements of an Army in front but did not know its strength or destination.

The guard was strengthened and as night came on we returned to camp. *Not a man in the camp but knew we had an enemy to the front before he slept that night, but even I had to guess its purpose* [emphasis added]. No general could have detected or reported the approach of an enemy more promptly than was done. (Here was read extracts from letter book 40 which are marked D). Thus while Buckland's Brigade in the execution of its proper duty was guarding safely our front, a colonel of another brigade in a safe corner was "looking for an attack every hour" [*Court Martial Record*, 6–18].

This strange comment by Sherman demands some examination. If Colonel Buckland were properly doing his duty as Sherman claimed in his testimony, why did Sherman on the day of the battle chastise him for ordering reconnaissance and "bringing on an engagement"? Sherman suggested it was somehow Worthington's fault that he had been deployed on the extreme right of Sherman's division, when it was Sherman himself who determined which brigades would occupy what areas upon the division's arrival at Pittsburg Landing. Worthington never asked to be placed on the right flank. Sherman's suggestion that Worthington was somehow in a "safe corner" presumes that Worthington had some choice in his positioning, which he did not. Where the enemy would choose to first strike the Federal camp at Shiloh was hardly a matter to which Tom Worthington would have been privy. Accusing him of playing it safe is not only ridiculous, but it demonstrates just how deep ran Sherman's personal animosity toward Worthington. In a similar tone, Sherman continued his testimony:

> As to the journal entry of April 5th 1862 I have but little to say. He [Worthington] found at Mrs. Howells two rebel pickets, the same reported by Buckland. As to the three guns on Hildebrand's left he could have heard no such thing, for our troops crossed and re-crossed the very ground all day Saturday. The battery came into position after daylight on Sunday after the pickets had been driven in.
>
> I say it was impossible for him to have heard as to the three guns on our left across the valley. The position is well known and was within our pickets. If he did hear so, it was his sworn and bound duty to have reported the fact to his commander, which he did not do.
>
> For days, weeks, and months after Shiloh the most foolish reports were published and traced to military men, vaguely alluded to as authority and never quoted by name.[8] Many persons stated they had seen what purported to be a journal of events, kept by Col. Worthington, containing   dates   and [they] warned me against him. I paid no attention to it, little dreaming that one who knew so well would do so much. I had enough of other things to do.
>
> I have given a history of events during the week preceding the Battle of Shiloh, and state further that from the 31st of March to the 5th of April, with part of my division, I was up the Tennessee River to Eastport. From the 2nd to the 7th April I have given an account.
>
> On the 8th my division pursued the enemy over the same ground 6 miles on the 9th, 10th, and 11th April I was up the Tennessee and broke the Bear Creek Bridge the original object of the expedition. I therefore repeat that my command did neglect no proper precautions, but was as industrious as vigilant and patient as any part of the troops consisting the Army of Tennessee. (Witness here introduced General Order No. 19 April 4th 1862 marked E) [*Court Martial Record*, 18–19].

The court then adjourned until 3:00 P.M. It is interesting that after Sherman's statement was taken, the full weight of it rested on the members of the court, unchallenged, without cross-examination, for three days until the next meeting.

FRIDAY, AUGUST 15, 1862

> The court convened by General Order dated August 12th 1862, whereof Brig. Genl. S. A. Hurlburt is President will set after this date without regard to hours—
>
> > By order of Maj. Genl. W. T. Sherman
> > J. H. Hammond, A.A.G.

At 8:00 A.M. the court met again, at which time the above order from General Sherman was read by the president, Brigadier General Hurlburt (*Court-Martial Record* 14). The order clearly indicates Sherman's intent to get this nasty business over with as soon as possible. Sherman was sick and tired of Worthington's behavior undermining, as he believed, his command authority. Sherman knew that Worthington would attempt to put him, Sherman, on trial for Shiloh, and he probably entertained little doubt that Worthington would make the affair as long and painful as possible. Sitting "without regard to hours" likely meant going as long in session as necessary, starting again the next day as rapidly as possible, getting a verdict, and getting rid of Worthington as expeditiously as possible.

The primary event of the second day was Worthington's cross-examination of General Sherman, but first Worthington moved that the witnesses on the charge of drunkenness be examined before he proceeded to cross-examine Sherman. Exactly why Worthington did this presents a difficult question. Three days had already elapsed since Sherman's damaging testimony. In such a trial, three days constitutes a long time for the members of the court to consider a witness' testimony before hearing rebuttal. Perhaps Worthington figured a few more hours would not make any difference. Maybe he wanted Sherman to steam a while longer. Worthington might have even sought more time to better prepare his own questions, though this seems unnecessary given that he had months to prepare for this moment. Did Worthington fear the drunkenness charge would actually be his downfall? If he did, perhaps he believed he could rebut that testimony first, then concentrate all his time and effort on grilling Sherman. Whatever his reason, the court refused his request to deal first with the drunkenness charge as "contrary to all precedent and injurious to the public service," thereby forcing Worthington directly into his long-awaited one-on-one with William Tecumseh Sherman.

Worthington Cross-Examines Sherman

Question by the Prisoner — Where were you when you saw me in a state of disgraceful intoxication at Lafayette?

Answer — Within the breastworks near the northwest corner of the woodshed. You were talking to Major Sanger. I was looking for you. You were on foot at that time — afterwards I saw you on horseback.

Prisoner — Did you see me that morning when you came in near the east part of the works?

Answer — I did not that I remember.

Prisoner — From what did you infer that I was drunk?

Answer — From your manner and your loud and boisterous words. I did not speak with you at that time.

Prisoner — Have you never seen my manner singular and my voice loud when I was sober?

Answer — I have.

Prisoner — Did you see me conversing with Col. Corse that day?

Answer — I think not.

Prisoner — What was the subject of my conversation?

Answer — I could not hear — I kept away purposely.

Prisoner — How long afterward did you see me on horseback?

Answer — In about 20 minutes or ½ an hour on a white horse outside of the shed in the woods. You rode off. I observed you unsteady in the saddle.

Prisoner — Did you see me again during the day?

Answer — I think not. I do not remember to have seen you on the march that day. If I did I have no recollection.

Prisoner — You state you saw me drunk on the 19th. Where was it?

Answer — I think it was at White Station west of the Depot just before the storm and about 4 or 5 P.M. You were on horseback.

Prisoner — Do you know whether or not the 22 axes ordered on requisition were delivered?

Answer — I do not.

Prisoner — Do you know whether or not there was a sledge or crowbar in the division?

Answer — Crowbars are only used to repair bridges and break Railroads — we afterward had them when engaged in that business — we had four battery wagons attached to a Division which contained sledges and other tools necessary to repair carriages and for blacksmith work. There were four sledge hammers in the Division with the batteries.

Prisoner — Were there any iron wedges?

Answer — I don't know. There were plenty of iron and wood in that country.

Prisoner — The entry of Thursday April 3rd you say is false and libelous — in what is it false?

Answer — In this — "Sherman has forbidden his quartermaster to receive anything" is false. There were indications of an attack is false — That our pickets were only out a mile is false — That we covered too much ground is false — That we should have had six batteries on our right is false — The assertion as to the cost of the floating store boats is calculated to give a false impression of extravagance — The boat supplied four Divisions nearly 30,000 men — no warehouse built on shore with the difficulties of unloading could have supplied that army. Pittsburg was only a temporary base of operations as the result has shown.

Prisoner — Did you hear of any artillery being near the Howell House Saturday evening the 5th of April?

Answer — I did not.

Prisoner — Did you hear of a force of 500 to 2000 men — cavalry and infantry being a mile beyond the Howell House?

Answer — I heard of the enemy's cavalry pickets being about 3 p.m. in the woods west of the hospital a mile beyond Mrs. Howell's (known as Wood's house) and heard of infantry through my scout near   Lane on Owl Creek about five miles from McDowell's camp which I supposed to be a part of the enemy's infantry which Col. Buckland had come in contact with the night before. On Saturday I had no cavalry subject to my command but about dark that evening eight companies of the 4th Ill. Reported to me for duty and I ordered [them] to be ready for a scout at daylight next morning in   with one regiment from McDowell and from Stewart [sic] on the right and left.

Prisoner — At what time on Saturday did you hear of the pickets being driven out of the Howell House?

Answer — The pickets were not driven out of the Howell House on Saturday — that ground was picketed by Col. Buckland who was out in person all Saturday afternoon and evening superintending the posting of his guards and pickets — the house which I call the Widow Howell's House was in a field near a lane in Buckland's front about three-fourths of a mile from his centre, used by the enemy as a hospital and where we found Capt. Polk wounded after the battle. Our pickets were a mile in front of that house. There was some cavalry skirmishing in that field on Saturday, but no infantry or artillery — on that Saturday Col. McDowell sent one company of infantry out to fields[?] nearly up to Meek's Lane four miles beyond and to the right of Mrs. Howell's. I gave my personal attention to our left flank which had become partially exposed by the falling of Lick Creek—the ford had become passable making it very important that it should be watched.[9] In company with Col. Stewart [sic] commanding that brigade and Col. McPherson of Genl. Grant's staff—I crossed that ford and looked to the approach by the Bark Road. Confirming Col Stuart's disposition of his pickets and guard which had been doubled since the developments of Friday before. I was perfectly willing the enemy should attack us and think Beauregard made a fatal mistake when he did it, but I deny that the enemy had a battery near the Howell House that Saturday afternoon. It was reported to me on Thursday that Mrs. Howell said there was to be a big fight in her field.

Prisoner—Did you know that the pickets of the 46th Ohio were at Mrs. Howell's House for a week before the battle?

Answer—I did not. If they were there they were entirely out of their place—Buckland and Hildebrand's pickets were a mile ahead of that. The house was in a large field and no place for pickets. It was not a picket station and if they were then they were of no use. The fork of the road in front was the key point of the attack and that point was watched. Woods'[?] house ¾ of a mile ahead was the point where the guards of Hildebrand and Buckland were stationed.

Prisoner—Did you know that the pickets were driven in from Baker's House on Saturday?

Answer—I know of no such house—no such house was a picket station—none of the pickets were driven in.

Prisoner—What do you mean by stating that "a man who knew so well, should do so much?"

Answer—I meant that it was strange that a man who had received a military education,[10] and who claims to know more than Halleck, Grant or Sherman his superiors in rank—and who boasts of his superiority to everybody—should be boring and perplexing every body who would listen to his stories—minding every body else's business but his own—intruding his opinions where they were unsolicited, and making himself so offensive that even Genl. Smith threatened to arrest me if I permitted him again to come on board his boat. That one who ought to know the proprieties of life should pay so little regard to them. His habit has been to wander about camp miles away from his regiment, without uniform, dressed in a grotesque manner attracting the remark of everybody.[11] An illustration of which I call his mind to the circumstances of his coming alone riding a broken down horse without any appearance of an officer,[12] carrying an old flintlock musket, six miles from his regiment on the 8th April to where Buckland and Hildebrand's Regiments were engaged with Forrest's Cavalry [Fallen Timbers]. I then reproached him, as I have done on many occasions, but because he "graduated at West Point," before I did, he professed to know more than any body else and disregarded all admonitions, advice, or reproof on the subject. I will here state that from my respect for the memory of his father, and for his family, I hoped that a returning sense of shame would make him mind his ways and return to the plain and honest duties of a Colonel without having recourse to a court martial. I knew that Col. Worthington knew his duties well and wondered that he should disregard them. That is what I meant by the statement that "one who knew so well could do so much."

Prisoner — How many times have you seen me a mile from my regiment?

Answer — At least a hundred times on the march and in camp, the dates I do not pretend to recall.

Prisoner — Have I to your knowledge ever neglected any specific duty in my regiment?

Answer — I will allege none, except such as are charged here. I leave that to his Brigadier.

Prisoner — Has any officer outside my regiment complained of me for meddling with other people's business?

Answer — Col. McDowell commanding the brigade has complained repeatedly.

Prisoner — Did you approve of an arrest made by Col. Hicks at Savannah for not getting my report over the river in time?

Answer — I do not recall the circumstances, but I think not.

Prisoner — Did you approve of an opinion of Col. Hicks that I ought to be arrested for purchasing corn at Savannah?

Answer — I have no recollection of any such opinion.

The court has decided that questions of this kind were improper and irrelevant. And the cross-examination closed.

— W. T. Sherman, Maj. Genl.
[*Court Martial Record*, 15–23]

With the above declaration, Sherman put an immediate end to Worthington's attempt to hold him accountable for his actions at Shiloh.

Sherman had heard all he intended to hear and, as commander, exercised his authority to stop any further cross-examination of himself. Worthington's line of questioning right before Sherman's sudden termination of the cross-examination seems completely appropriate. He sought to rebut Sherman's assertions and implications that he was unfit for command. Worthington must have been sorely disappointed when the court agreed with Sherman that the questions were "improper and irrelevant."

Next in the proceedings, Major Sanger, 55th Illinois Volunteer Infantry and formerly General Sherman's aide, testified regarding the diary extract and Worthington's alleged drunkenness at Lafayette. Worthington cross-examined him. Then Captain Dayton, aide-de-camp to Sherman, testified regarding Worthington's drunkenness in Memphis, and Worthington cross-examined him as well.

SATURDAY, AUGUST 16, 1862

Testimony Continues

The court met at 8:30 A.M. with Major Hammond testifying regarding Worthington's behavior on July 18. Worthington cross-examined Hammond and then listened to Lieutenant Colonel Corse, 6th Iowa, testify that he and Colonel McDowell encountered Worthington on July 17 near the depot at Lafayette and that "[we] were informed that Old Tom was drunk and having a fight with an Irishman" (*Court-Martial Record* 33). By the time they arrived on the scene, the two men had been separated and the crowd dispersed. About ten minutes later, Corse saw Worthington on the railroad platform in an altercation with a soldier, whom Worthington had ordered to the guardhouse. When the man refused to go, Worthington got some men and the officer of the guard and tried to force him to the guardhouse. Both the officer of the guard and the men refused Worthington's order, so Worthington began to physically force the man toward the guardhouse, again drawing a crowd of angry soldiers. Corse says that during the incident Worthington exhibited "intense excitement and strong indications of intoxication" (*Court-Martial Record* 34). Worthington disappeared for several minutes, then reappeared and again attempted to arrest the same man, but he was unsuccessful. Corse testified that Worthington was sober when he saw him the following day.

Next, Col. Kilby Smith, 54th Iowa Infantry, testified regarding seeing the diary extract, and Worthington cross-examined him. He was followed by Worthington's executive officer, Lieutenant Colonel Walcutt,

46th Ohio, who testified that he had not seen the diary extract until the previous Sunday (10 Aug.), but he had on occasion heard Worthington read extracts from it. Walcutt indicated he declined to sign a "statement" Worthington drew up about the battle. Walcutt confirmed Worthington's intoxication in his quarters at Fort Pickering on August 6 and on the 17 of July in Lafayette.

For some reason, Worthington only asked Walcutt one question in cross-examination and that was a minor clarification as to when Walcutt had seen him intoxicated. If the questioning had ended there, Worthington would have been much better off, but the judge advocate questioned Walcutt further, and the resulting testimony was quite damaging to the colonel of the 46th.

When pressed by the judge advocate, Captain McCoy, to further explain his testimony that he had seen Worthington drunk, Walcutt stated that on the 6th of August he returned from Memphis and stopped at Worthington's quarters where he found:

> a large crowd of officers and soldiers of different grades there laughing—when I looked in the door I found Col. Worthington standing in the floor in his shirt and pants, and in his bare feet making a sort of speech to the crowd. He was making violent gestures—the crowd were poking fun at him—calling on him, calling on him to make more of a speech. He was talking all the time to the crowd—I cannot recollect what he said. [I] remained but a few moments and went to my quarters [*Court-Martial Record* 39].

Walcutt delivered what is perhaps the most detrimental testimony of the entire trial, for as Worthington's second-in-command, he clearly demonstrated that his colonel had become a mockery of a commander. One can easily imagine the men crowded around Worthington, chuckling at his drunken tirade and urging him on to ever more outrageous statements.

"Come on, Colonel. Tell us more!"

"We want to hear what *really* happened!"

There seems little doubt that Worthington's behavior as described under oath by his executive officer constituted conduct unbecoming an officer. But Thomas Worthington was hardly the first officer to ever exhibit such behavior in an age when drinking, and drinking to excess, was an accepted part of the life of a soldier, so long as that drinking did not influence actions on the battlefield. The extent to which Worthington felt betrayed by his second-in-command cannot be determined. But Worthington's cross-examination of Walcutt seemed to be considerably less severe than his questioning of the other witnesses.

His brigade commander, Colonel McDowell, testified next that Worthington was unfit for military duty on July 18 when his regiment was preparing to leave Lafayette. He confirmed Corse's account of the platform incident, and McDowell said he was "mortified" by what he observed. He says Worthington, having failed to get the man arrested, wanted McDowell as senior commander to do it. McDowell took the matter under advisement in an attempt to calm Worthington, then urged him to go to his quarters.

Lieutenant Rice, 46th Ohio, testified that he saw Worthington drunk on horseback with another man (Tom Hunter) on July 25. Captain Sharp then testified that Worthington was "what we could call 'tight.' He was under the influence of liquor" on the day the brigade went into Memphis (*Court-Martial Record* 44). The trial was steadily unraveling on Worthington, who now faced some of his own men confirming what he heretofore might have portrayed as the division commander, his aides, and the brigade commander's attempt to get him. Relative to the platform incident, Worthington claimed he was simply doing his duty as division officer of the day that day, although that seems in no way to mitigate his actions.

Next he cross-examined Captain Sharp and, in light of the previous testimony, asked the amazing question, "Do you recollect how much 'bounce' there was in a bottle you gave me?"

Sharp answered, "The bottle was more than half full." "Did you urge me to take the bounce because you did not like it?"

"I told you the mess did not like it — and gave it to you — you took it" (*Court-Martial Record* 45).

First Lieutenant Jacob Lohrer, 46th Ohio, provided further damaging testimony confirming the incident involving the crowd on August 6 in Worthington's quarters. He said that Lieutenant Watts "was trying to get him to bed, and succeeded in laying him down." When Lieutenant Barber arrived from a leave at home, Worthington tried to stand up and shake his hand.

> [Worthington] finally succeeded in getting up. He was staggering a great deal. Col. Worthington said, "let me alone — I am not drunk. I am only slightly intoxicated. I can walk." And then [Worthington] began abusing Genl. Sherman saying he was not a Union Man, his heart was not in the cause [*Court-Martial Record* 46].

Lohrer then stated that the "privates around the quarters were making fun of him and he was cutting up with them."

Lohrer was followed by Capt. Phillip Crow, 46th Ohio, who testified that he had previously seen Worthington drunk, as well as on the day the regiment left Lafayette (the platform incident). And in perhaps the only moment that brought a chuckle to the court, Crow said that, after Worthington's speech to the crowd, he "thanked them for their presence, and told them he would now thank them for their absence" (*Court-Martial Record* 47).

TUESDAY, AUGUST 19, 1862

The court reconvened at 9:00 A.M. and began with Capt. Thomas M. Hunter, Company K, 1st Tennessee, who testified that he met Worthington in Memphis, accompanied him on horseback (on the same horse) to his quarters, and later returned to Memphis. He says Worthington was drunk. Worthington cross-examined Hunter by asking him, rather strangely, "Did I remonstrate against you being behind me?" Hunter said that he did but added that Worthington later invited him to "get on."

"Do you remember me stating it would raise reports and create observation?" Worthington asked. Hunter indicated he did not recall him saying that.

With this testimony the prosecution closed. Worthington then immediately objected to proceeding further, and in raising what would turn out to be a critical point of order, he insisted that the trial should not continue "without [his] knowing by whom the charges were drawn or advanced" (*Court-Martial Record* 50). The court overruled his objection and ordered Worthington to proceed with his defense. Even to the most casual observer, this aspect of the trial seems highly irregular, and it ultimately constituted some of the grounds for the Army's judge advocate general to later examine the proceedings. The right to face one's accusers is a fundamental guarantee under not only the nation's civilian judicial system, but under the rules of military justice as well. Certainly, Worthington was facing his accuser in the sense that Sherman testified against him in open court and endured Worthington's cross-examination. But at no time had the court declared officially that Sherman was the author of the charges against Worthington, and while there is little doubt Worthington knew who was producing this show, he still had the legal right to have such information officially declared and noted in the record. The information would shortly emerge in testimony, but the court's effort to avoid publicly naming Sherman as author of the charges seems an overt attempt to cover up what legal minds like Sherman's must have known full well to be an insult to jurisprudence.

Major Hammond was called to testify for the defense, and Worthington spent most of his time asking him questions about Shiloh. Major Sanger was then recalled by the defense to testify as to when the order was given to move Behr's battery from his position with McDowell's brigade (9:30 A.M., April 6). Worthington then called Col. Ralph Buckland to also testify about Shiloh. His testimony did not serve to bolster Sherman's version of events. In fact, Thomas Worthington was now in full effect, eliciting a chronology of events to support his claims that Sherman was derelict in his duties at the Battle of Shiloh. The proceedings had now evolved into what Sherman must have feared most — a close examination of his leadership, or lack of it, at Shiloh. Matters grew even worse when the tenacious Worthington recalled Sherman and asked him, under oath, one very direct question: "Will you tell me who drew the charges against me?"

"The charges were drawn substantially by me," Sherman admitted. "I placed the subject matter in the hands of the Judge Advocate for trial" (50). With that answer, the witness was excused from the stand, and Worthington, satisfied that everyone knew officially what they had known all along unofficially, continued with his defense.

Captain Sharp testified to the presence of artillery before April 6. In some of the most damaging information developed to refute Sherman's initial testimony, Sharp said:

> There was a piece of artillery near the Howell House to the right on Saturday evening. I suppose it was Rebel [since] it pointed to our camp. It was first observed in the early part of the afternoon. I did not see it until 5 p.m. I reported the circumstance to both Col. McDowell and Genl. Sherman. Genl. Sherman said he would have the artillery in readiness [57].

Sharp declared unequivocally that he was at the Howell House on picket with his company of 40 men. He also said he reported to McDowell "habitually." Sherman never admitted hearing a report of artillery at the Howell House on Saturday, April 5, but if the report was delivered as Sharp testified, it would have certainly constituted the kind of information "any intelligent mind" (as Sherman arrogantly testified) might have used to piece together the enemy's intent to attack his camp. What motive would Captain Sharp have to lie under oath? Clearly, it would not have been to protect Worthington — for Sharp had already damaged his colonel with his testimony of Worthington's intoxication.

First Lieutenant Emanuel Giesy, quartermaster of the 46th, then testified about the supplies the 46th did *not* receive before the Battle of Shiloh. He was followed by the 46th Ohio's sergeant major, George Gorman, who testified that he was present at the Howell House when a

Confederate prisoner told him his regiment was only three miles away. That was on Saturday morning, April 5. Worthington was hard at work developing information that indicated Sherman could have known, indeed, that he *should* have known, that his camp was on the verge of being attacked by a massive Confederate force. The court adjourned after Sergeant Major Gorman's testimony, leaving Worthington, perhaps for the first time in the trial, with a sense that he was getting his message on the public record.

WEDNESDAY, AUGUST 20, 1862

The court met in session at 8:00 A.M., and Worthington continued to develop information regarding the debacle at Shiloh. Colonel Hildebrand testified, as did Capt. J. C. Smith, division quartermaster. Lieutenant George Crary, Company B, 46th, testified to being three miles out from camp, hearing artillery Saturday afternoon opposite Hildebrand's brigade, and knowing "there were infantry in front of our pickets, the cavalry advanced first, then they brought up infantry." He heard drum rolls from what he suspected was more than one regiment.

Worthington then recalled Lieutenant Colonel Walcutt. When asked relative to the diary extract if he took a note from Worthington to Sherman, Walcutt answered, "I took a note from you to General Sherman the night before the Division left Lafayette for Moscow. He told me you must be careful what papers you sent him or he would arrest you" (*Court-Martial Record* 63). Walcutt also testified, "I never knew of you neglecting any duty on the march or elsewhere in consequence of intoxication." He then confirmed Worthington's claims of inadequate supplies upon leaving Paducah.

Worthington next presented James Chensworth, a cotton buyer from Memphis, who testified that he saw Worthington mounted with "a young man" (Hunter) and indicated that he thought the young man to be intoxicated, but that he did not believe Worthington to be intoxicated. This civilian was followed by William Graham, assistant surgeon of the 40th Illinois, who testified he never saw Worthington drunk except in his quarters, their two units being habitually encamped together. Worthington continued trying to rebut the drunkenness charges by questioning Lt. Col. J. W. Boothe, 40th Illinois, who said he had not seen Worthington "at any time since we left Corinth so tipsy as to be unfit for duty." Another civilian, Edward Silvey, a sutler in Memphis, indicated he "never saw [Worthington] unfit for business." One wonders what manner of "business" caused Silvey to so regularly see Colonel Worthington.

Worthington's presentation of his defense witnesses seems rather disjointed, for he next turned back to the issue of Shiloh, questioning Capt. Michael Miller, 4th Indiana Battery, as to the position of his forces on April 5. Then Worthington recalled his brigade commander, Colonel McDowell. Under oath, McDowell claimed not to remember Captain Sharp's report of artillery on Saturday afternoon at the Howell House. McDowell then testified that he had not seen Worthington "intoxicated so as to be unfit for duty since we came to Memphis" (*Court-Martial Record* 67). And lastly, relative to Shiloh and Sherman's testimony that Worthington was constantly predicting the Union Army's defeat and all manner of dire consequences, McDowell admitted, "I never heard you predict any actual disaster. On Monday or Tuesday before the battle you insisted that we would be attacked and complained of the want of tools" (67).

In an attempt to mitigate the testimony of his drunkenness, Worthington presented Dr. A. S. Shaw, surgeon of the 6th Iowa, who testified:

> I have not seen you unfit for duty by reason of liquor since I became acquainted with you. Your reputation is that of a restless, sleepless man, unquiet. Persons not intimately acquainted with you might perhaps suppose you tipsy when not so [68].

He was followed by Capt. A. W. Walder, Company D, 6th Iowa, who testified he never saw Worthington intoxicated.

Worthington's defense lacked a consistency in presentation, being disjointed and difficult for the members of the court to follow. What was his counsel, Capt. J. W. Alexander, doing all this time? Was it not the responsibility of Captain Alexander to help the colonel of the 46th shape his defense into a coherent presentation? Actions by Alexander by and for Worthington's defense are strangely absent from the court-martial record, and outside of the initial mention of Alexander at the beginning of the trial, he does not appear again in the proceedings. He might have made suggestions and given advice for some of the objections that appear in the proceedings, or he might have suggested some of the questions Worthington asked in cross-examination, but the record does not indicate such participation. Then again, Worthington's personality and his dogged determination to do things his own way might have rendered Captain Alexander a mere prop on the stage of this judicial drama. At any rate, Worthington again changed the focus of his presentation to Shiloh, as he questioned Lt. J. A. Fitch of Waterhouse's Artillery regarding the location of his batteries. Fitch was followed by Howell Parsons, quartermaster sergeant of the 46th, who confirmed Worthington's axe story.

Again addressing the issue of drunkenness, Worthington called a member of the court, Brigadier General Denver, whose headquarters hosted the trial, evoking from him testimony that in the limited times he had seen Worthington he had never seen him intoxicated. Next Worthington offered a paper marked Exhibit G, a handwritten request that the court allow him to go into evidence outside the times set forth in the specifications and in his printed document (the diary extract). He wanted authorization to question the witnesses, specifically Sherman, on events from the 6th of March, when the division left Paducah, through the 10th of May. The court overruled the motion — an action Worthington must have realized was a significant defeat for his effort to expose Sherman.

He turned again to defending the drunkenness charge and called Timothy H. Ward, hospital steward of the 46th Ohio. Ward said he *had* seen Worthington at the hospital unfit for duty due to intoxication, but he then said he had not seen anything unbecoming. That was testimony Worthington might well have done without. Conrad Leckleiter, private in the 46th Ohio, said he did not see Worthington drunk the morning the unit left Lafayette. In an effort to reduce earlier damaging testimony that alleged Worthington was drunk when his horse lay down in a ditch with him on it, Private John Wheeler said Worthington's horse liked to roll in the ditch when he got the chance. Private Homer Hoover, Worthington's orderly at the time of the alleged drunkenness, testified that he saw Worthington's horse lie down with him in Wolf Creek at Lafayette but added, to Worthington's consternation, that he "thought he was intoxicated." And while the pronoun reference (he) is technically ambiguous, it is doubtful Hoover meant the horse.

Thursday, August 21, 1862

The court began at 9:00 A.M. with Col. David Stuart, 55th Illinois, taking the stand to answer more questions about Shiloh. He was followed by 2nd Lt. John Lute, Company C, 46th, who testified that he saw Worthington on July 17 and that he gave coherent instructions about a bridge the unit was to build. But he stated that he thought Worthington was "under the influence of liquor" (*Court-Martial Record* 76). When Henry M. Person, a teamster for the 46th, was asked if he heard Worthington using violent or profane language about the time the 46th Ohio left Lafayette, he stated that he did not and that Worthington seemed in "a better humour than usual." Continuing in the disjointed presentation of his witnesses, Worthington then recalled Colonel Kilby Smith, 54th Ohio, and questioned him about the 18th of July and about Shiloh.

At the end of the session, the testimony for the defense was closed, and Worthington requested one week to prepare for his closing argument. "The court refused his request, but granted him until Monday morning the 25th i[n]s[ta]nt. at 9 o'clock" (*Court-Martial Record* 79).

Monday, August 25, 1862

On this, the final day of the trial, Colonel Worthington immediately asked for more time to finish his defense. Keeping in mind Sherman's instruction that the business of the court should be rapidly conducted, "the court unanimously decided that the request could not be granted as an unusual time had already been given" (*Court-Martial Record* 80). After the proceedings had been read to the court, Worthington took the floor and offered an address in his defense (marked Exhibit H). In beginning his delivery of a 50-page defense treatise, Worthington declared immediately that he had sought the court-martial:

> Mr. President and officers of the court, candor as a soldier and integrity as a man compel me to admit that this trial has been of my own seeking. I deemed it a duty to myself, to my regiment, to the Army of the Tennessee, [and] the Army of the Republic, a duty to the people of the United States, to truth and the perpetuity of the government that I should do my humble part in staying to some extent that flood of negligence, incompetence, and improvidence that is bearing us onward to that gulf of military despotism which has been the grave of all such government[s] as ours in all past times.
>
> The sacrifice of my commission, of my life, even my honor were nothing if I can in the least degree develop that utter disregard of all common sense that — contempt of all martial principles and law which has defeated the zeal and   of our troops, the efforts of the government and the liberal contribution of the people general in the prosecution of this deplorable war. To Genl. W. T. Sherman the country and the army will also be under obligation for calling this court by its means some little light ... may be thrown upon ... our disgrace not only at Shiloh but many other fields before and since that bloody day; causes and practices which have called for a double installment of blood....
>
> And here let it be distinctly understood that it is not I, T. Worthington of Ohio a humble and unfortunate field officer

(1)

Mr President and officers of the court

Candour as a soldier and integrity as a man compels me to admit that this trial has been of my own seeking. I deemed it a duty to myself, to my state, to the army of Tennessee, the army of the Republic; a duty to the people of their United States, to truth and the perpetuity of the Gov't. That I should do my humble part in staying to some extent that flood of negligence, incompetence & improvidence that is hurrying us onward to that gulf of military ruin which has been the grave of all such Governments as ours in all past time.

The sacrifice of my commission of my life, even my honor, were nothing if I can in the least degree developp that utter disregard of all common sense, that seeming contempt of all martial principles, a weak which has despoiled the scale bravery of our troops and the efforts of the government and the liberal contributions of the people generally in the prosecution of this deplorable war — To Gen'l W. T. Sherman this country above the army will also be under obligation for willing this court by means of which some little light in any authentic shape may be thrown upon these events which may stain our disgrace not only at Shiloh but many other fields before and since that bloody day, citizens & practices which have called for a double instalment of blood & tears bearing desolation to myriads of happy homes and destitution to the credit of the nation —

And here let it be distinctly understood that it is not of J. Worthington of Ohio, an humble and unfortunate field officer of volunteers, who is now on trial before you — (no, gentlemen, your victim is of a higher order). It is Major Gen'l W. T. Sherman who is now on trial before you — not Gen. Sherman

95

of volunteers, who is now on trial before you. No, Gentlemen, your mission is of a higher order. It is Major Gen. William T. Sherman who is now on trial before you.

Worthington went on to argue against Sherman's claim that he circulated the diary extract to gain a "popular reputation," submitting instead that the entire matter had held him up to ridicule and court-martial. Worthington claimed that the charges against him were motivated by Sherman's "personal feelings toward the prisoner of the court. Feelings of aversion or enmity ... originating in natural, opposite idiosyncrasies" from the day of his arrival in Paducah and "resulting in numerous attempts at [Worthington's] degradation" (*Court-Martial Record* 4). To support his competence as an officer, Worthington discussed the redoubt he built in Lafayette and again referenced Halleck's *Elements of Military Art and Science*, page 43, providing a list of quotes that sounded more like a lecture on defense and fortifications than a defense summation. In what seems almost a diatribe on fundamental tactics, Worthington talked about the Federal defenses north of the Potomac River in the east, as well as the Battle of Bull Run. He defined for the court the meaning of "logistics" and explained Sherman's failures in that area. He even attacked Sherman's practice of taking "sick men forward" during the Tennessee campaign. In a series of rhetorical questions, he sought to drive home his claims against Sherman:

> Who will not believe an attack is imminent with a superior enemy an hour's march off? Who will not believe an attack is imminent though the enemy's artillery is ... before his camp?

He reminded the court of Sherman's lack of scouts in the hours immediately before the attack on April 6, and he again discussed how Sherman had ignored the reports of prisoners, which clearly indicated a large army not far away.

> It is at any rate notorious in Gen. Sherman's Division that he has paid little or no attention to the health, comfort, or good condition of his troops. He has generally issued the requisite orders of a Division commander and something more but has paid no personal attention at all to their fulfillment except in the case of Brigade Drill for a few days about the time of his promotion at Shiloh [*Court-Martial Record* 42].

Opposite: PHOTOGRAPH 7.3 The first page of Worthington's 50-page closing statement.

Worthington then claimed that quick action by Sherman might have thwarted the Confederate attack or, at a minimum, have disrupted their initial efforts on the morning of April 6.

> Had Sherman's three batteries been posted on the high ground in front of Buckland's right, fifty thousand men taken in flank could have been swept away in the two hours before the center fell back at 9:00 A.M. [*Court-Martial Record* 49].

In Worthington's mind there existed "no greater evidence of [Sherman's] negligence than leaving Appler's left exposed as it was," and he stated so in his summation. He denounced "the manner in which this trial was gotten up," as well as Sherman's "manner and language towards him," closing with the comment that "there was an invitation to the enemy to make an attack — where, how, and when he chose that invitation was given to the Rebel Army on the 5th and 6th of April 1862 by Major Gen. W. T. Sherman" (*Court-Martial Record* 51).

Following Worthington's final argument, the court closed to further testimony and began deliberation. How long the members of the court deliberated is uncertain, but they returned that day with their findings.

Findings

Given the nature of the testimony against him, Tom Worthington was probably not surprised when the officers hearing the case returned with this verdict:

> The Court after mature deliberation find the prisoner Col. Thomas Worthington, of the 46th Regiment Ohio Infantry Volunteers as follows:
> Of the 1st Specification of 1st Charge [drunkenness on duty] — *Guilty*.
> Of the 2nd Specification of the 1st Charge, so much as charges drunkenness on the streets of the City on the 6th day of August 1862 — *Not Guilty*. The latter clause "and at his own quarters within the limits of Fort Pickering in such condition" — *Guilty*.
> Of the 1st Charge — *Guilty*.
> Of the 1st Specification of 2nd Charge [habitual drunkenness] on the following dates: July 17th, 18th, 19th, 21st, and 25th, and August 6th, 1862 — *Guilty*.
> Of the other dates named in this specification — *Not Guilty*.
> Of the 2nd Charge — *Not Guilty*.
> Of the 1st Specification 3rd Charge [conduct unbecoming an officer and a gentleman] — *Not Guilty*.

Of the 2nd Specification 3rd Charge — *Guilty*.
Of the 3rd Specification 3rd Charge — *Not Guilty*.
Of the 3rd Charge — *Guilty*.
And the court do therefore sentence him the said Col. Thomas Worthington, of the 46th Regiment Ohio Infantry Volunteers, to be "Cashiered" ["General Order No. 86"].

TIMING AND MOTIVATION FOR A COURT-MARTIAL

Worthington knew beyond a doubt that publishing that diary extract would likely get him court-martialed. He admitted as much and declared that he courted the confrontation. And if the trial had just been about the truth or falsity of Worthington's allegations, he might have stood a reasonable chance of a less harsh verdict. But the clear insubordination of publishing the diary extract, coupled with Worthington's alcohol abuse, proved sufficient to prompt his removal from the service. Yet perhaps worst of all for Worthington, the issue of drunkenness on duty and conduct unbecoming an officer had provided the legal cover Sherman needed to silence one of his severest critics. That Sherman would convene a court-martial to get rid of an officer who would not be silenced should surprise no one considering his own admission regarding newspaper reporters in a letter to his wife just one week after the Battle of Shiloh:

> I now have the lawful right to have a Court Martial, and if I catch one of these Cincinnati newspapermen in my Camp I will have a Court and *they will do just as I tell them* [emphasis added]. It would offer me a real pleasure to hang one [Hirshson 124].

During his testimony, Sherman suggested that Worthington fabricated part, if not all, of his diary after the battle. While that claim is possible, it was neither proven at the court-martial nor can it be proven today. The language and the actions described on the various dates in the diary extract appear completely consistent with the arrogant meddling and constant second-guessing that Worthington demonstrated throughout his association with General Sherman. Even Sherman admitted that Worthington had been predicting attacks for days prior to the actual battle, so the entries prognosticating an impending attack make sense. Sherman did not contest the fact that Worthington hunted up and down the landing in search of axes and clothing in the days prior to the battle. Also, Worthington's concern about the shabby economics of the supply system is fully consistent with his experience as a successful businessman. Last, but perhaps most important, it is completely within character for a man like Tom Worthington to meticulously record his actions, particularly if he believes himself smarter and better qualified for leadership than the man appointed over him. Having such a record would be critical to his usurping Sherman at some future date.

WORTHINGTON GETS WHAT HE WANTED

The issue of why Worthington behaved as he did in the months after Shiloh must be addressed in any discussion of his charges against Sherman. As a West Point graduate familiar with Army regulations, protocol, and conduct, Worthington knew full well that to continue to stir the controversy over Sherman and Grant's culpability at Shiloh would be flirting with disaster. In his writings after the war, indeed, in his own defense at the court-martial, Worthington claimed that he sought his own court-martial as the only means by which he could expose the truth about Sherman and Grant's incompetence at the Battle of Shiloh. Writing about himself in the third person, as he frequently did after the war to create the semblance of distancing himself from the issues, Worthington declared, "The ... court-martial [was] provoked by him [Worthington] as the only means of obtaining official evidence of the criminalities of two or more Union commanders at Shiloh" (Worthington *Facts* 1).

It would be perhaps easier for the modern reader to believe that Worthington did not intend to be court-martialed. Certainly, many of his contemporaries questioned his resorting to such an extreme measure. It would be easier to dismiss Worthington as simply a disgruntled subordinate, angry about being placed under the command of men he believed inferior to himself in talent and experience. It would be simpler to believe that he was so enraged by what he saw as the senseless loss of Federal lives at Shiloh that he just lost control, letting his mouth outdistance his brain, exposing himself to the charge of insubordination. It would be convenient to believe that his abuse of alcohol clouded his judgment, loosed his tongue, and made him say and do things he would later regret. But Tom Worthington was a much more complicated and deliberate man than any of the above explanations of his behavior, taken by themselves, can explain.

If Worthington could have made his case short of a court-martial, he would have done so. Nothing in his writings demonstrated any desire to leave the service, i.e., he was not weary of the war and looking for a way to get back home. On the contrary, his life was no longer "a blank" as he had described it prior to the outbreak of hostilities. He seemed to revel in his wartime service, deeming himself possessed of the kind of military expertise that the Army — and his country — needed at the front. When the newspapermen and the politicians began to lose the scent of Sherman's trail in favor of more immediate game, he saw no other way, short of putting Sherman under oath and on the witness stand, to keep under scrutiny what he believed to be the facts. He had to keep the pot boiling if he ever expected Sherman to be held accountable, and he did so by distributing the extract from his diary. Marking his diary extract "private and confidential" seems a sophomoric effort to cover himself when the document was clearly intended for publication and distribution.

Worthington was, indeed, a disgruntled subordinate, angry about being placed under the command of men he believed inferior to himself in talent and experience. He detested Sherman from their very first meeting in Paducah, resented Sherman's position, disliked his command attitude, and despised what he believed to be his neglect of duty. But his dislike of Sherman seems to be no greater than Sherman's dislike of him; in fact, the two men seemed to feed off their mutual animosity. Worthington would have loved nothing more than to see Sherman removed from command. When Major Sanger, 53rd Ohio Infantry (at the time of the court-martial, he was on Sherman's staff), was asked under oath what he knew of Worthington's published diary account, Sanger testified:

> Shortly before leaving camp at Shiloh Col. Worthington called to see me to get the exact time of our falling back from our first line, and stated that he was preparing a history of the Tennessee Expedition. He offered to read me portions, and did read some extracts. ... my understanding was he was getting up a statement for publication to reflect upon Genl. Grant and Sherman. He said, "I want to make a Report of the Tennessee Expedition and throw the responsibility of our defeat where it belongs." He stated that it rested upon Genls. Grant, C. F. Smith, and Sherman and he was determined to show them up [*Court-Martial Record* 25].

Worthington's open solicitation of a court-martial was designed to show up his superiors. Sherman, in turn, took the opportunity that Worthington provided him to dispense with a man who kept pointing to the latest blot on his record. Stanley P. Hirshson in his biography of Sherman cites the opinion of Col. Walter Q. Gresham, one of the jurors who heard the case. Worthington issuing the diary extract was exactly "what Sherman wanted," for he was now able to arrest Worthington and try him for insubordination.

Yet dislike of Sherman, no matter how intense, hardly seems justification enough to sacrifice the Army position and title that Worthington so enjoyed. Martyrdom at the hands of the truth appears noble enough — but perhaps a bit too noble for a man of Worthington's ego and definitely too noble to serve as the *only* justification for Worthington's actions. Quite simply, Worthington was truly enraged by what he believed was the senseless loss of Federal lives at Shiloh. His were not crocodile tears. His feelings of sadness, loss, and betrayal appear everywhere from his angry treatises to his eloquent war poetry written after Shiloh. That powerful sense of loss drove him to demand that someone — and in his mind the "someone" was easily identified — suffer the consequences. Yet sadness and righteous indignation alone do not explain why he would sacrifice his future as an Army officer and expose his family name to potential disgrace through the vehicle of a court-martial. The influence of the Worthington name — a name which Sherman himself respected as he stated in his testimony — certainly would have bought him an audience for his charges outside of the realm of court-martial.

The court-martial testimony establishes that Worthington did abuse alcohol to the point that it clouded his judgment, loosed his tongue, and made him a public spectacle. But many soldiers abused alcohol, Grant not the least of them, and they did not find themselves sitting before a jury of their officer peers. The testimony against Worthington paints the picture of a raving drunk. Major W. D. Sanger of the 55th Ohio Infantry, then on Sherman's staff, testified to seeing Worthington

> on the 18th July about 11 a.m.... disgracefully drunk. He had citizens by the buttonhole, and was giving what purported to be a history of the Campaign. He was running about the works. I saw him talking with Mr. Wallace of Chicago and others — He was giving Wallace his account of the battle of Shiloh and the march to Corinth — also the labor of the division on the railroads, up to Lafayette, and what he termed "our disgraceful retreat to Moscow." Severely criticizing the conduct of Genls Halleck, Grant, and Sherman. I afterward saw him several times, during our halt at Lafayette, in loud and indecent conversation, cussing and swearing at teamsters, sutlers, and citizens — I also saw him with difficulty mount his horse [*Court-Martial Record* 24].

The court-martial produced ample evidence from a variety of witnesses that Worthington was, on perhaps a half dozen different occasions,

Seven. Court-Martial of Thomas Worthington

intoxicated. But so were hundreds of other commanders at some point in the war. That fact, by itself, would hardly have been grounds to cashier the man from the service. But Worthington's behavior was not just the ramblings of a drunk. *What* he was saying, not how he said it, got him court-martialed. Sanger and others testified:

> On one or other occasions near that time [July 18], perhaps the next day or day following, in Memphis he was marking with a stick, talking very loud to a crowd of citizens and soldiers, and giving an account of some battle, moving troops. I remember to have seen him three or four different times since our arrival in Memphis [*Court-Martial Record* 25].

Is there any doubt regarding upon what battle he was instructing the good citizens and soldiers of Memphis? This behavior, Sherman reasoned, was contrary to the good order and discipline of his command, and it had to be stopped. The fact that Worthington was drunk simply added fuel to the fire for the court-martial. But what is interesting about the alcohol abuse alleged against Worthington is that it never seems to have occurred prior to Shiloh. Every instance of intoxication alleged against Worthington seems to have occurred during July. Sherman testified that he never previously had cause to believe that Worthington neglected any of his duties, nor did he have any doubt that the colonel knew his job. Now if Worthington were a chronic abuser of alcohol during March in Paducah, and Sherman knew of it, he must have concluded that his drinking did not affect his ability to command. What aspect of Worthington's drinking in July suddenly made him unfit for command? The answer is not the drinking. The answer is the language out of Worthington's mouth — language that was accusatory of Sherman. Some might argue that Worthington, who imbibed with restraint prior to Shiloh, was so disturbed by the events of Shiloh and what he believed to be Sherman's responsibility for those tragic events that he turned to alcohol for solace. Others might say he drank to ease the pain, and his drinking to excess, in turn, led him to behaviors that prompted the court-martial. On the latter point, others might even suggest that Worthington's drinking was no more severe than most of the other officers and men stationed in Memphis during a time when Sherman himself encouraged alcohol abuse by allowing the proliferation of taverns and collecting taxes for the city on each of them.

The answer to the question of why Worthington behaved as he did is a confluence of all of the above issues.

SITTING ON THE PAPERWORK

Based upon the verdict of the court-martial, Sherman wasted no time getting rid of Worthington. Within two weeks Sherman relieved Worthington of command of the 46th Ohio Infantry, stripped him of his status as a volunteer officer in the U.S. Army, and sent him home to Ohio. Effective September 15, 1862, Thomas Worthington "ceas[ed] to be an officer of the Volunteer Army of the United States" (*Court-Martial Record* 16). Sherman's acting adjutant general, Capt. S. M. Dayton, referred Worthington's court-martial proceeding through General Grant to the War Department, declaring that the case should be referred to the president of the United States under the 65th Article of War. But he added that "in time of war" the "approval of the sentence in such cases by the President is not requisite but is within the power of the officer assembling the Court" (*Court-Martial Record* 19). Roughly translated, Sherman's judge advocate was saying that General Sherman could charge a soldier, appoint the court, testify against that soldier, enforce the sentence of the court-martial, and cashier an officer without an outside set of eyes ever passing judgment on the matter. Sherman did precisely that with General Order No. 86, dated October 1, cashiering Worthington.

While Sherman had wasted no time getting rid of Worthington, he did not feel an equally expedient need to process the court-martial results through his commander, General Grant, and ultimately to a review by the War Department's judge advocate general. Worthington's court-martial proceedings remained within the district of West Tennessee until October 14, when they were forwarded along with two other court-martial results through General Grant to the War Department. During that time, Worthington attempted through official channels to call attention to the irregularities of the trial. Sending a letter to the U.S. Army's adjutant general on September 17 through Lt. Col. Walcutt (then acting commander of the 46th) and Colonel McDowell, Worthington requested the proceedings be examined against Section 65 of the Article of War, dated May 1830. In his endorsement on Worthington's request, Sherman tried to assure the government that Worthington knew the subject matter of the charges and that the charges were made by him and "placed in the hands of the judge advocate." Hence, according to Sherman's attached note, Worthington should have "excepted to [the charges] before pleading." Rather, Sherman observed, Worthington actually "courted the trial and waived all objections on this point" (Worthington *Blunders* 4). The latter statement by Sherman is clearly false, for Worthington never waived his right to know who preferred the charges; in fact, he insisted upon and finally got an admission from Sherman regarding the matter — an admission that came well toward the end of the trial.

"THESE FINDINGS ARE A NULLITY"

By the end of October Worthington's request for review of his court-martial had reached the Army adjutant general, who replied to the district of West Tennessee that "the Secretary of War will direct what order shall be issued in this case." On November 19, 1862, Joseph Holt,[13] judge advocate general for the Army, wrote his review findings to Edwin M. Stanton, secretary of War. He summarized Worthington's claim that Sherman had acted as both "accuser and prosecutor" and outlined Worthington's request that the findings be disregarded. Wrote Holt, citing the Articles of War:

> The objection seems to me well taken. Whenever a general officer commanding an army, or a colonel commanding a separate department, shall be the accuser or prosecutor of any officer in the army of the United States under his command, the general court-martial for the trial of such officer shall be appointed by the President of the United States" [Worthington *Blunders* 6].

Holt cited Worthington's objection during the trial to proceeding further "without knowing by whom the charges were drawn or advanced." Worthington's objection being overruled, Holt concluded, "was irregular." He also forcefully rejected Sherman's argument that if Worthington thought the proceedings were illegal, he should have protested at the beginning of the trial. Sherman had argued that Worthington's attempt to have the charges set aside constituted a "plea in abatement," but Holt did not concur:

> The irregularity suggested, does not call into question merely the jurisdiction of the court to try Colonel Worthington, but its existence as a legally organized body.

And in a stinging rejection of Sherman's logic, he wrote:

> It is never too late [for an accused person] to insist on so radical and fatal a defect as this. It is of the highest importance that the administration of public justice, as well in the military as in the civil service, should be not only pure, but unsuspected. This, however, could not be the case where a commanding general, with all

To Mother
Ap 7/62

Memphis Sept 7th 1862
6 am

Recd yours of 31st ult
yesterday. The stuff will
answer for pants but overcoat
will soon be new. Have not
been at the express office. Think I shall
assign shortly. My Regt has done
more and better work in and out
of battle than any other from Ohio
or in Hallicks army, and as officers
I can [show] as good and better subs-
-titute at home. Yet I have been
kept studiously out of view especially
by Sherman in whose military capacity
I have have little confidence and
more in his loyalty to the present form
of gov't or indeed the union. I may write
further in a week or so, we are not much
safer here than at Shiloh. Love to
[all]
Yours T. Worthington

the moral power which belongs to his position, is permitted at once to prefer charges against his officers and to organize courts-martial for their trial [Worthington *Blunders* 6].

Sherman's court-martial of Tom Worthington was therefore pronounced "without color of authority, and its proceedings and findings ... a nullity."

Worthington would later claim that Sherman, Grant, Sherman's judge advocate, McCoy, and others acted in disobedience of the Articles of War by retaining the record of his court-martial for at least six weeks after the trial and two weeks after Sherman executed the sentence. They knew, Worthington argued, that what they had done was illegal, and by sitting on the proceedings until the sentence was endorsed by Grant and carried out by Sherman, they could effectively be rid of Worthington before anyone was the wiser. The delay in sending to Washington the court-martial proceedings, Worthington further argued, resulted in his inability to get himself reinstated into the Army once the findings were declared null and void by Judge Advocate Holt.

Even though the judge advocate general of the Army had sided with Worthington in his charge of an illegal court-martial, the damage had been done. Worthington was out of the Army and out of Sherman's way. His long road to regaining his honor and what he believed to be his rightful place as an officer in the Army of the United States now began. Sherman biographer Hirshson reminds us that even one of the men on Worthington's court-martial realized the unsavory nature of what had happened to Thomas Worthington:

> Gresham and his wife always maintained that Sherman tried to cover up this sorry episode. The published Official Records of the war ignored it. With the exception of Gresham's the biographies and autobiographies of the officers involved did the same [Hirshson 132].

Of Sherman and his court-martial of Worthington, Hirshson writes, "for someone who had practiced law, Sherman possessed primitive ideas about justice" (132).

Even after the court-martial, a defiant and proud Tom Worthington wrote home to a family member from Memphis:[14]

Opposite: PHOTOGRAPH 7.4 Worthington used some of this same Union stationery to write portions of the defense he presented as his closing argument at his court-martial. Upon the findings, he sent this letter home, indicating his intention to resign (courtesy Ross County Historical Society).

> Think I shall resign shortly.... [M]y regiment has done more and better work in and out of battle than any other from Ohio or in Halleck's Army, and as far as I can [tell] has as good or better reputation at home. Yet I have been kept stubbornly out of   by General Sherman in whose military capacity I have but little confidence and none in his loyalty to the present form of govt or indeed the Union. I will write[?] further in a week or so, we are not much safer than at Shiloh [Worthington 7 Sept. 1862].

At this dark moment in his life Tom Worthington might have reflected back upon the inspiring words that Thomas Reed delivered upon his graduation from West Point:

> But be assured, your country will every where meet you with approbation, and open to you the prospects of useful and honorable pursuits [Reed 39].

Worthington must certainly have felt like someone had crept into his life in the night and switched what Reed had predicted as "the present pride ... of the country" for his current shame and discredit.

Chapter Eight

In Search of Honor

LONG JOURNEY HOME

For a West Point–educated man whose life had been a 55-year effort to live up to the expectations associated with coming from Ohio with the family name of Worthington, the court-martial findings and his resultant dismissal must have devastated Worthington. The reader will recall the Worthington family motto: *Virtute Dignus Avorum,* or "in virtue worthy of one's ancestors." That his dishonor did not prompt him to take his own life is a testament to his inner strength and to his determination to redeem his dignity. Still, saying good-bye to the regiment he had raised, drilled, and led into heretofore the greatest battle of the Civil War must have been one of the most difficult tasks of the old colonel's life. The long journey back to Ohio afforded him several days to figure out what he would say to the many questions sure to be waiting for him. Of course there would be the doubting glances, the whispers behind his back, the rumors running rampant regarding his dismissal. Somehow he found the courage to face his accusers, his family, and his friends, and the obstinate streak that worked to get him into so much trouble with Sherman might have been the very characteristic that saved him. For he lost no time mustering support for what he expected to be a triumphant return to active duty.

It would have been convenient for Sherman, Grant, and the entire War Department if all the soldiers who had known and served with Tom Worthington had unanimously affirmed that he was, indeed, an arrogant, eccentric drunk who was unfit for command and a disgrace to the Army.

Unfortunately, at least for those who wanted most to be rid of him, Worthington still possessed some powerful, influential, and ardent supporters who weighed in on his behalf. The ink on the judge advocate general's nullification of the court-martial verdict had scarcely dried before Tom Worthington was petitioning the government to be reinstated in the Army in some capacity. What follows is some of the correspondence Worthington orchestrated to plead his case.

To copies of their original letters of recommendation for Worthington issued early in the war, Brig. Gen. Catharinus P. Buckingham and Maj. Gen. Robert C. Schenck added notes of continuing, unqualified support:

> I still entertain the opinion expressed in the above letter without discrimination or qualification.
> Washington, Feb 9, 1863
> — C. P. Buckingham, Brig. Gen.[1]
>
> Feb 25, 1863
> I still entertain the same opinion and recommend that Col. Worthington be restored to service.
> — Robert Schenck, Maj. Gen.[2]

The court-martial verdict had shaken neither Buckingham nor Schenck's confidence in Worthington, nor did it deter Brig. Gen. W. S. Rosecrans and others from voicing unqualified support for Worthington to be reinstated in the Army:

> I have known Col. Worthington but nine months but have observed those qualities of mind and body mentioned by Gen. Buckingham and cheerfully add my testimony and wishes for Col. Worthington's success in the service.
> — W. S. Rosecrans, Brig. Gen., U.S.A.

Others added their support as well:

> The undersigned cheerfully concur in the opinion of Gens Buckingham, Schenck, and Rosecrans and would say further that the diary extracts referred to by Col. Worthington in his letter to Gen. Halleck of July 11th 1862 evince a degree of providence, vigilance and military aptitude which should not be lost to the govt. at the present time.
> Feb 9th 1863
> — V. B. Northon[?] Ohio
> — Crofts Wright, late Col.[3]
> — B. F. Wade
> And many others [*Court-Martial Record*].

By specifically referencing the diary extracts and Worthington's "vigilance" and "aptitude," it appears from this letter that these officers not only believed in Worthington the man, but also believed in the credence of his claims relative to Sherman and the Union Army's lack of preparedness at Shiloh. Ultimately, the intercession on Worthington's behalf took the form of a direct appeal to the secretary of War. In a letter to Worthington, Gen. J. G. Swift announced his intent to lobby on Worthington's behalf, and he provided him a copy of the correspondence to the secretary of War:

>26th Feb 1863 —
>Col. Thos Worthington
>
>I have conversed with Gen. Robert Anderson [Worthington's West Point roommate] and Col. Ja[mes] Monroe on your subject and also with Gen. Scott and am fully satisfied that the govt. would find material benefit in offering you employment in the US Army, and that a good mode of satisfying the Secy of War on this subject would be his instituting an inquiry by a board of officers as to your merits and as to the legality of the proceedings of the court-martial in your case.
>
>That you were educated at West Point is an   to your having there acquired   information and your military conduct evinces this fact. In these days of seeming   of generalship in our army it behooves the govt. to seek the gentlemen who do possess that ability to conduct our good soldiers to victory and I heartily wish you may find the employment you seek — not from personal motives on your part but from devotion to our Union and our   .
>
>J. G. Swift
>
>P.S. Enclosed is a note to the Hon. Secy. of War. Gen Swift formerly of the U.S. Army presents his compliments to the Hon. Mr. Stanton. Gen. S[wift] having accidentally become acquainted with the facts that relate to the character and ability of Col. Thos Worthington late a General officer in the Ohio Militia is of the opinion that he possesses qualities amply fitting him for the position of a general officer. In the days when such abilities are not readily found Gen. Swift suggests respectfully to Mr. Stanton the institution of such inquiry as may satisfy Mr. Stanton as to the actual merits of Col. Worthington.
>
>City of New York
>26th Feb 1863 [*Court-Martial Record* 102].

But for all of Worthington's high-powered support, Secretary of War Stanton was in no hurry to reinstate him. Stanton had, after all, still to deal with Grant and Sherman — two officers who were winning battles for a change. The old adage that "to do nothing is, in fact, to take action" applies in the case of Worthington's petitions, for Stanton simply let them languish while he and his generals prosecuted the war. Worthington waited throughout the summer of 1863 for the weight of his supporters' recommendations and the gravity of his illegal court-martial to move Stanton and the Army leadership to return him to duty. When nothing happened by the fall, he again took matters in his own hands. He seems to have believed that he would, in time, be returned to duty, but in the meantime he saw no reason to let up on the pressure against his nemesis, General Sherman. Thus Worthington wrote S. A. Hurlburt, president of his court-martial, to get the details of the proceedings so he might use that information against Sherman:

> Morrow Warren Co. Ohio Sept 7th 1863
> Maj. Gen. Hurlburt
> On receipt of your letter last fall   . I wrote to Mr. Henry Buchanan whom I had left in Memphis to get a copy of such part of your memoranda of my trial as I wanted. I have however, left the city and I now wish to say that I wish if possible to get the testimony of Lt. Col. Walcutt and my order of dismissal[?] in this case. This letter will probably find you at home and having misplaced your letter I have forgotten the address. Under obligation to your former   you will further oblige me by your   in this matter which   . The Judge Advocate Genl. (Holt) has declared the trial a nullity under the 65th Article of War but I am not returned to service. Will you also oblige me to favor to say (if you recollect it) that I filed my resignation or also a copy of the   from a diary as part of my defense.
> Very respectfully yours,
> T. Worthington [*Court-Martial Record* 105]

Ready Once Again—
Morgan's Raid into Ohio

While Worthington was unable to return to the war during the summer of 1863, the war came to him in the form of Confederate General John Hunt Morgan's raid into Kentucky and Ohio. From Burkesville, Kentucky, on July 2, Morgan with 2,460 men dashed north, destroying railroad tracks and communication lines in the heart of Federally occupied territory. Upon reaching Brandenburg, Kentucky, he crossed the Ohio River and began moving northeast through Indiana toward the Ohio line. The route of Morgan's bold raiders would take them within 20 miles of Worthington's home in Morrow, Ohio. General Ambrose Burnside, in command of Federal forces in Kentucky, believed Morgan would attempt to recross the Ohio River somewhere south of Cincinnati. Thus, on July 8, he declared martial law in the city and called out the militia in 32 southern Ohio counties. Worthington, formerly a brigadier general in the Ohio Militia, likely saw a chance to redeem his honor in this call-up of home guards, and he offered his services. Never bashful about his own ability, Worthington threw his energies into orchestrating a force to stop and, if possible, trap John Hunt Morgan and his men in Ohio.

But organizing poorly trained militiamen and mounting them in time to stop the veteran southern cavalry would have been a challenge to any leader. Morgan had not crossed the Ohio until July 8, thus Worthington could not have been afforded more than a day to assist in rallying the militia in Warren County. By the afternoon of July 9, Morgan's main body had already skirted north of Cincinnati, skirmished with the pickets in the vicinity of Camp Dennison (where Worthington had subsidized the water supply), passed through Batavia, and reached Williamsburg, some 28 miles east-southeast of Cincinnati. Other than some ineffective ambushes and guerrilla-style sniping, the militia could offer little resistance to Morgan's men as they cut through the heart of southern Ohio. As to Worthington's role in the hasty defense of his native state, we find only the following statement in the West Point *Biographical Register of Officers and Graduates*: "July 11–20, 1863, he joined the Indiana and Ohio volunteers raised to repel General John Morgan's Rebel Raiders" (Cullum 393).

While battling for reinstatement in the Army and chasing Morgan across southern Ohio, Worthington's woes were compounded in 1863 by the deaths of two of his sisters: Eleanor (Ellen) Worthington Watts and Margaret (Maggie) Worthington Mansfield.

ANOTHER OFFER OF SERVICE

General Robert Schenck, still confident that Worthington could make a significant military contribution to the war effort, prevailed upon Tom during the spring of 1864 to request an audience with the president himself. The court-martial had been deemed "a nullity," and since Worthington had resigned under honorable circumstances, no regulatory prohibitions stood in the way of his reinstatement as an Army officer. The previous letters of support from Schenck and Rosecrans had availed little, and since

PHOTOGRAPH *8.1* Worthington also blamed Ulysses S. Grant for Grant's complicity in the surprise Confederate attack, yet he sought his help when trying to reclaim a commission and return to active duty (Library of Congress).

normal military channels had failed to gain him restoration to the service, Worthington agreed to Schenck's request. Worthington traveled to Washington and gained his audience with Lincoln during the last week of March. Given Worthington's personality, one can envision the meeting starting out with the usual courtesies. Raised with class and dignity and never lacking for eloquence, Worthington likely laid out the details of his illegal dismissal and probably even restrained his overwhelming urge to elaborate on Sherman and Grant's mistakes at Shiloh. His arguments on his behalf, however, were not sufficient to convince Lincoln to reinstate him in the Army. In fact, Lincoln appears to have researched the matter and received negative recommendations from both General Halleck and, surprisingly, Judge Advocate General Holt—the man who declared Worthington's court-martial illegal. An adverse recommendation by Holt would seem to suggest that his declaration of a nullity in Worthington's trial had not prevented him from digesting the evidence that pointed to the colonel being unfit for service. In his meeting with Lincoln, Worthington heard the president declare him, on advice from Halleck and Holt, unfit to be a colonel. The Worthington temper flared upon hearing those words and, according to Lincoln, Tom made the "urgent" request that the president "put it in writing" (Basler 276). Lincoln obliged him. Furious at his rebuff, Worthington wrote Lincoln on April 12:

> I will never reenter the Army while that terrible and degrading law under which I have had no official notice of being dismissed continues to disgrace the statute book [Basler 276].

Worthington seems to be citing here a technicality used by Halleck and Holt to block his return to service. But Worthington's quarrel was with far more than an interpretation of Federal statutes regarding court-martial proceedings. His quarrel remained, as it had been before, during, and after Shiloh, with the men under whom he had been compelled to serve.

> I saw something of ... [abuse of court-martial law] ... at Memphis ... where a General ... scarcely ever clear of liquor staggered into his court room to decide on the cases of men better and abler than himself" [Basler 276].

Despite all that had happened, Worthington still considered himself a better officer and a better soldier than William T. Sherman, and he refused to be intimidated even by President Lincoln himself, declaring in his April 12 letter that he would, perhaps, return to the Army someday on *his* terms:

When Holt and Halleck ... are in their proper places, if the war should still be on hand I may possibly request a removal of that disability under which by their advice and initiation, I must for the present remain, hoping for better luck next time. With a very respectful request that this document may be referred to either or both of these distinguished "Field Officers" [Basler 276].

In spite of his disastrous meeting with Lincoln in March, Worthington decided by the summer of that year that he had waited long enough for government leaders to change their attitude toward him. Again he traveled to Washington and again he brought the matter of his reinstatement to President Lincoln. But on this trip he carried a letter of recommendation written by Ohio Governor Dennison to Lincoln, dated August 24, and expressing the hope that Worthington's "differences with General Sherman and his dismissal from the service, may not be allowed to prejudice his present application to your Excellency." The letter also bore the endorsement of Thomas Corwin, who suggested that Worthington "be placed in some military position where the country may enjoy the benefit of his services" (Basler 524). The letter was no doubt hand delivered by Worthington, and based upon the strength of its advocacy, he received an audience with the president. Worthington even planned to request an audience with Grant himself, should the president grant him reinstatement into the Army. His plan was to travel down to Virginia and find some position of service with the Army operating against Richmond. Lincoln immediately telegraphed Grant from the Executive Mansion on August 29, 1864:

Lieutenant-General Grant:
Colonel T. Worthington of Ohio is here, wishing to visit you. I will send him if you say so, otherwise not.
— A. Lincoln.

Considering the ferocity with which Worthington had denounced not only Sherman's performance at Shiloh but also Grant's, it comes as no surprise that Grant would avoid a meeting with a man who had become his nemesis. In response to Lincoln's telegram, Grant wired a succinct response that same day:

Your dispatch of 1:40 P.M. in relation to permitting Col. Worthington to come here is received. I should be very sorry to see the Colonel. He has nearly worried the life out of me at times when I could not prevent an interview [Basler 524].

Grant's telegram indicates that Worthington had on a previous occasion traveled directly to the Army in the field and cornered Grant with questions about his reinstatement. If Worthington harbored any hope that Grant might intervene on his behalf, that hope must surely have vanished with the August visit to Lincoln. In fact, no record exists that Worthington ever again attempted to rejoin the Federal Army. This final rebuke might have been the crushing blow that began Worthington's rapid descent into his reclusive lifestyle back at Yamoyden in Morrow, Ohio.

CHAPTER NINE

After the War

When the war ended in April 1865, Worthington was back in the business of agriculture on Edward D. Mansfield and the late Margaret Worthington Mansfield's Yamoyden estate in Salem Township, or Morrow, Ohio. But the war years had left Tom Worthington with not only a devastated reputation he would struggle to regain but also with a decimated family, as Anna McAllister points out in her biography of Sarah Worthington:

> Death had taken sad toll among the ten Worthington children who used to play together so happily at Adena. Only Sarah and her two brothers [James and Tom]... remained of all the merry family [332].

Tom's younger brother, Dr. Francis Worthington, had succumbed in 1849 in Cincinnati of typhus. Elizabeth Worthington Pomeroy had died in December 1855 at age 38. Margaret Worthington Mansfield had died at Yamoyden in March 1863. And just one month after Maggie, Tom had lost another sister, Eleanor, who died in Chillicothe (McAllister 332–333).

Angered and embittered at his treatment by Sherman, Grant, Halleck, Holt, Lincoln, and a host of others, Worthington closed himself off from the world in a small cabin at Yamoyden. But while he isolated himself physically, Worthington was far from through attempting to tell his version of history, to identify the culprits of the disaster at Shiloh, and to find some degree of redemption for himself and his family name. He began his quest for justice by tracking down the records of his own court-martial and trying to elicit from the government the admission that he had been wrongfully dismissed from service.

On January 8, 1867, Special Order No. 11 was issued by the War Department in Washington officially revoking Worthington's cashiering and declaring him honorably discharged upon tender of his resignation to date from November 21, 1862. This little-noted piece of War Department administrative action was a major step toward Worthington regaining his honor. The refusal to officially revoke his removal had been the technicality that Halleck and Holt had used to prevent him from reentering the service in 1864. And while this action came too late to help him during the war, it became a central truth around which he would wrap a series of arguments and accusations, some sound and some ridiculous, that would continue to appear in print for the next 15 years.

One can find in Worthington's correspondence during this period increasing mention of his physical ailments—ailments that parallel those of his father in his later years. Some of the more persistent references are to "inflammatory rheumatism" and various gastric difficulties. But his physical maladies might have been overshadowed by the mental anguish he suffered as a result of his dismissal from service, anguish that took the form of his subsequent all-consuming hatred of Sherman and Grant. Responding to another of the West Point "circulars" seeking information on graduates, Worthington wrote on December 14, 1867, complaining of gastric fever, influenza, and rheumatism. Yet his ailments were not so severe as to prevent him from planning a trip to Washington the following month—the sole purpose of which would be to pursue his investigation into his court-martial proceedings and to gather information with which he could continue his verbal assault on Sherman and Grant.

Thus, over the next five years, Worthington maintained a regular correspondence with the War Department. Characteristic of that correspondence is his March 20, 1868, letter to Edwin M. Stanton requesting a copy of the proceedings of his separation from the Army. Again in August of that year he wrote for extracts from his court-martial hearing, which would confirm the judge advocate general's declaration of his trial a nullity per the 65th Article of War. Worthington busied himself during the postwar years with a near-obsessive effort to clear his own name and to damage that of Sherman and, to a lesser degree, Grant.

"My Bitterest Enemies"

Finally satisfied that he had gathered enough information to make his charges in writing, Worthington published with his own money the first of many pamphlets designed to inform the public of what he perceived as blunders and mistakes of military leadership during the late war. In March 1869, Worthington arranged for publication in Washington of the elaborately titled *No. 1 of the Blunders of the Rebellion and Their Dead-Sea Fruit in Six Numbers: Being a General Review of the Causes which Protracted the War, Quadrupled Its Expense, in Waste of Life, Money, and National Credit, and by the Rejection of All Method, Plan, or Providence in and out of the Army, Has Precipitated Present Results and Future Danger to the Union.*

In this and other works, Worthington's attacks on Sherman and others he believed had been inept leaders began to broaden well beyond a discussion of Shiloh. In a letter to J. A. Garfield extracted in the above-mentioned pamphlet, Worthington even attacked Sherman for what amounted to a power grab in his postwar position as general of the Army.

By the end of the decade Worthington published two more pamphlets detailing what he believed to be mismanagement of forces and failures of military leadership. Still, he was not satisfied that he had made his case against Sherman and Grant. As mentioned previously, his works employed an often-humorous third-person narrative in a thinly veiled effort to gain some objective distance from the subject he addressed. Most certainly a man of Worthington's education knew that only the most casual observer would be taken in by this awkward literary device, yet he persisted in using it with each subsequent publication. But hints of paranoia amid increasingly less believable charges and accusations began to emerge in Worthington's correspondence and publications by the mid–1870s. The war had been over almost a decade, and Worthington had published several pamphlets purporting to offer the true history of the Battle of Shiloh. Still, his version of the story remained known to relatively few people, and he had expended considerable personal funds to get that little amount of information into print.

He wrote to West Point on December 14, 1874, in response to its request for updated information on graduates. In that letter he claimed that "the Shermans [were] trying to defeat" his efforts to publish a complete history of the Battle of Shiloh and suggested that they had written "a Military History of Colonel Worthington" in retaliation.[1] He made no attempt to curb his animus, informing West Point chroniclers that their circular:

> finds me 72 years of age and in exceeding poverty for service at Shiloh which made Sherman and Grant what they are — and for that service they have been my bitterest enemies ever since — as they are now [Worthington 14 Dec. 1874].

by Union Commanders at Shiloh; only to be obtained by a Court Martial, after all efforts for an inquiry had failed, August, 1862.

Col. Tom Worthington as he received the First Fire at Shiloh, at

HORSE REARS AT A SHOT THROUGH THE WITHE

By Gen. TOM WORTHINGTON, late Col. 46th Ohio Vols.

This portrayal of himself as a penniless, pitiful, old man mistreated by lesser men who rose to prominence at his expense was a recurring theme of his writing and speaking starting in the mid–1870s. He leaned heavily upon the sympathy factor in later attempts to gain a pension and to gain monetary reimbursement for his work on the Army's water supply at Camp Dennison in 1862. The drawing of Worthington that appeared on the cover of several of his pamphlets pictures him sitting alone, his clothes crumpled, a crutch in his hand, and a look upon his face that can only be described as one of desperation and pain.

PHOTOGRAPH 9.2 This drawing of an aging Worthington appeared on the cover of more than one of his inflammatory pamphlets (photograph by author).

The case of Tom Worthington became a cause through which others who opposed Sherman or Grant, for reasons other than their performance at Shiloh, could attack these celebrated war heroes. On March 24, 1878, an article appeared in the Washington newspaper the *Capital* presenting a picture of Worthington not unlike that he had developed for himself. The article began, "One of the saddest spectacles to which kind hearts can be presented is that of helpless old age abandoned to the hard necessities of life." It continued with a depiction of Worthington as a pitiful, old man standing beside a passing parade where William T. Sherman was riding in a carriage.

> There is an old man who appears here from time to time, whose infirmities are aggravated by a keen sense of wrong; for while a fire

Opposite: PHOTOGRAPH 9.1 One of Tom Worthington's early pamphlets charging Sherman and Grant with incompetence at the Battle of Shiloh (photograph by author).

of wrath, at the abuse he suffers, burns within until he is half-crazed, his efforts to right himself are pitiable in their feebleness ["A National Disgrace" 1].

The article asserted that Worthington "saved … our army from utter annihilation" at Shiloh and praised him for "soldierly instinct" and "high courage." But it also pointed out how obnoxious his behavior had become since the close of the war, painting a distressing picture of a man obsessed:

> We met him upon the Avenue last Thursday. We made no effort to escape him, although, God knows, he holds one as the dreadful old mariner held the wedding guest in Coleridge's wild poem. He goes over the late war again and again. He has all the facts with a fearful tenacity in his mind, and only forgets that he has given them to you over and over before. His pale, ashy face, once so strong in its setting of full forehead, Roman nose and square, prominent and solid chin, has nothing left but the gleam of an eye in which there lurks a touch of insanity. His slouched hat is pulled over his white head, as if it were a night-cap. His clothes, of a past fashion, are ragged and threadbare, while his feet are clad in heavy shoes, good for ten years' wear, that he greases and wears without socks ["A National Disgrace" 1].

The writer indicated that in the middle of his retelling of Shiloh, Worthington stopped midsentence and cast "as ugly a gleam as we ever care to see from his gray eyes." Worthington was described as realizing that Sherman was passing in a carriage, "sitting back with arms folded, as if he felt that the eyes of the world were on him in grateful admiration." Worthington lifted a trembling arm, fist clenched, and screamed at Sherman, "There goes the damned scoundrel — the damned cowardly, lying scoundrel — the damned traitor! There he goes, damn him!"

The writer of the editorial restated in broad terms most of Worthington's claims:

- žthat the action of the 46th Ohio after being repositioned on McLernand's right saved the Federal Army at Shiloh
- žthat Worthington failed to receive due consideration for promotion due to politics
- žthat his financial claims against the government had been unjustly denied
- žthat Grant and Sherman conspired to rid themselves of an honest man

The author then continued to carry Worthington's banner:

> Grant and Sherman ought to have been court-martialed and shot. Instead of this Colonel Tom Worthington was court-martialed and cashiered. Had the old man — like Buell, Nelson and a thousand others — held a discreet silence, his gallant achievements would have been rewarded with promotion; but his honest wrath and indignation knew no bounds. On all occasions he denounced in the most profane manner the conduct of the inebriates, his superior officers, and he was disgraced ["A National Disgrace" 3].

The court-martial, the writer charged, was "packed," and though its verdict was overturned by the staff judge advocate, Worthington's subsequent dismissal by Lincoln was "instigated ... by Halleck" ("A National Disgrace" 3). The article then quoted a letter from Confederate General P. T. Beauregard, who appeared to support Worthington's claim that the hearty defense of the Federal right between noon and two o'clock:

> delayed [the Confederate] advance sufficient to prevent an earlier rout of the Federal Army ... thus giving time for part of Buell's reinforcements to arrive on the field at Pittsburg Landing just prior to the last Confederate assault at 5:00 P.M. on April 6th ["A National Disgrace" 3].

Worthington believed he had found a postwar ally in Beauregard who clearly suggested in his correspondence with the colonel the importance of the fight put up by the 46th Ohio Infantry and other units against the Orphan Brigade on the Federal right. Through his incessant lobbying for a "true history" of the battle, Worthington had won over some believers; and though many of them were friends and family, they would declare, as did Dr. Leonard Mounts of Morrow, Ohio, for decades to come that "I believe, and I think also my father and Gen. Beauregard believed, he [Worthington] saved the day [at Shiloh]" (Wells 26 June 1999).

Though the Beauregard letter was reprinted in the *Capital* editorial, the letter was written originally to Worthington apparently in response to a query that he generated to Beauregard in an effort to bolster his claims about Shiloh. How this letter fell into the hands of the editor of the *Capital* becomes apparent when one considers that the editor was Donn Piatt, the brother of Worthington's sister-in-law Martha Piatt Worthington, the wife of Tom's brother James. Donn Piatt was a harsh and vocal critic of both Sherman and Grant during Reconstruction, often using his newspaper to attack them. Having the occasion to do so on behalf of the family would have been an opportunity too appealing to resist. Still, the fact that the editorial was printed by a man sympathetic to Worthington does not by itself make the accusations false or erroneous. It does, however, help to explain the tone of the article, particularly the concluding paragraph:

> And now while Sherman rolls by in his equipage — the fool of luck, paid an enormous salary for doing nothing — and is followed and flattered by the crowd, this brave old man, whose past glitters with an achievement that saved an army, and perhaps the republic, is left to penury and rags. He can not even get an honest claim paid, based on service of an important sort rendered the Government in the beginning of the war. Can the republic afford to treat its children in this unjust and inhuman manner? ["A National Disgrace" 3].

For a decade after the war, Sherman seemed content to allow Worthington's pamphlets and declarations to be viewed as either sour grapes from an unfit officer or the vain ravings of a near-madman. But the appearance of this 1878 editorial in the *Capital* newspaper, with its apparent endorsement of both Worthington's cause and his claims, forced Sherman to reply. He chose to do so in a letter to the *Washington Post*, reprinted with an endorsement on April 6 in the *U.S. Army and Navy Journal*. His reply began with the information that Piatt was the author of the editorial and, therefore, Sherman argued, must be compromised in his views because of his familial relationship with Worthington. The article continued by saying, "The colonel has been around Washington of late boring everyone who will listen to him about his wrongs, in having been dismissed from the volunteer Army for drunkenness" ("Slanderer" 1).

Sherman stated that the carriage incident was "pure fiction," spending a lengthy paragraph describing how he was not on that street in his carriage during the week so claimed and how he usually made that trip on foot or on horseback. He further asserted the entire tale was made up to support (a) Worthington's claim for government reimbursement (for the water supply at Camp Dennison) and (b) his claim that he was the victim of a West Point conspiracy to prevent his promotion. Of Worthington's claim that he saved the Federal right at Shiloh, Sherman was quick to note that the key point of the defense was the "causeway across Owl Creek at Shiloh meeting-house, covered by Hildebrand's [brigade]," rather than the bridge at Owl Creek. This comment seems to suggest that Hildebrand's brigade was somehow more responsible for the delay of the Federals than was McDowell's brigade of which Worthington was a part. Certainly, at the beginning of the battle, McDowell's brigade was hardly engaged; however, the beginning of the battle was not the time frame referenced by either Worthington or Beauregard. And nowhere, before or after this letter, did Sherman ever claim that Hildebrand saved the day ("Slanderer" 2).

Next, Sherman explained the conduct of the court-martial of Worthington. First, he quoted the specifications of drunkenness on duty, habitual drunkenness, and conduct unbecoming an officer. Second, he declared the verdict and named the members of the court-martial. He said that most of his court members "are now living and occupy important positions in civil life," adding that "not one of them was a graduate of West Point." Sherman indicated that he had not met Worthington since the court-martial, but that he had received numerous letters from him, and he acknowledged that Worthington had produced several publications in newspapers and in the form of pamphlets. To support his position and to further marginalize Worthington, he even quoted Lincoln's 1864 "put it in writing" dismissal of Tom's request for reinstatement in the army. At no point in his rebuttal did Sherman ever address the illegality of the court-martial he ordered, convened, appointed, testified to, and for which he administered the findings and carried out the sentence. Instead, by way of defense, Sherman spent the remainder of his rebuttal patronizing Worthington and continuing to paint him as a pitiful eccentric whose wild charges should not be believed by any reasonable person:

> Colonel Worthington is now an old man, in trouble and affliction, and I think the editor of the *Capital* should not expose his weakness and foibles. If he has any claim for compensation for services of any nature on the part of the Government, I have not and will not interpose an objection, but I understand he has been paid in full, in the same manner and to the same extent as all other officers ["Slanderer" 2].

While Worthington must certainly have been pleased to read that Sherman would not object to his legitimate claims for reimbursement for the Camp Dennison water supply, he would have been much happier to see Sherman admit, at least in some part, his complicity in the defeat at Shiloh or in the illegal court-martial he ordered and conducted. But such an admission was not, nor would it ever be, forthcoming from Sherman. Whitelaw Reid described Sherman as a man who

> was still always right in his own eyes. He was right when he depreciated defensive works before Pittsburg Landing. He was right when he eulogized Halleck's refusal to move without defensive works every half mile in his advance upon Corinth. He was right when he assaulted Kenesaw [Reid, *Ohio*, Vol. I, 491].

PHOTOGRAPH 9.3 From this depot in Morrow, Ohio, Worthington abandoned his life as a recluse just long enough each year to travel to Washington during congressional session to lobby for reimbursement for the Camp Dennison water supply and to continue his attacks on Sherman (photograph by author).

To Reid's observation, one must add that Sherman still believed himself right when he court-martialed Worthington.

The remainder of Sherman's rebuttal attacked Piatt for what amounts to jealousy, poor judgment, political infighting, and the suggestion of cowardice:

> During the war I never heard of him at Shiloh, Vicksburg, Chattanooga, Atlanta, or elsewhere, where there was fighting and danger. I understand he belonged to that noble army of martyrs who suffered as provost marshals, judge-advocates and sutlers at the rear ["Slanderer" 4].

Physical Afflictions

Worthington's last surviving sister, Sarah Worthington King Peter, philanthropist and humanitarian, died on February 6, 1877, in Cincinnati amid the company of the Catholic sisters she had supported so faithfully her entire life (McAllister 379). James Taylor Worthington, eldest son of Governor Worthington, died at Adena on August 11, 1881. All of his siblings having died, Tom now found himself alone in his generation. And while he maintained sporadic contact with nieces and nephews, he drew further and further into personal isolation. The following timeline demonstrates Worthington's continuing efforts to build a case against Sherman and for his own exoneration. When he was not writing letters and pamphlets from isolation in Morrow, he was traveling to Washington at least once a year during congressional sessions to lobby for reimbursement of the funds he had spent to procure a water supply for Camp Dennison, as well as to press his attacks against Sherman and Grant. A review of government documents provided with his court-martial records, as well as publication data from the Library of Congress, presents a rather busy Worthington.

April 1878 Worthington requested a copy of his court-martial record from the War Department and insisted on a "printed proof" of Exhibit A, his diary extract. The War Department replied that they could not certify the document they sent him as a "printed proof."

June 1, 1878 Worthington published "Brief Record of Colonel Worthington's Service during the Civil War" and through his remaining political contacts had the document submitted to Congress. On the same trip to Washington, Tom paid Thomas McGill & Company to publish an 18-page pamphlet entitled *Col. Worthington Vindicated: Sherman's Discreditable Record at Shiloh on His Own and Better Evidence*. The work amounted to a rehash of his earlier claims supplemented with extracts from his court-martial proceedings.

April 29, 1879 Worthington requested through the House Committee on Military Affairs a copy of the correspondence, dated November 19, 1862, between Judge Advocate General Holt and Secretary of War Stanton regarding his case. That same year, during another visit to Washington, Worthington published at his own expense a 13-page pamphlet that he made available to Congress. This work he described as "being a statement of official oppression and misconduct involving treasonable practices by Gen. W. T. Sherman."

February 18, 1880 Worthington requested from the War Department yet another copy of the record of his trial. Again in Washington to plead his case, he had the War Department mail the requested copy to his temporary residence: 208 7th Street SW, Roth's Saloon. It would appear that for Worthington old habits died hard.

The year 1880 would prove a busy one for Worthington. The Ohio

Census for Warren County that year lists Thomas Worthington, aged 73, living in Salem Township as a "fruit grower." Living in the house with Worthington was a 12-year-old boy named William Kelley, listed as a "boarder." He was likely the son of next-door neighbor Nancy Kelley, aged 62. She was sole parent to three daughters and two sons aged 21 to 29. Since the Kelleys were farmers, young William might have resided with Worthington as a hired hand, assisting the elderly man in tending his fruit trees.

Despite all the controversy he had stirred after the war, despite his being court-martialed, and despite his being cashiered, the troops that served under Worthington never seemed to turn against him. Even in the court-martial they had tried to testify in a truthful, yet supportive, manner. And after the war they never shunned him; in fact, they often sought him out as a speaker for their veteran gatherings. In 1880 Worthington was invited to address such a gathering of Union volunteers in Columbus, Ohio, August 10–12. He took that opportunity to call, once again, for a thorough investigation of the conduct of the Civil War "without regard to party preferences, to have the truth established through the intervention of a congressional commission or a military court of inquiry" (Worthington *Address* 2). Of course Worthington was primarily interested in the world coming to accept his version of the truth about Shiloh, but he also outlined a number of other issues that he believed should be investigated. First, he believed the call-up of 1.5 million men to suppress the rebellion had been unreasonably expensive, ending up in money disappearing into the hands of private profiteers. He suggested that no organized effort to train, arm, and equip the militia had been seriously attempted. He argued that southern ports should have been blockaded "in the first rather than the fourth year of the war" and, lastly, that the government had suppressed his official report of Shiloh along with the official records. In his third-person narrative style, and with an appeal for sympathy in his old age, Worthington made what had become an all-too-frequent call for inquiry, this time to his fellow veterans rather than to the government:

> For eighteen years the colonel of the 46th Ohio has urged upon the government an inquiry ... [and] ... could not have gone quietly to his nearly approaching grave without asking an opportunity to answer these pertinent questions [Worthington *Address* 3].

Worthington continued to publish his versions of history during 1880, but he began to widen his net of accusation. Where Sherman had been the

Nine. After the War

primary recipient of his animus in most of the earlier pamphlets, with Grant receiving mention of culpability, his newer works reflected a tighter focus on Grant and other leaders beyond Sherman. In his 1880 pamphlet *A Correct History of Grant at the Battle of Shiloh*, Worthington narrowed his shot group to Grant, reproducing a letter he had sent to the general. In that letter Worthington bemoaned the fact that the military authorities had failed to investigate the malfeasance within the Army.

> Five Oaks, near Morrow, Ohio, Dec 8, 1879
> ... The Military authorities which could then have been held responsible [for investigating the "unexplained mysteries" of Shiloh] have all passed away. Lincoln, Stanton, Halleck, Henry Wilson of the Senate Military Committee, and Senators Wade and Chandler, who entirely controlled ... the Committee on the Conduct of the War, which in a great measure controlled the War Department and the course of the Government towards McClellan, Halleck, and other commanders east and west, are no longer personally responsible to any human tribunal [7].

Having survived almost everyone he thought had a public responsibility to get at the truth, Worthington took it upon himself to "address letters of inquiry to the most prominent army officers engaged on the above-named days [April 6–7, 1862], and now living, who have made official reports or other reliable statements on the subject." In his letter to Grant, he asked a series of questions to which he, no doubt, felt he already knew the answers. The purpose of the letter appears to have been to get in yet another jab at his "bitterest enemies," hoping that might generate yet another response in which Worthington could find contradictions of fact or observation:

> While in expectation of an attack at Shiloh, on your own evidence and Sherman's, from the 3rd to the 7th of April, 1862, why were the division commanders of the Army of the Ohio at Columbia, Tennessee, on the evidence of Generals Buell and Ammen, notified that they were not wanted at Savannah, Tennessee, before the 7th April, 1862?
> Why on the 4th of April, when Hardee and Bragg were in line, or approaching closely with 20,00 men, two miles from your front, and the rest of the Confederates near at hand, — why did you notify General Nelson, twenty miles off, that he could not be sent to Pittsburg Landing for want of transportation before the 8th April, while there were many idle boats at Pittsburgh and Paducah? If these notifications or orders, calculated to keep the Army of the

> Ohio out of the battle, were not intended for that purpose, what was their intention?
> ... Why, contradicting this statement to Nelson that you expected no attack, did you write to General Buell on the 6th, at 7 a.m., that you had expected an attack, but not before the 7th or 8th of April, except for future evidence that you had not been surprised by the attack? [*Correct History* 10].

Worthington was clearly baiting Grant in this letter to respond to his charges, thus keeping a controversy stirred that Grant hoped had long ago been put to rest. Throughout the letter Worthington pointed out inconsistencies and outright falsehoods in Grant's past comments and writings about Shiloh, particularly when compared with the recollections, testimony, and reports of other officers present at the time. Worthington's questions indicate the degree to which his charges, both against Grant and Sherman, had escalated beyond mere incompetence. He was now talking about Grant being involved in a conspiracy to lose the battle:

> After Major Ricker's information [cavalry reconnaissance that revealed a growing Confederate force] (well known to Sherman and by him admitted) on the afternoon of the 5th, that the Confederate advance was at hand, why, with the knowledge that Hardee and Bragg were but two miles off, were the Union cavalry pickets withdrawn from Sherman's front? And if it was not thereby the intention to conceal the presence of the enemy from the troops, leading to their surprise on the morning of the 6th, what was the intent of an act unheard of in the history of war?
> Why were there four gaps in the Union line,[2] aggregating over a mile on a front of two and a half miles, between Shiloh Church and Lick Creek ford, unless to facilitate the turning of one or both flanks of three Union divisions at the moment of attack (as occurred accordingly) and the consequent defeat of the army? [*Correct History* 13].

In this pamphlet, Worthington raised some tough questions that to him and to many military historians were never satisfactorily answered by Grant. He reproduced the publication, promising to prepare and publish a second part containing similar questions directed to Sherman, and he tried to get it into the hands of congressmen and general readers as well. He told his readers to

> please enclose ten cents to me, at the city [Washington] post office for this number [pamphlet one], or one dollar or more for full

copies, at fifty cents each, when the work is finished — over 100 pages. Till my legal and admitted claims are in whole or in part paid, by act of Congress, I am next to helpless in getting means to illustrate my work, —capable of more varied and striking illustration than any battle of historical record. And if any material error is expressed or implied in this number, I will forfeit all dues now claimed by me and all claim to the character of a soldier or an honest man. And for an inquiry into the incidents and events of the battle, I will give up all claim upon the Government,[3] except what Congress may be willing to bestow for a service which has cost me over seventeen years of poverty and obloquy for doing my duty on the battle-field of Shiloh, and holding my position for hours, after my regiment and the field, or their positions on the same, had been deserted by my three immediate commanders on April 6, 1862.
T. Worthington
46th Ohio [*Correct History* 15]

Another of Worthington's pamphlets, *Report of the Right Flank March to Join McLernand's Right at 9 a.m. and Operations of the 46th Reg't Ohio Vols, 1st Brigade, 5th Division, on the Extreme Union Right, at Shiloh, April 6th, 1862*, appeared in 1880. It also contained reports called "The March to Corinth" and "A Brief History of the 46th Ohio Volunteers" for a total of 39 pages written in his classic third-person style. In this publication Worthington continued to expand his charges beyond that of military incompetence or dereliction of duty at Shiloh to include the vision of a vast conspiracy to prolong the war. Worthington charged, among other things, that Grant, Halleck, and Stanton were members of a devious cabal whose purpose was to suffer a deliberate defeat at Shiloh so that the war might last long enough for them to achieve power and position. What was originally described as a plot to get *him* had now evolved into a plot to get the entire country. While Worthington's later pamphlets became long on accusation and tirade and often short on direct evidence, they make fascinating reading as Worthington, realizing he had few years remaining to make his case, attempted to present a systematic view of the blunders that led to the disaster at Shiloh. Drawings of Worthington frequently graced the cover of these works (see Photograph 9.1 and Photograph 9.2).

After 1880, the steady stream of pamphlets slowed, replaced instead by Worthington's appeals and submissions directly to Congress. Already in 1879 he had published his *Memorial to Congress Being a Statement of Official Oppression and Misconduct involving Treasonable Practices by Gen. W. T. Sherman*. He followed that effort with a submission to Congress in 1881 outlining "the expediency of correcting the present drill" (*Military*

Bibliography 122). The next year he filed what he claimed was his official report from the Battle of Shiloh, a report "suppressed by the Union commanders in 1862 and the War Department now."

Worthington did at last receive a modest pension from the government in 1882, and that token of appreciation for his Federal service might have, at least for a time, assuaged some of his anger (McCormick 39). Soon after, however, Worthington petitioned Congress for an increase in his pension and accompanied that request with "a brief record of his civil and military service during the Civil War" (*Military Bibliography* 122). Between 1880 and 1883 Worthington published *Ballad of the Rebellion with a Sketch of His Service in the Civil War, and Evidence of Treachery by Union Commanders at Shiloh; Only To Be Obtained by a Court-Martial, after All Efforts for an Inquiry Had Failed, August 1862*. And while he never backed off his claims of treachery among the Union leadership, this work, unlike previous ones, contained some rather elegant poetry, which Worthington wrote in honor and commemoration of the men who died at Shiloh.[4] Yet even in his poetry he managed to alternate between eulogizing the combatants and attacking Sherman. In "A Ballad of Shiloh," Worthington declared:

> Azalea buds, young April's pride,
> Bloomed o'er glade, vale, and lea
> Where Shiloh's battle-field spread wide
> Down by the Tennessee ...
>
> Two, three, four Generals rearward fled,
> And marching all alone
> The 46th towards danger sped,
> Its time and place unknown ...
>
> Our Colonel — needs not here to say —
> Lives in their memories well.
> Whose lives and fame were saved that day
> Of storms of shot and shell [*Ballad* 38–39].

By 1884 Worthington realized he was running out of time, so he renewed his assault on the forces he believed had wronged him. But his approach seems somewhat mellowed by time and mortality. On January 11, 1884, he wrote to Judge Advocate General Swain trying to get Swain to "certify the correctness" of extracts from his court-martial, which address Col. John McDowell being present at Lafayette, Tennessee, on July 17–18, 1862. Since these dates coincide with the dates when he was charged with drunkenness, his inquiry suggests that Worthington might have turned at least some of his attention from the Shiloh debate to mount an assault on his "conduct unbecoming" charges and conviction. What literary offering might have emerged from his latest research will never be known, for Worthington had issued his last damning declaration against Sherman or any other soldier in the war.

"So the Old Colonel Had to Give It Up"

Worthington's January letter to Judge Advocate General Swain would turn out to be one of his last attempts at recognition and redemption, for on Saturday, February 23, 1884, Tom Worthington, last of Governor Worthington's children, died in Washington, D.C., at 77 years of age. He was pronounced dead in his room at 1007 E Street NW in Washington. He apparently died broke and alone, the cause of death being listed as "senile gangrene." As Worthington's body was prepared for return to the family cemetery in Chillicothe, Ohio,[5] an obituary appeared in the *New York Times* describing him as popular for "his outspoken independence." The obituary outlined his schooling at West Point and his leadership of the 46th Ohio during the war. The better part of the text was given to an explanation of his claims of instrumentality in the salvation of the Federal Army at Shiloh, his court-martial, and its nullification. The writer noted, however, that as Worthington's claims became more outlandish, he lost the respect of many who had previously supported him:

> A few years ago he published a second account in which he went so far as to charge Grant and Sherman with deliberately conspiring to betray the Union army into the hands of the rebels. The extreme bitterness and venom with which he attacked these officers recoiled upon himself, and had the effect to antagonize all his former friends ["Letter" 4].

Worthington had recently revised his last will and testament with specific instructions regarding how the proceeds from his claim against the government for reimbursement for the Camp Dennison water supply should be used if the claim were settled in his favor. First, Worthington directed "payment of a mortgage held by Rufus King [Sarah's son] to erect a monument to the 46th Ohio at a site he selected in the village of Morrow." Ever meticulous, Worthington had even prepared sketches of what the monument should look like and plans for its emplacement. The inscription he wrote for the planned monument read:

PHOTOGRAPH 9.4 Upon his death in Washington in February 1884, Worthington's body was returned to Chillicothe, where he was buried near other relatives in the Worthington family plot (photograph by author).

This monument was erected by Col. Thomas Worthington in honor of the dead of the 46th O.V.I. Regiment who fell and lay at Shiloh when Grant and Sherman ran away [Opes 2].

Second, Worthington indicated that, with the Rufus King land debt paid off, the property should "become a public picnic or playground and should be maintained as such." Third, the colonel intended a small sum to be set aside as an endowment the proceeds from which would be used to maintain the picnic grounds (Opes 1).

Upon Worthington's death, his lawyer, E. P. Dudley, pursued the merits of his claim against the government, but he ultimately concluded that since Worthington had died, he would likely never receive any settlement relative to Camp Dennison. Worthington had, several years previous, received from the government a check reimbursing him for expenditure of personal funds to buy axes and grindstones "in defiance of instructions of General Sherman at the Battle of Shiloh." When he received payment from the government, Worthington was "vastly pleased ... because he considered that it practically vindicated the course taken by him in that Battle" (Opes 2).

Nine. After the War

Since no additional settlement from the government was forthcoming, and since Worthington had spent almost everything he had in his relentless pursuit of the justice he believed he deserved, the wishes expressed in his will could not be followed. Instead, after conferring with the Warren County Court, Dudley determined to sell the property Worthington had purchased for the monument to the 46th Ohio Infantry and apply the funds toward payment of the Rufus King mortgage claim. With what little money remained, Dudley purchased the tombstone that now stands at the head of Worthington's grave in Grandview Cemetery in Chillicothe, Ohio.

Many of his contemporaries knew Tom Worthington's tortured postwar life as indicated by his obituary in the *Scioto Gazette*:

> He died, at last, a poor, disappointed, heart-broken man, no nearer the accomplishment of his hopes than twenty years ago ["His Disappointments" 1].

Worthington's body reached Chillicothe on Monday night, February 25, 1884, and services were held for him at the First Presbyterian Church at 2:00 P.M. on Wednesday the 27th. The old colonel was buried that afternoon in the family plot with Chillicothe's Sill Guards and the A. L. Brown Post of the Grand Army of the Republic (G.A.R.) providing full military honors ("His Disappointments" 1).

Chapter Ten

Conclusion

Sherman Changes His Tune

The story of Thomas Worthington is ultimately a story of command, leadership, and how personality affects both. It demonstrates that neither the privilege of birthright nor the presence of talent can guarantee success either in life or in the military. But it is also the story of the pursuit of truth, or at least one man's view of the truth, and it demonstrates that even the claims of an obnoxious, willful, arrogant man might, at least at their root, contain the seeds of truth.

Consider this. For all the contempt Sherman showed for Worthington and his ideas about defense at the court-martial trial, he "appears to have been won over to the idea that an *abatis* might be valuable as protection to his camp" (Boynton 31). Shortly after the battle, Sherman issued an order for each brigade commander to

> carefully examine his immediate front; fell trees to afford his men a barricade, and clear away all underbrush for two hundred yards in front [modern term is *clearing fields of fire*], so as to uncover any approaching enemy; with these precautions, we can hold our camp against any amount of force that can be brought against us [Boynton 31].

"These precautions" are precisely what Worthington had lobbied for in the days prior to the battle. Yet in August 1862, during the court-martial, Sherman made fun of Worthington for wandering about the landing in search of axes and for constantly predicting "the worst." During his testimony, Sherman had defiantly declared that defenses would invite an enemy attack. As Boynton points out, "there is no indication that General Sherman considered this post-Shiloh order either an evidence of weakness, or an invitation to attack, or as calculated to make his 'raw men timid'" (31). Shiloh seems to have changed Sherman's tune but not enough to admit it during the court-martial of Worthington four months later, and he certainly never came close to admitting culpability during Worthington's 22-year campaign to hold him responsible for the debacle of April 6, 1862.

THE ISSUE OF SURPRISE

Any objective examination of the many studies of Shiloh will lead one to inevitably conclude that most of the Union Army, and William Tecumseh Sherman in particular, was indeed surprised by the attack of Albert Sidney Johnston's Confederate Army on April 6, 1862. The operative word is most, for Colonels Tom Worthington, Jessie Appler, and Everett Peabody, as well as numerous others seem not to have been taken off-guard to the extent that their division commander was. After the war, General Prentiss, in what appears to be an effort to avoid further damage to Sherman and Grant's reputations, preferred to characterize the situation on the morning of April 6 as one of "unpreparedness" rather than surprise. Even accepting Prentiss' euphemistic description, which the facts do not support, the blame falls squarely in the laps of Generals Grant and Sherman.

Shiloh was a company and regimental commanders' battle, and while the generalship of Sherman, Prentiss, McLernand, and Hurlburt contributed to the survival of the Federal Army, it was the actions of small-unit commanders that kept the Union troops from being swept into the river on the first day. Where leadership at the division and army level had failed to prepare the troops for a surprise attack, which should have been no surprise at all, many company and regimental leaders stood resolute in their defense once the fighting began, contesting every inch of ground and buying valuable time for Buell and Nelson to arrive with reinforcements. Andreas quotes one of his contemporaries, who makes a strikingly lucid summation of the situation on Sunday, April 6: "[The Confederates] outgeneralled us; but we outcolonelled them" (114). Andreas points out that because of the surprise, the confusion, and the nature of the wooded terrain, at Shiloh "no one man knew much more of the battle ... than what was going on within the reach of his vision" (115). Or, as a soldier stated who in the midst of the fight Sunday morning had been ordered to go to the rear and get a wound treated, "Captain, this fight ain't got any rear" (Dawes 40).

> It seems to me the facts show that [Sherman] was either surprised, which was a mistake in judgement, or that he knew the enemy [was] coming, and did not make the usual military preparations for defense, and thus placed in jeopardy a great army [Andreas 120].

Andreas' comments appeared well after the war, and while they seem temperate when compared to the images of a tipsy Tom Worthington drawing diagrams in the dirt, telling "the true story of Shiloh" to anyone who would listen and publishing written accusations against Sherman, they represent fundamentally the same charges Worthington made:

> But for the foresight of General Prentiss in sending out Colonel Moore on Sunday morning so very early, the Rebels would have reached Sherman's and Prentiss' camp before six o'clock, their approach would hardly have been known, and the results must have been far more disastrous [Andreas 122].

Colonel Jacob Ammen commanded the 24th Ohio Infantry and a brigade under General Nelson at Shiloh. He arrived at the fight late in the afternoon of the first day, and after clearing the way with bayonets through the skulkers and deserters cowering along the river bank, Ammen's men came ashore and helped solidify Grant's position with the coming of darkness. A fighter, not a journalist, and certainly no enemy to Sherman or Grant, Ammen stated unequivocally in a letter on April 8:

> Our forces were surprised [on the morning of the 6th], driven back from their camps and thousands deserted their colors, moving to seek their own safety huddling together on the steam boats, under the bank, and generally impeding the progress of those that were trying to meet the foe [Ammen 2].

Sherman's behavior in the days and hours leading up to Sunday morning, April 6, were just as imprudent and neglectful in *underestimating* his enemy as his actions in Kentucky and Missouri had been in *overestimating* his enemy. But the greatest difference in these circumstances, and the aspect of Sherman's neglect that troubled and haunted Worthington for the rest of his life, was that where Sherman's bad military judgment simply alarmed people during his tours in Kentucky and Missouri, his gross errors in judgment cost thousands of lives at Shiloh. Once the decision was made not to allow troops to dig in and fortify their camp — perhaps the only outward sign that might have swayed Johnston to call off the attack at his famous council of war on Saturday night — nothing Sherman could have done with the available intelligence would have thwarted the Confederate attack. But had Sherman acted immediately and decisively upon the overwhelming evidence of an impending enemy assault (e.g., a reconnaissance-in-force, artillery placed well forward and at the ready), many of the Union soldiers who went to their graves that fateful day might well have lived. Whitelaw Reid wrote in his book *Ohio in the Civil War*:

> It must ever seem inconceivable to those not actual witnesses to the fact, that officers, with military education, and professing to understand war and war's conditions, should have lain for weeks in the vicinity of an enemy he believed to outnumber him, without a spadeful of earth thrown up for defense, without even an obstruction of fallen timber, and finally, without pickets a mile beyond his own tent! [432].

Sherman never expected Johnston to leave his base in Corinth and attack the Federal Army. And it is fair to say that Sherman did not trust the analyses of militia and volunteer officers like Worthington, Hildebrand, and Buckland and, hence, did not heed their warnings. But Larry J. Daniel, in his book *Shiloh: The Battle That Changed the Civil War*, accurately identifies the "root cause" of Sherman's lack of decisive action on the Friday and Saturday before the Confederate attack:

> When [Sherman] had fallen victim to exaggeration back in Kentucky, he had been labeled insane. To have appeared shaken and overly alarmed would have subjected him to a similar criticism — "they'd call me crazy again," he wrote Ellen [his wife] [Daniel 138].

Worthington's actions in command of the 46th Ohio Volunteer Infantry did not single-handedly save the Federal Army at Shiloh, as he claimed until his death. He bravely fought and adeptly led his troops under fire, and his participation in countering Trabue's flank movement around noon on April 6 and, perhaps even more important, his stubborn defense between noon and two o'clock northeast of Crescent Field substantially contributed to the salvation of the Union Army at Shiloh. One might argue that by delaying Trabue's advance, McDowell's brigade kept the Kentuck-

PHOTOGRAPH 10.1 In 1991 the author (second from right) taught U.S. Military Academy cadets on the Battle of Shiloh and shared with them the story of Thomas Worthington (photograph by author).

ians from gaining the rear of Prentiss in the Hornet's Nest. If Trabue had succeeded in getting behind Prentiss before late afternoon, the Hornet's Nest might have been surrendered sooner, giving the Confederates time to sweep the Federals away from Pittsburg Landing by perhaps 3:00 or 4:00 P.M. Had that occurred, Grant might have found his position untenable, and perhaps he might have been compelled to surrender before help could arrive.

The Federal Army remained in camp at Pittsburg Landing and vicinity from March 13 through the Confederate attack on April 6. That amounts to three weeks available for improving the Federal position. Sherman's argument that defensive preparations, such as an abatis or hasty breastworks, would somehow have invited an enemy attack must go down in the history books as one of the most ridiculous defenses of a commander's actions ever recorded. To Colonel Tom Worthington, commissioned and trained as an engineer at West Point, it must have seemed ludicrous beyond all belief:

> No degree of admiration for the brilliant genius he subsequently displayed, can blind impartial observers to the *criminal foolhardiness* [emphasis added] and blundering which made the first day of Pittsburg Landing a slaughter, and well-nigh an irreparable calamity [Reid 432].

In defense of his actions at Shiloh, Sherman stated that it was "necessary that a combat, fierce and bitter, to test the manhood of the two armies, should come off, and that was as good a place as any." To this might-as-well-be-here mentality about Shiloh, Sherman added, "it was not a question of military skill and strategy, but of courage and pluck" (Reid 432). Reid rightly concludes:

> When the military student of another generation comes to read such words from the man who took Atlanta, in apology for neglect of pickets, lack of any regular formation of line, and absence of the slightest defensive works, against a foe supposed to be superior, he will find it as difficult to believe that the Lieutenant-General Sherman of history wrote the excuse as that he was guilty of the blunders [433].

Second only to the absurdity about inviting an attack was Sherman's arrogant comment uttered during Worthington's court-martial, "What business is it of [Col. Worthington's] whether his superior officer invited an attack or not?" Is it not the business of *every* commander to take all possible precautions against the destruction of his force? Surely, regimental commanders must question their leaders when their efforts appear to threaten good order, discipline, and the safety of their troops. The division commander need not heed his regimental commanders' warnings or advice, but no one can seriously argue against the regimental commanders' right to ask tough questions and raise issues.

Most historians, perhaps unfamiliar with the analysis of military intelligence, have given Sherman a free pass on yet another issue. During Worthington's court-martial, Sherman seemed satisfied with his reconnaissance efforts during the period of April 1–5, arguing that since his pickets and patrols uncovered only enemy cavalry, albeit in strong force, he did not put credence in peripheral reports of the size or intention of the enemy force. Only the presence of infantry and/or artillery, Sherman argued, provided grounds for him to determine the presence of a large enemy force intent on attack. But significant flaws exist in Sherman's reasoning. By the time infantry and artillery are uncovered by reconnaissance, it is too late to be proactive in the defense. Sherman's comment is the modern warfare equivalent of saying, "I didn't know Hitler would invade Poland until I saw the tanks coming." Such was the case at Shiloh, for the Federal troops found themselves *reacting* to Confederate initiatives rather than acting in their own defense. Even if one accepts Sherman's fallacious argument regarding infantry and artillery, ample evidence existed well before the battle of enemy cavalry in force much larger than necessary for the enemy to place outposts or present a screen. Historians have often failed to take Sherman to task over his analysis of the information available and the production of battlefield intelligence. Exclaiming, "My God, we are attacked!" as his orderly is killed beside him by an enemy infantry brigade in battle formation less than 500 yards away hardly amounts to effective battlefield intelligence on Sherman's part.

> It remains true that [Sherman] was out-generaled before Shiloh. His opponent planned his destruction almost within his hearing, and without arousing him from his slumbers. There is one cloud on his horizon, one blot on his escutcheon, — he was surprised at Shiloh [Andreas 123].

Sherman likely had several "blot[s] on his escutcheon," but Worthington would spend the rest of his life calling attention to one particular stain.

Consider again Worthington's claims against Sherman:

1. Utter disregard of the immediate and obvious indications of an attack after Friday noon, as shown by leaving all things as they were; [definitely true]

2. Utter disregard for his artillery, with respect more especially to its ammunition; [possibly true]

3. Failing to make any provision for his own wounded and sick men; [partially true]

4. Fatuity in leaving useless his right brigade, to say nothing of his left, either of which might, if thrown on either rebel flank, have driven back the first attack even as late as 8:00 A.M.; [doubtful but possible]

5. Unaccountable sacrifice of five guns of Behr's battery, when the whole might have been, as one gun was, preserved with the first brigade; [not true]

6. Useless and reckless waste of life in the charge by Colonel Hicks' 40th Illinois regiment; [probably not true] and

7. Hastily leaving the weakest and most exposed part of his line, where his presence would seem most needed; [untrue]

How could a man who had only three months prior to Shiloh been "throwing the army in a panic" and predicting doom and gloom even suggest that Thomas Worthington was "an alarmist" always predicting the worst?

In the final judgment, if such ever comes on these matters, it is not Sherman's behavior in command while under hostile fire that Worthington's accusations—and his subsequent treatment at the hands of Sherman—call into question. Even Whitelaw Reid grants that Sherman's "conduct [under fire] did much to vent an abandonment of the field under the shock of the first disaster" (432). Rather, it is Sherman's tactical analysis *prior to* the attack on the morning of April 6, 1862, together with his expedient disregard for the rule of law in the aftermath of Shiloh that should disturb future generations as they consider Sherman's place among military leaders in the Civil War.

Outside of the half dozen witnesses at his court-martial who testified to occasional incidences of drunkenness, no evidence exists that Worthington's men ever spoke ill of him in terms of his competence or ability as a leader. But for all of his West Point training, his experience in the Mexican War, his time with the Ohio Militia, and his service during the Civil War, the one aspect of leadership that Worthington never seemed able to grasp was the fact that leadership is measured not only by how one handles subordinates, but also by how one handles superiors.

LIKE FATHER, LIKE SON

The proximity of Tom Worthington's sapling to his father's tree cannot be ignored. Tom showed behaviors throughout his life that were strikingly similar to his father's behaviors. Scholars have debated for years whether nature or nurture dominates in determining how we will behave as we grow older, and the answer is quite likely a hearty dose of both. Still, Tom Worthington's life seems to argue strongly for nature; while Tom did not gain anything near the success of his father, he was in many ways very much like the governor. Also, one cannot ignore the indicators of Worthington's future behavior to be found within his cadet experience at West Point. If character can be defined as how a person behaves under pressure, then the pressured environment at West Point brought out actions and attitudes in Worthington that would eventually lead to his downfall. A quick review of his demerit list in Chapter Two will indicate a young man who, not unlike his father, was headstrong, willful, and slightly arrogant and who had trouble dealing with his superiors. His father warned him in a letter in 1826 that "nothing was so important to any one as a complete control of temper and actions," and the governor urged him to "avoid meddling officiously in the affairs of others or by our folly with unbridled tongues give others an opportunity if not an invitation to meddle in our affairs" (Governor Worthington, 24 Dec. 1826). Even Worthington's affinity for alcohol might have been tied to genetics given the excessive drinking of two of his brothers and his uncles. Is the fabric of our nature woven so tightly early in our life that there is little we can do to change the texture? The concept seems to apply to Worthington.

Many terms may be arguably applied to Tom Worthington—cantankerous, arrogant, presumptuous, contemptuous of authority, bitter, perhaps even slightly mad in his later days—but one term that cannot be applied to the colonel is liar. He was, in fact, a competent tactician, a talented writer, a skilled debater, and a brave soldier. But history is replete with men who were solid tacticians, masters of maneuver, and calm under fire. Yet for lack of interpersonal skills and the ability to deal with the chain of command, their military potential and martial gifts were never fully realized.

Sherman was multifaceted as well. Insecure, vengeful, accusatory, sometimes mad—but one term that cannot be applied to him is ineffective. He did, despite his mistakes at Shiloh, manage to hold on until nightfall of April 6 and, with the help of Buell and Nelson, he regained the ground he lost on Sunday and with it the opportunity for further advancement in the ranks of the U.S. Army. But history is replete with men who advanced in rank and enjoyed future successes in the war. Yet for lack of careful attention to the military rule of law and their responsibilities, they might have been relieved of duty and rendered unable to fully realize their potential.

SEEDS OF HIS OWN DESTRUCTION

Tom Worthington would swear until the day he died that the greatest enemy in his life was William Tecumseh Sherman. But the sad truth is that the greatest enemy to Tom Worthington was Worthington himself. When he had failed to rise to a position of prominence during the Mexican War, Worthington had blamed "circumstance—that unspiritual god of misdirection." Yet an objective examination of the facts of his life must admit of his own authorship of many of those circumstances. For example, Tom Worthington's early charges about Sherman and Grant's lack of preparedness at Shiloh were grounded in fundamental truth, but his abuse

PHOTOGRAPH *10.2* The author at the grave of Thomas Worthington (photograph by author).

of alcohol and the subsequent erosion of his credibility sowed the seeds of Worthington's own destruction. The inability to control alcohol seems to have been a recurring theme in the Worthington family, for Tom's brothers Albert and William drank to excess, as did several of his uncles. Family papers suggest that Tom's father, the governor, was a teetotaler, perhaps as a result of having too often seen his brothers drunk (Brown 1). Did Tom's overindulgence come as a rebound effect, as is often the case in a family where the parents allow no alcohol? Whatever the reason for his drinking, it was, in fact, the alcohol and his subsequent behavior that created for Sherman the circumstances and the legal cover to get rid of Worthington, a man who called a little too much attention to a truth Sherman would rather forget.

The obituary writer in the *Scioto Gazette* summed up the Worthington situation with considerable clarity when he observed:

> In spite of certain eccentricities which probably injured his cause in Washington, the Colonel was at heart a gallant old man. Finely educated, upright, and talented, he might under happier circumstances, have made a brilliant record ["His Disappointments" 1].

McCormick references an obituary that reflected Worthington's lifelong determination to seek vindication:

> It will be characteristic of him to carry his grievances to the highest Court of the universe, to the Commander-in-chief, where there will be no disguising the fact as to who should wear the nation's honor in justice, if death does not end it all [39].

Somehow, the scene of Tom Worthington still defiantly arguing "the correct history of the Battle of Shiloh" before the judgment throne of God is not all that hard to imagine.

Notes

Chapter One

1. One of the governor's daughters, Margaret, wrote in her diary that spending time with New Englanders was like "being bound in boards and cold pressed" (Brown 1).
2. Governor Thomas Worthington and his wife had ten children. James was the eldest son and fathered nine children himself. Governor Worthington's next oldest boy was Albert, then Tom, followed by brothers William and Francis. Neither Albert, Thomas, nor William ever married. Tom's older sisters were Mary and Sarah Anne. His younger sisters were Eleanor, Margaret, and Elizabeth (*Genealogy Forum*).

Chapter Two

1. It appears rather odd that an inspection would be scheduled after lights out, but this was most probably not an everyday occurrence. Rather, the cadre likely reserved this time to spring a surprise inspection or to leave the expectation of an inspection ever-present in the cadet's mind — a technique still employed with good effect at the academy.
2. Saratoga, New York, features mineral springs with a high sulfur content, which are claimed to have medicinal properties. It was a frequent gathering spot for the idle and the wealthy who came there to "take the waters."

3. Tom's sisters Margaret and Eleanor were attending Mrs. Emma Willard's Academy in Troy, New York. Since the late fall of 1825, James had been traveling in Europe on behalf of his father, examining European manufacturing. "Board[ing] in a French family with five other Americans," James wrote to Tom in December of that year that he was "about to cross the Alps and [travel] on to Lyons, Turin, Lighorn, Florence and then to Rome" (James Worthington, 14 Dec. 1825).

4. Since leaving West Point, James had adopted much of his father's characteristic travel and interfaced with noteworthy businessmen and leaders. In the late spring of 1825, James had sailed to Europe to tour the manufacturing towns and learn any mechanical techniques that might improve production back in Ohio. While in France, James helped his father set up an itinerary for the U.S. visit of none other than Lafayette himself.

5. The *Register of Merit* is contained in several narrow, old binders maintained in the Special Collections at the U.S. Military Academy Library. The volumes contain the academic scorings and conduct ratings of all cadets during the period referenced. The pages, worn and yellowed, must be handled with great care, and the musty-smelling ancient books reveal that, for some people, there is no hiding the deeds and misdeeds cataloged in one's "permanent record." What is particularly interesting about Worthington's entry is the presence of a penciled note at the extreme right edge of the margin — a note added many years after the examination results by some diligent recorder of events who saw the need to annotate that this particular cadet had been "dismissed by sentence of court-martial."

6. Due to the availability of positions in the regular Army they also received concurrent commissions as second lieutenants.

CHAPTER THREE

1. Fort Monroe would, after the Civil War, hold — without ever trying him for a crime — a prisoner who had been one of Worthington's fellow cadets at the academy: Jefferson Davis.

2. Worthington underlines the word *honor* in his letter apparently to lend a satirical tone to his comment.

3. The dichotomy between citizen-soldiers and regular Army troops remains prevalent today. Some of the finest soldiers the author has ever worked with were Army National Guard and reservists. But the attitude among some active duty soldiers that somehow these volunteer troops are less than competent is still evident. Some studies, and some practical experience in the Gulf War, indicated that, in fact, many of the Guard and

reserve "round out" units *were not* ready to deploy for action in the gulf. That lesson proved true in Vietnam and in World War II as well. And while modern "militia," or National Guard, soldiers do drill regularly, they often have less than state-of-the-art equipment, they might not drill enough, and the system still appears ripe for political patronage.

4. A running argument for the past 150 years has revolved around whether or not the war with Mexico was truly a defense of American soil and the right of self-government or whether it was a "shameless land grab" germinated in the minds of President Polk and his advisors. That argument, coupled with claims that the war was a not-so-veiled attempt to extend slavery into the West, helped to fuel the controversy that surrounded not only the nation's entrance into the war but also the historical interpretations of the outcome.

5. There is some evidence that Worthington was transferred back to Company D (the Hocking County company) as a lieutenant after losing the election to Morgan (McCormick 28), but the records of Ohio soldiers in the Mexican War clearly shows Worthington as adjutant during the Monterey campaign.

6. Worthington underlines the words *sick leave* in his letter to West Point perhaps to preclude anyone from suggesting that he returned to Ohio because he was simply weary of the war or dissatisfied with his rank and position.

CHAPTER FOUR

1. Capt. George Cullum was instrumental in creating the biographical file on West Point graduates during the mid-1800s. As an example of his thoroughness, he sent an inquiry in January 1860 to S. W. Thatcher of Chillicothe, Ohio, concerning information on graduates Thomas Worthington, Thomas McArthur, and J. W. Scott. In a reply to Cullum, Thatcher informed him of his research in Ohio to develop the military record and the whereabouts of the subjects. McArthur's records could not be verified due to what Thatcher called the "utter confusion" of the state records, and Scott was described as having moved to Beattie [?] County, California, in 1848 (coincidentally the year John Sutter discovered gold and prompted a general gold rush). Thatcher reports that Scott practiced law there until his death in January 1959. Of Worthington, Thatcher wrote, "Genl Thomas Worthington raised a company of volunteers and went to Mexico with them during our war with that Country under Genl. Taylor."

2. Worthington planned to approach "General Scott," presumably Winfield Scott, who he hoped would use his influence on behalf of Worthington regarding position and rank in the coming conflict.

3. H. S. and J. Applegate had operated a publishing company in Cincinnati since 1850, and while they concentrated on such standards as Plutarch's *Lives*, Rollin's *Ancient History*, and Lyon's *Grammar*, they were not afraid to tackle Worthington's manual as well as some later controversial commentaries on the conduct of the war (Ford and Ford 278).

4. In retrospect, one can see Worthington applying a principle of training used by the U.S. Army today. Rather than issue a soldier a book that contains training information for basic skills and all skill levels above the entry-level soldier, the Army tailors its "job books" and soldier's manuals to teach only what a soldier needs for a given skill level and, perhaps, one level higher.

5. Among the units being rapidly organized were Cincinnati's River Guards, the Cleveland Grays, the Columbus Videttes, the Lancaster Guards, and the Dayton Light Guards.

6. Sarah Worthington King Peter was a philanthropist, art connoisseur, and lifelong advocate for the poor, the sick, and the disenfranchised in society. Appearing in the bibliography are several books that detail the life of this fascinating, progressive woman of the nineteenth century. As one individual knowledgeable of the Worthington family told the author, "Sarah probably made more of her life than any of the Worthington children" (Brown 1).

7. Private Christian Zook's account indicated that the 46th arrived at Paducah on Friday night the 21st, but considering that he described being on the river "three nights and days," the arrival time calculated from Cincinnati comes out to the 20th, which is the date Worthington indicated they arrived.

8. Private Christian Zook was born in Fairfield County, Ohio, in 1842. He enlisted in the 46th on October 18, 1861, at Camp Lyon.

9. Hicks was removed as brigade commander and replaced with Col. John A. McDowell when the brigade was reorganized to include the 46th Ohio, 40th Illinois, Morton's Battery, and the 6th Iowa Infantry.

10. An interesting description given Worthington's own background in the militia. Still, in Worthington's mind, there was one big difference between the men — West Point.

11. Henry Wager Halleck, a New York native, wrote the *Elements of Military Art and Science* in 1846 — a volume Worthington quoted when later registering his complaints against General Sherman in a letter to Halleck.

12. This book does not claim to provide anything approaching a full biographical sketch of William Tecumseh Sherman. Several excellent biographies of Sherman, e.g., Marszalek and Hirshson's (see bibliography), were used to develop a picture of the man who would be the lightning rod for Worthington's wrath before, during, and after the Battle of Shiloh.

13. While Halleck was publicly insisting that Sherman was not losing his mind and that he was simply in need of some rest, he was privately singing a different tune. In a letter to his wife, Halleck wrote that "certainly" Sherman had "acted insane" (Marszalek 167).

14. Ormsby MacKnight Mitchell was an underclassman to Tom at West Point (Class of 1829) and a prominent Cincinnati attorney before the war. A gifted and talented man in astronomy and mathematics, his differences with Gen. Buell eventually resulted in him being sent to an outpost in South Carolina where he died from yellow fever in October 1862.

15. In an interesting historical coincidence, the "burned railroad bridge" Sherman mentioned in his memoir constituted the remains of the bridge over the Tennessee River at Danville. That particular bridge had been guarded for the Confederacy by Capt. J. B. Williams' Independent Cavalry up until its destruction in the face of the massive Federal advance from Paducah. Lewis Washington Moody, a private in Williams' cavalry and the great-grandfather of the author of this book, was at that bridge in the fall of 1861.

16. What a great line! What a revealing comment! Everyone can relax now, the West Point officer is on the scene. Yet, having deemed himself vanguard for the entire army and sallied forth ahead of his division commander, Worthington had every right, even a responsibility, to assume command upon arrival at Savannah. In his memoirs Sherman chided Worthington for dashing about giving orders, when, in reality, he was fully justified in doing just that — at least until Sherman or someone who outranked him arrived. It is difficult to view his action as malicious any more than the modern instance of another West Pointer, Gen. Al Haig, declaring, "I'm in charge" when asked who was running the White House after President Ronald Reagan had been shot.

CHAPTER FIVE

1. John Adair McDowell of Keokuk, Iowa, was the brother of General Irvin McDowell, who commanded the Union forces at the Battle of Bull Run.

2. Appler did serve as a lieutenant in a company of Portsmouth Guards (approximately 80 men) during the Mexican War.

3. No one should have been surprised that an infantry regimental commander, commissioned originally as an engineer, would want to dig in and fortify against a possible enemy attack.

4. Worthington was a businessman. Recall that he acted with his own money to obtain a water supply for troops at Camp Dennison when none could be had. He understood capital, and he understood cost and economy, but on April 3, 1862, he best understood that he could not get what he felt he needed, and he was clearly bothered by the idea that the government supply system was being administered inefficiently.

5. Imagine the loneliness of being the only competent person in the Army!

6. In testimony against Worthington in August, Sherman seemed to credit Buckland for keeping him "positively informed," but his behavior that night heaped anything but credit upon the Ohio colonel.

7. Hildebrand, well past 60 years of age and formerly a major general in the Ohio Militia, operated with neither a staff "nor even a mounted orderly" (Dawes 2).

8. Gen. C. F. Smith was in a sick bed deteriorating rapidly from a tetanus infection contracted by scraping his leg in a minor incident while getting into a skiff. General McLernand, who outranked Sherman, was now at Pittsburg Landing and should have technically assumed command of all forces camped in the vicinity, but he appears to have deferred to Sherman, and Grant seems to have been perfectly satisfied with that arrangement. Grant regarded Sherman as "in command of all troops at Pittsburg Landing" during Grant's absence, with the exception of McLernand's division. Sherman was the only division commander in the Army of the Tennessee who was a West Point graduate and who had served in the old Army (Dawes 3).

9. Even given the emerging vegetation and undergrowth in April, Worthington, occupying a point of observation on the high ground near the Widow Howell's house, could well have seen elements of the first wave of Confederate forces pressing in the general direction of Shiloh Church.

10. This brigade was made up of the 3rd Kentucky, the 5/9th Kentucky, the 6th Kentucky, the 31st Alabama, the 4th Alabama Battalion, Crews' Tennessee Battalion, Cobb's and Byrne's batteries, and Morgan's Cavalry Squadron. They were nicknamed the "orphan" brigade because, being primarily made up of Kentuckians, they would not be able to return to their Federally occupied home state for the better part of the war. They wandered the Confederacy as "orphans."

11. This statement is a half-truth, for while one or more of Sherman's aides might have escorted McDowell, his staff, and the 40th Illinois to reposition in Crescent Field, the 46th Ohio and the 6th Iowa were left behind to make their own way without guides.

12. This sudden facing movement to confront Trabue and elements of the Kentucky Orphan Brigade is the specific action Worthington would point to after the war as evidence that he "saved the Federal right at Shiloh." While his quick action — the result of his emphasis upon drill and discipline — and the subsequent stubborn defense did for some two hours halt a major Confederate initiative against the Federal right, the defense of the hillside was not solely the work of the 46th Ohio. Rather, McDowell's entire brigade, together with the 13th Missouri, contributed to the Federal success, albeit temporarily. Worthington's rapid engagement of Trabue might have indeed saved his own regiment and perhaps even the 6th Iowa nearby. But to argue that it saved the entire Federal force might be a reach. Still, Worthington's quick recognition of Wharton's cavalry attempting to flank the Federal right at Owl Creek Bridge on Sunday morning might have kept the Confederates from positioning a force behind McDowell's brigade and cutting off their retreat. Without McDowell's forces during the 12:00–2:00 P.M. fight, the Federal right might have collapsed.

13. The late George Reeves, former superintendent of Shiloh National Military Park, explained to a group of West Point cadets, whom the author took to Shiloh, exactly how devastating was the Union artillery at Duncan Field. Reeves indicated that once the Federals had expended all their grapeshot (close range artillery rounds containing dozens of grape-sized iron balls in what resembles a coffee can), they began double-loading canister rounds in their cannons and setting the fuse for "zero" so the rounds would explode immediately upon firing and disperse shrapnel. Reeves further stated that an artillery piece manned by a competent crew and fired as rapidly as possible could shoot approximately three times a minute. Thus, with the explosive capacity of the double canister rounds, and the rapid loading, the Federals spit forth from each cannon enough shrapnel to roughly equal the cyclic rate of fire for a modern M-60 machine gun, or 1,100 rounds per minute. Multiplying that figure times the 40 or more cannon along the sunken road, it is no wonder so many Confederate soldiers lost their lives in multiple charges across Duncan Field. The author timed the cadets in a dead run from the wood line on the Confederate side to the sunken road — a run that had the young men carrying no rifle or pack. It took one minute and five seconds to cross the exposed fire area. Imagine doing that in the face of such terrible fire, and one gets

an idea of the bravery and determination of both sides in this horrible conflict.

14. Among the officers mortally wounded at this point on the field was Capt. W. Lee Harned of the 6th Kentucky. The author met Capt. Harned's grandson, the late Albert Harned, in Hardin County, Kentucky, in 1980 while researching another book describing Morgan's Christmas raid into central Kentucky. As it turned out, Albert Harned was a wealth of information about the battle at the Rolling Fork River on December 28, 1862. Albert's father, a ten-year-old boy at the time, had been orphaned upon Capt. W. Lee Harned's death at Shiloh the previous April. While sharing the story of his father's encounter as a boy with Morgan's cavalry, Albert lamented that the family had never known exactly where or how Captain Harned died at Shiloh. After some research, the author was able to explain to Albert Harned not only where on the battlefield his grandfather died, but the approximate time and circumstance. It seems that during the assault on the 46th Ohio, Capt. Harned kept sticking his head up from behind cover to monitor the enemy situation and keep an eye on his troops. One of his men had just urged him to keep his head down, but apparently Capt. Harned peeped once too often and took a round squarely through the forehead.

CHAPTER SIX

1. The letter cited is a badly mangled fragment kept at the Ross County Historical Society in Chillicothe, Ohio. No address markings are present to identify the intended recipient, however, the letter appears in the Worthington family papers and may be presumed to have been mailed to either brother James or the husband of some other family member.

2. This figure comes very close to 246 casualties, which is the figure listed on the monument to the 46th Ohio at their defensive line between 12:00 and 2:00 P.M. on April 6.

3. Ewing's letter did not appear until October — almost seven months after Stanton's findings.

CHAPTER SEVEN

1. An interesting choice as senior officer on the court-martial board, Hurlburt himself was shadowed with charges of drunkenness and corruption during the postwar years (Welsh 180). It is highly unlikely he devel-

oped his taste for and propensity to consume alcohol only in the years after the conflict. Thus, the man sitting in judgment of Worthington might have been guilty of the same drunkenness with which Worthington was charged.

2. James William Denver had experienced a broad career as a surveyor, schoolteacher, lawyer, newspaper editor, and Mexican War veteran. He had participated in the California gold rush, killed a man in a duel, been secretary of state for California, secretary of the Kansas Territory, and governor of the territory that included the present state of Colorado. For him the city of Denver is named (Warner 120).

3. In command of a brigade under Hurlburt at Shiloh, Veatch sustained 650 casualties among his four regiments, and he later in the war saw his career jeopardized when he ran afoul of Gen. O. O. Howard.

4. Walter Quintin Gresham, a lawyer, practiced in southern Indiana near Cordyon and in Elizabethtown, Kentucky, before the war. He would be the only member of the court-martial proceedings to question the motives of Sherman and the legality of the hearing (Warner 188).

5. All quotations dealing with testimony and/or cross-examination of witnesses are taken directly from *Court-martial Record of Proceedings against Col. Thomas Worthington, 46th Ohio Infantry (Volunteer), Held at Camp Pickering, Memphis, Tenn., Aug. 14–20, 1862.* National Archives, Court-martial Records.

6. This comment and the one shortly following in italics, made under oath, might be the most ridiculous statements Sherman would ever make regarding his lack of preparedness at Shiloh.

7. Not only did Sherman not prove such a statement in the court-martial, he never successfully proved it during his entire life, as questions regarding surprise and lack of preparedness at Shiloh dogged him until his last days.

8. Bear in mind that all the reports were not the "foolish" ramblings of shirkers and cowards, e.g., Foster's letter home.

9. Sherman had, just three days before, testified that the camp at Shiloh was likely the most defensible ground on earth.

10. There is in the modern army a concept called the WPA, or the West Point Protective Association. A belief held by many officers who are non–West Point graduates, the WPA supposedly means that West Point graduates "look out for one another" to the exclusion of other officers. Though belief in a WPA is unsubstantiated by any research or study, the simple truth is that men who have graduated from the intense experience of West Point feel a kinship and a duty to one another that they do not share with other officers. Sherman's stinging comments about Worthington "knowing better" constitute what amounts to a lament that his fellow

West Point graduate let him down in terms of his appreciation for loyalty, discipline, chain of command, and general military order.

11. The father of Dr. Leonard Mounts of Morrow, Ohio, treated the wounded on a hospital boat at Pittsburg Landing. Dr. Mounts indicated in a conversation with Tom Worthington's great-niece (Helen Dudley) in 1948 that his father told him of seeing Worthington at the battle wearing "a linen duster over his uniform." "It was raining hard [and] you can imagine how he looked" (Wells 26 June 1999, 4).

12. Sherman himself was frequently and consistently described as being disheveled in appearance and only loosely resembling an officer.

13. Joseph Holt had been appointed judge advocate general on Sept. 3, 1862, having briefly served as President Buchanan's secretary of War during the escalating Fort Sumter crisis. As chief of military justice per Lincoln's appointment, his rulings were the final authority for jurisprudence in the Federal Army. A man who understood the law, he used the power of his office, with Lincoln's approval, to suspend the writ of habeas corpus so that the government might arrest individuals outside of the military for crimes against the nation during time of war (Sifakis 316).

14. As is the case with his April 17 letter fragment from Shiloh, the letter resides with the Worthington papers held by the Ross County Historical Society, and the recipient of this letter cannot be positively identified. The stationery shown in the reproduction of this letter is the same Union stationery that Worthington used to write out the lengthy closing defense statement he presented at his court-martial.

CHAPTER EIGHT

1. Buckingham had known Worthington at West Point, graduating two years ahead of Tom and, like Worthington, returning to run a business in Ohio after a brief stint with the regular Army. In November 1862 he delivered the order that removed George McClellan as commander of the Army of the Potomac.

2. Schenck was another Ohioan, who Lincoln made a brigadier general in payment for his political support. While he held field commands in Virginia up to Second Bull Run, a serious wound in that battle relegated Schenck to a desk job. He was elected to Congress in 1863 and made chair of the Committee on Military Affairs, a committee that Worthington would target to expose the abuses of command and leadership in the Army. Schenck's recommendation was a powerful influence in Worthing-

ton's case, but not powerful enough to overcome Lincoln, Halleck, Grant, and Sherman combined.

3. Col. Wright had led his regiment in concert with McDowell's brigade's defense of the Federal right between noon and 2:00 P.M. on April 6.

CHAPTER NINE

1. The author has found no trace of any retaliatory publication authored either by Sherman or any member of his family.

2. The four gaps Worthington mentions likely refer to the separation between the Tennessee River and Stuart's brigade, between Stuart and Prentiss, between Prentiss and Appler's 53rd as it advanced ahead of Sherman's division, and between Appler and the remainder of his brigade.

3. This "claim" likely refers to his attempt to get a monetary settlement from the government for furnishing the water supply to Camp Dennison during the mobilization and deployment from Ohio.

4. Worthington was a gifted writer, not only of treatises and pamphlets, but also of verse. His poems, while not artistically equal to the premier poets of the day, reflect a solid grasp of meter, rhyme, and verse and represent some quality examples of period rhyme. His work has largely been overlooked by literary historians and collectors of Civil War verse.

5. Arrangements for shipment of Worthington's body back to Chillicothe were made by General Rosecrans, who seems to have remained his supportive friend until the bitter end.

Bibliography

American Heritage Dictionary. 2nd College Ed. Boston: Houghton Mifflin, 1982.

Ammen, Col. Jacob. Letter to A. B. Martin, Esq. 8 Apr. 1862. U.S. Military Academy Special Collections.

Andreas, Alfred T. "The 'Ifs and Buts' of Shiloh." 12 May 1887. *Military Essays and Recollections — Papers Read before the Commandery of the State of Illinois, Military Order of the Loyal Legion of the United States*, Vol. 1 Chicago: A. C. McClurg, 1891.

Annual Report of the Board of Visitors to the United States Military Academy — Made to Congress and the Secretary of War for the Year 1826. U.S. Military Academy Press & Bindery, 1894.

Baltimore Sun, "Death of Col. Worthington," 24 Feb. 1884.

Basler, Roy P., ed. *The Collected Works of Abraham Lincoln*, Vol. 7. New Brunswick: Rutgers University Press, 1953.

Bering, John A., and Montgomery, Thomas. *History of the Forty-eighth Ohio Vet. Vol. Inf*. Hillsboro: Highland News Office, 1880. www.ben2.ucla.edu/-worth/oh48hist.html.

Bioguide. http://bioguide.congress.gov.

Bogan, Dallas R. *Warren County's Involvement in the Civil War*. Middletown, OH: U.N. Printing, 1991.

Boynton, H. V. *Sherman's Historical Raid: The Memoirs in the Light of the Record*. Cincinnati: Wilstatch, Baldwin, 1875.

Brown, Mary Anne. Personal interview. 17 June 1999.

Calhoun, John C. Letter to Sylvanus Thayer. 14 Aug. 1819. U.S. Military Academy Special Collections.

Catton, Bruce. *Grant Moves South*. Boston: Little, Brown, 1960.

———. *Terrible Swift Sword: The Centennial History of the Civil War*, Vol. 2. Garden City, NY: Doubleday, 1963.

Civil War Homepage. www.civilwarhome.com/Andersonbio.htm.

Cozzens, Peter. *The Darkest Days of the War: The Battles of Iuka and Corinth*. Chapel Hill: University of North Carolina Press, 1997.

Combined Military Service Record for Thomas Worthington, Colonel, 46th Regt. Ohio Infantry. National Archives, Military Service Records.

Court-Martial Record of Proceedings Against Col. Thomas Worthington, 46th Ohio Infantry (Volunteer) Held at Camp Pickering, Memphis, Tenn., Aug. 14–20, 1862. National Archives, Court-Martial Records.

Cullum, George W. *Biographical Register of the Officers and Graduates of the U.S. Military Academy at West Point, New York: 1802–1890*. Cambridge, MA: Houghton, Mifflin, 1891.

Daniel, Larry J. *Shiloh: The Battle That Changed the Civil War*. New York: Simon & Schuster, 1997.

Dawes, E. C. "My First Day Under Fire at Shiloh." *Sketches of War History 1861–1865. Papers Prepared for the Ohio Commandery of the Military Order of the Loyal Legion of the United States 1890–1896*. Ed. W. H. Chamberlin. Cincinnati: Robert Clarke, 1896.

Evans, Nelson W. *A History of Scioto County, Ohio*. Vols. 1 & 2. Portsmouth, OH: 1903.

Ewing, Thomas. Letter to Benjamin Stanton. 24 Oct. 1862. Ohio Historical Society.

Ford, Henry A., and Ford, Kate B. *History of Cincinnati*. Cleveland: L. A. Williams, 1881.

Foster, John H. Letter to B. F. Foster. 17 Apr. 1862. Author's collection.

Galloway, William A. *Old Chillicothe*. Xenia, OH: Buckeye Press, 1934.

Gardner, Col. Hamilton. "The Class of 1827." Unpublished manuscript, U.S. Military Academy Special Collections. 1951.

Genealogy Forum. http:/genforum.familytreemaker.com/cgi-g…thomas, worthington

"General Order No. 86." Headquarters, District of West Tennessee, Jackson, TN, 1 Oct. 1862. GSA Division of Military Records, National Archives.

The Graduates of the U.S. Military Academy. New York: W. H. Graham, 1847.

Grant, Ulysses S. *Personal Memoirs of U.S. Grant* (in 2 volumes). New York: Charles L. Webster and Company, 1885.

———. *The Papers of Ulysses S. Grant: Vol. 5: April 1–August 30, 1862*. Ed. John Y. Simon. Southern Illinois University Press, Feffer & Simons.

Gresham, Martha. *Life of Walter Quintin Gresham, 1832–1895*. Chicago: Rand McNally, 1919.
Henry, Robert Selph. *The Story of the Mexican War*. Indianapolis: Bobbs Merrill, 1950.
Hicks, Roger W., and Shultz, Frances E. *Battlefields of the Civil War*. Topsfield, MA: Salem House, 1994.
Hirshson, Stanley P. *The White Tecumseh: A Biography of William T. Sherman*. New York: John Wiley, 1997.
"His Disappointments Past." *Scioto Gazette*. 27 Feb. 1884.
Hocking Sentinel. Sept. 1991. Chillicothe, OH: Hocking County Genealogical Society.
_____. Sept. 1994. Chillicothe, OH: Hocking County Genealogical Society.
_____. Mar. 1995. Chillicothe, OH: Hocking County Genealogical Society.
Johannsen, Robert W. *To the Halls of the Montezumas: The Mexican War in the American Imagination*. New York: Oxford University Press, 1985.
Kelton, [?] General. *Memo to George W. Cullum regarding the Record of T. Worthington's Civil War Service*. 12 Dec. 1865. U.S. Military Academy Special Collections.
"The Late Col. Thos. Worthington." *Scioto Gazette*. 5 Mar. 1884.
"Letter from Washington." *New York Times*. 25 February 1884.
McAllister, Anna Shannon. *In Winter We Flourish: Life and Letters of Sarah Worthington King Peter 1800–1877*. New York: Longmans, Green, 1939.
McCormick, Robert W. "Worthington vs. Sherman." *Timeline*. June–July 1991.
McDonough, James Lee. *Shiloh: In Hell before Night*. Knoxville: University of Tennessee Press, 1977.
Mansfield, Edward D. *The Mexican War: A History of Its Origin*. New York: A. S. Barnes, 1848.
Mansfield, Jared. Letter to Governor Thomas Worthington. 21 June 1819. Ross County Historical Society.
Marszalek, John F. *Sherman: A Soldier's Passion for Order*. New York: Free Press, 1993.
_____. "William T. Sherman and the Verbal Battle of Shiloh." Article excerpt. Columbus: Ohio Historical Society, n.d.
Medert, Pat. Personal interview. 23 June 1999.
Memo on War Department Stationery regarding the Career of T. Worthington. 14 Jan. 1866. U.S. Military Academy Special Collections.
Military Bibliography of the Civil War, Vol. 4. Dayton, OH: Morningside House, 1987.

Military Service Records of Thomas Worthington. Washington: National Archives, Military Service Records.

More, Frank, ed. *The Civil War in Song and Story: 1860–1865*. New York: P. F. Collier, 1892.

Mounts, Dr. Leonard. Letter to Miss Helen Dudley. 5 Mar. 1948. Collection of Mrs. Charlotte W. Wells.

"A National Disgrace." *Capital*. 24 Mar. 1878.

Official Register U.S.M.A. — Registers of the Officers and Cadets of the U. S. Military Academy. June 1827. U.S. Military Academy Special Collections.

Ohio History. www.ohiohistory.org/places/adena

Opes, Warren. Letter to Mrs. [Elizabeth Phipps Mansfield] Dudley. 11 Mar. 1910. Collection of Mrs. Charlotte W. Wells.

Peter, Sarah Anne Worthington King. Letter to Rufus King. 25 May 1862. Ross County Historical Society.

Pollock, T. A. Letter to Col. Crofts Wright. 6 May 1881. Ohio Historical Society.

Record of Delinquencies, 1822–1828. U. S. Military Academy Archives.

Reed, Hon. Thomas B. *Address to the Cadets at West Point, June 20, 1827*. New York: J. Seymour, 1827.

Register of Merit, 1817–1835, Vol. 1. U. S. Military Academy Archives.

Reid, Whitelaw. *Ohio in the Civil War: Her Statesmen, Generals & Soldiers*, Vol. 1. New York: Moore, Wilstatch & Baldwin, 1868.

_____. *Ohio in the Civil War: Her Statesmen, Generals & Soldiers*, Vol. 2. Cincinnati: Robert Clark, 1895.

Richards, Channing. Letter to Col. Crofts Wright. 10 Apr. 1862. U. S. Military Academy Archives.

Roman, Alfred. *The Military Operations of General Beauregard*. Vol 1. New York: DaCapo, 1994.

Roseboom, Eugene H. *The Civil War Era*, Vol. 4 of *The History of the State of Ohio*. Ed. Carl Wittke. Columbus: Ohio State Archaeological and Historical Society, 1944.

Sears, Alfred Byron. *Thomas Worthington: Father of Ohio Statehood*. Columbus: Ohio State University Press, 1958.

Sherman, William T. *Memoirs of General William T. Sherman*. New York: Appleton, 1904.

Sifakis, Stewart. *Who Was Who in the Civil War*. New York: Facts on File, 1988.

"A Slanderer Answered." *U.S. Army and Navy Journal*. 6 Apr. 1878.

Sword, Wiley. *Shiloh: Bloody April*. Dayton, OH: Morningside, 1974.

Thatcher, S. M. Letter to George W. Cullum. 16 Feb. 1860. U.S. Military Academy Special Collections.

Thirteenth Annual Reunion of the Association of Graduates of the United States Military Academy — West Point, New York — 12 June 1882. Philadelphia: Times Printing House, 1882.

Thompson, Ed Porter. *History of the Orphan Brigade*, 2nd Ed. Dayton, OH: Morningside, 1999.

Thorndike, Rachel Sherman, ed., *The Sherman Letters: Correspondence between General and Senator Sherman from 1837 to 1891.* New York: Charles Scribner's Sons, 1894.

Walden, Geoff. "Cheer, Boys, Cheer!" *The Kentucky Brigade at Shiloh, 6–7 April 1862.* http://www.rootsweb.com/-orphanhm/shiloh.htm.

The War of the Rebellion: A Compilation of the Official Records of the Union and Confederate Armies. Prepared under the direction of the secretary of war by Bvt. Lieut. Col. Robert N. Scott, Third U.S. Artillery and published pursuant to act of Congress approved June 16, 1880. Washington: Government Printing Office, 1884.

Warner, Ezra J. *Generals in Blue.* Baton Rouge: Louisiana State University Press, 1988.

Weisenburger, Francis P. *The Passing of the Frontier*, Vol. 3 of *The History of the State of Ohio.* Ed. Carl Wittke. Columbus: Ohio State Archaeological and Historical Society, 1941.

Wells, Charlotte W. *Miscellaneous Card File References on Col. Thomas Worthington.* Walpole, MA: 1999.

_____. Letter to James D. Brewer. 26 June 1999. Author's collection.

Welsh, Jack D. *Medical Histories of Union Generals.* Kent, OH: Kent State University Press, 1996.

Wilcox, General Cadmus M. *History of the Mexican War.* Washington: Church News Publishing, 1892.

Williams, T. Harry. *McClellan, Sherman and Grant.* New Brunswick: Rutgers University Press, 1962.

Worthington, James. Letter to Thomas Worthington. 14 Dec. 1825. Ross County Historical Society.

Worthington, Margaret. Excerpts from unpublished manuscript "The Diary of Margaret Worthington 1836–37." Transcribed by Charlotte W. Wells and Laura Prieto.

Worthington, Sarah. Letter to Rufus King. 19 Feb. 1862. Ross County Historical Society.

_____. Letter to Rufus King. 18 May 1862. Ross County Historical Society.

Worthington, Thomas. *Address to the Union Volunteers, August 10, 1880.* Morrow: Warren County Free Press, 1880.

_____. *Ballad of the Rebellion with a Sketch of His Service in the Civil War and Evidence of Treachery by Union Commanders at Shiloh; Only To*

Be Obtained by a Court-Martial, after All Efforts for an Inquiry Had Failed, August 1862. Independently published by the author, 1880?. Ross County Historical Society.

_____. *Blunders of the Rebellion and Their Dead-Sea Fruit*. Washington: 1869. Ohio Historical Society.

_____. *A Brief History of the 46th Ohio Volunteers*. Independently published by the author, 1878.

_____. *Brief Record of Colonel Worthington's Service During the Civil War*. Washington: 1878. Thomas McGill and Company.

_____. *Colonel Worthington Vindicated: Sherman's Discreditable Record at Shiloh on His Own and Better Evidence*. Washington: 1878. Thomas McGill and Company.

_____. *A Correct History of Grant at the Battle of Shiloh*. Washington: 1880. Thomas McGill and Company.

_____. *Facts Developed as to the Battle of Shiloh by Colonel Worthington's Court-Martial, August 1862*. Published independently by the author as the second part in a ten-part series generally titled "The Battle of Shiloh," 187?.

_____. Letter to James Worthington. 6 Feb. 1826. U.S. Military Academy Special Collections.

_____. Letter to James Worthington. 24 June 1826. U.S. Military Academy Special Collections

_____. Letter to Col. James Swearingen. 17 Jan. 1839. Ross County Historical Society.

_____. Letter to Col. James Swearingen. 11 Feb. 1839. Ross County Historical Society.

_____. Letter to Col. James Swearingen. 27 Feb. 1839. Ross County Historical Society.

_____. Letter to Dr. L. Joodah. 21 May 1846. Ross County Historical Society.

_____. Letter to Lt. Reeves, Adjutant. 6 Nov. 1847. U.S. Military Academy Special Collections.

_____. Letter to Lt. Reeves, Adjutant. 26 Nov. 1847. U.S. Military Academy Special Collections.

_____. Letter to George W. Cullum. 8 Feb. 1850. U.S. Military Academy Special Collections.

_____. Letter to Ellen Worthington. 25 Apr. 1856. Ross County Historical Society.

_____. Letter to George W. Cullum. 29 Feb. 1860. U.S. Military Academy Special Collections.

_____. Letter to Unknown Family Member. 15 Apr. 1862. Ross County Historical Society.

_____. Letter to Unknown Family Member. 7 Sept. 1862. Ross County Historical Society.

_____. Letter to West Point. 14 Jan. 1866. U.S. Military Academy Special Collections.

_____. Letter to George W. Cullum. 25 June 1867. U.S. Military Academy Special Collections.

_____. Letter to George W. Cullum. 14 Dec. 1867. U.S. Military Academy Special Collections.

_____. Letter to George W. Cullum. 12 July 1874. U.S. Military Academy Special Collections.

_____. Letter to George W. Cullum. 14 Dec. 1874. U.S. Military Academy Special Collections.

_____. *Memorial to Congress Being a Statement of Official Oppression and Misconduct Involving Treasonable Practices by Gen. W. T. Sherman.* Washington: 1879. Thomas McGill and Company.

_____. *Report of the Right Flank March to Join on McLernand's Right, at 9 A.M. and Operations of the 46th Reg't Ohio Vols, 1st Brigade, 5th Division, on the Extreme Union Right, at Shiloh, April 6th, 1862.* Washington, D.C.: 1880.

_____. Shiloh; or, The Tennessee Campaign of 1862; Written Especially for the…. Washington: McGill & Witherow, 1872.

_____. *The Volunteer's Manual.* 2 Vols. Cincinnati: Applegate, 1861.

Worthington, Governor Thomas. Letter to Thomas Worthington. 24 Dec. 1826. Transcribed by Charlotte W. Wells. Cleveland: Western Reserve Historical Center.

Zook, Christian, Pvt., Company F, 46th Ohio Infantry (Volunteer). *Letters to His Family: Feb 22–Apr. 5, 1862.* Civil War Miscellaneous Collection. Carlisle, PA: U.S. Army Military History Institute.

Index

Adams, Steamer 67–70
Adena 9, 10, 32, 193
Alexander, Capt. J. W. 157
Ammen, Col. Jacob 104, 205
Anderson, Robert 16 (photo), 17, 61, 175
Appler, Col. Jesse J. 81–96
army life on the march (Mexican War) 40

Barrett, Capt. Samuel E. 81
Bartley, Gov. Mordecai 36
Beauregard, Gen. P. G. T. 83, 92, 107, 108, 189, 203
Behr, Capt. Frederick 81
Behr's Battery 99–101
Bragg, Maj. Gen. Braxton 92
Brazos de Santiago (Mexico) 38, 39
Buckingham, Brig. Gen. Catharinus P. 174, 305
Buckland, Col. Ralph 86, 88, 155
Buckland's Brigade 81, 93, 84, 98
Buell, Maj. Gen. Don Carlos 105–107
Buford, (Cadet) Napoleon B. 15, 22
Burnside, Gen. Ambrose 177

Calhoun, John C. 14
Camargo (Mexico) 39–40
Cameron, Simon 54
Camp Chase 52, 55–56
Camp Dennison 52, 53

Camp Lyon 55
casualties at Shiloh 128–133
Cincinnati (Ohio) 53
Cleburne, Col. Pat 94
Clifton (Tenn) 68
Cooke, Phillip St. George 15, 19
Corinth (Miss.) 122–123
court-martial charges: against Worthington 139; findings of the charges 162–163; findings officially revoked 169
Cox, Major H. S. 79
Crary, First Lieut. George 156
Crow, Capt. Phillip 153, 154
Curtis, Col. Samuel R. 44

Darke, Gen. William 7–8
Davis, Jefferson 18, 216n
Dawes, Adjutant E. C. 86, 92, 95
demerits (at West Point) 23–25
Dennison, Gov. William 52
Denver, Brig. Gen. 137, 158, 223n
Dudley, E. P. 200

Elements of Military Art and Science 213
Ewing, Thomas 116

Fallen Timbers 111, 150
5th Ohio Cavalry 84, 86
53rd Ohio Infantry 81, 83, 86, 91–96

235

54th Ohio Infantry 80
55th Ohio Infantry 80
57th Ohio Infantry 81, 95
Fisher, Anne 45
Fisher, Sarah 45
Fitch, Lieut. J. A. 157
Forrest, Gen. Nathan B. 108, 111.
Fort Donelson 64
Fort Henry 65
Fort Pickering 124
Fort Sumter 50
40th Illinois Infantry 86, 88, 98
46th Ohio Infantry: at Paducah 59–64; at Shiloh 77–106; table of casualties (Shiloh) 128–132; up the Tennessee 65–76
48th Ohio Infantry 85, 86, 93
Foster, J. B. 55
Foster, Maj. John H. 114, 115
4th Kentucky Infantry 100
Fulton, Lieut. Col. R. A. 79

Garfield, J. A. 185
Giesy, First Lieut. Emanuel 55, 155
Gorman, First Sgt. George 155
Grant, Ulysses S. 64–65, 81, 103–108,112, 114–116, 120, 123, 164, 168, 171, 173, 178 (photo), 180–181, 195–197
Gresham, Walter Q. 223n

Halleck, Gen. Henry W. 62 (photo), 63, 65, 66, 120, 123, 125–127, 197, 218n
Hammond, Capt. A. S. 66, 151
Hardee, Gen. William J. 92
Hardee's Tactics 51
Hicks, Col. Stephen D. 57, 58, 73, 70, 78, 80, 127, 218n
Hildebrand, Col. Jesse 87–95, 220n
Hildebrand's Brigade 81
Holly Springs (Miss) 124
Holt, Judge Advocate General Joseph 169–170
Hunter, Capt. Thomas M. 153, 154

intelligence (battlefield) 208–209
Irvin, Col. William 44

Johnson, Capt. R. W. 50
Johnston, Gen. Albert Sydney 81, 82, 92, 103

Kelley, Nancy 194
Kelley, William 194
Kentucky Orphan Brigade *see* Trabue
King, Rufus 32

Lafayette (Tenn) 124
LaGrange (Tenn) 124
lanceros (Mexican) 41
Lee, (cadet) Robert E. 18
Lincoln, President Abraham 179
Lohrer, First Lieut. Jacob 153

McDowell, Col. John Adair 77, 218n, 219n
Malmborg, Lieut. Col. Oscar 80
Mansfield, Edward D. 32
Mansfield, Margaret (Worthington) 177
Mason, Rodney 80
Matamoros (Mexico) 40, 77
Memphis (Tenn) 124–125
Mexican War, cost to Worthington 42–43
Miller, Capt. Michael 157
Mitchell, Gen. Ormsby 65, 219n
Monroe, Maj. Thomas B. 171
Monterey (Mexico) 41, 32, 108
Morgan, Col. G. W. 37, 38, 217n
Morgan, Capt. John Hunt 108, 176–177
Moscow (Tenn) 124

Neil, Adjutant Jack 55
Nelson, Jesse (drummer boy), 48th Ohio Infantry 93
Nelson, General William 104
newspaper reports (about Sherman) 112–114

order of Battle for Sherman's Division at Shiloh 80–81

Paducah (Kentucky) 55–60
pamphlets, Worthington's post-war 195–197
Peabody, Col. Everett 86–89, 92
Person, Henry M. 158
Piatt, Donn 189, 190
Pittsburg Landing, 46th Ohio's arrival at 75–78
poetry, Worthington's 198
Polk, Leonidas K.: as a cadet 14, 15, 22; as a Maj. Gen. 83

Pond's Brigade 100
Pope, General John 65
Prentiss, Brig. Gen. Benjamin 88
Prentiss' Division 88, 104, 105

Rains, Gabriel 15
Reed, Honorable Thomas 25
Resaca de la Palma 37
Reid, Whitelaw: opinion of Sherman 206; report on Shiloh 112
Rice, Lieut. Col. A. V. 81, 95, 153
Ricker, Maj. (5th Ohio Cavalry) 86, 196
Rosecrans, Gen. W. S. 174, 175, 225n

Sanger (aide to Sherman) 151
Saratoga (NY) 18, 215n
Savannah (TN) 67–70
Schenck, Maj. Gen. Robert C. 174, 177, 224n
2nd Ohio Infantry (Mexican War) 37–41
70th Ohio Infantry 81, 86, 98
71st Ohio Infantry 80
72nd Ohio Infantry 81, 93
77th Ohio Infantry 80, 89
Sharpe, Capt. A. G. 88, 153, 155
Shiloh, role of the 46th Ohio Infantry at 77–110
Sherman, Senator John 117
Sherman, Maj. Gen. William Tecumseh: alcohol policy in Memphis 124; altercation with Worthington in Paducah, KY 67; at the battle of Bull Run 59; belief in value of drill 60; confrontation with Worthington over sick men at Savannah 71–72; convinces Grant to remain at Corinth 123; delays paperwork on courtmartial of Worthington 168; discovers enemy attack at Shiloh 96; duties at Paducah, KY 64; duties in Kentucky and Missouri 60–63; eccentric behavior 61; issue of insanity 63–64; praises Worthington's courage at Shiloh 117; pre-war activities 59; reprimands Worthington 70–72
6th Indiana Light Artillery 78, 81, 89
Smith, Gen. C. F. 65, 67–70, 220n
Smith, Capt. J. C. 156
Smith, Col. T. Kilby 80, 151, 159
Smith, Maj. William 55

Stuart, Col. David 149, 158
Stuart's Brigade 81
Sullivan, Col. Peter 81
surprise, at Shiloh 204–206
Swaine, Lieut. P. T. 50
Swearingen, James 30–34
Swift, Gen. J. G. 175

Taylor, Maj. Ezra 81
Taylor, Col. W. H. H. 84
Tennessee River, campaign along 66–72
Terry's Texas Rangers 97
3rd Mississippi Battalion (Hardcastle's) 92
13th Missouri/22nd Ohio Infantry 100
Thornton, Capt. Seth 36
Tigress (steamer) 103
Trabue, Col. Robert P. 100–103, 106, 221n
tracing incident at West Point 19
12th Michigan Infantry 89
25th Missouri Infantry 89, 92
Tyler (gunboat) 73

Virtute Dignus Avorum 173
Volunteer's Manual, Volumes 1 & 2 50–52

Walcutt, Lieut. Col. C.C. 55, 152, 156
water supply at Camp Dennison 53
Waterhouse, Capt. Allen C. 81
Waterhouse's Battery 93, 94
Watts, Eleanor (Worthington) 177
Wharton's Cavalry 97
Williams, Capt. John 78, 80
Worthington, Eleanor 177, 183, 216n
Worthington, Eleanor Swearingen (wife of Gov.) 29, 44
Worthington, Elizabeth 44, 45, 183
Worthington, Francis 183
Worthington, James 13, 14, 18, 29, 183, 193, 216n
Worthington, Julia 45
Worthington, Margaret 31, 32, 177, 183, 215n, 216n
Worthington, Sarah 56, 183, 199–120, 192–193, 218n
Worthington, Col. Thomas: academics 22–23; address to Union veterans 194, 195; adjutant (Mexican War) 33, 37–39; allegations against Sherman

at Shiloh 113–114; appeal to President Lincoln for reinstatement 179; appeals to the War Department 176–178; arrested and charged by Sherman 134; attempts reinstatement in the Army 174–180; battle for land and property 30–33; burial of 199, 201; Cincinnati (OH) 50; command at Lafayette (TN) 124; controversy with Sherman at Paducah, KY 67; court-martial findings overturned 169–170; court-martial of 137–163; death in Washington, D.C. 199; demerits at West Point 24; gambling 31; last will and testament 200; letter fragment from Shiloh 113, 114 (photo); march to Corinth (MS) 120–122; militia (OH) service 32–34; obituary 201; portrayal in the newspaper 190–191; praised by Sherman for courage at Shiloh 117; as a recluse 46; resigns commission 171–172; at Savannah (TN) 67–70; sentence of the court-martial 163; war poetry of 198

Worthington, Governor Thomas, Sr. 7–11, 20–22, 27, 30, 210–211; children of 215n

Wright, Col. Crofts 100, 225n

Yamoyden 181, 183

Yellow Creek Expedition 73–75

Zook, Pvt. Christian 77, 218n

www.ingramcontent.com/pod-product-compliance
Ingram Content Group UK Ltd.
Pitfield, Milton Keynes, MK11 3LW, UK
UKHW041941140426
5217IPUK00014B/606